For the wide-eyed believers, overzealous underachievers,
and dunce-cap-wearing dreamers. . . . Keep striving.

Taping myself to a pole in downtown Toronto—
a publicity stunt for the launch of our Comedy Network show.

ACKNOWLEDGMENTS

Thank you to my father and mother, Richard and Mary Jane Green. You have been great parents. Thank you for being as supportive and encouraging as anyone could ever hope their parents to be. (Sorry you are still mad about the statues.) My brother, Joe, thanks for not taking my shit too seriously. I am proud to be your brother. I think our best years together are yet to come.

Glenn Humplik. Thanks for being there during this crazy ride. I often miss those early days back on college radio when it was just you and me screwing around on-air with no idea of what we were doing. There have been a lot of good jokes at your expense. Not many people out there could have been such a sport.

Derek Harvie. Thanks for not selling out. If you hadn't pushed us into the darkness, I'm sure much of our absurdity would have never occurred. I'm sure there is a horse, and several cows, who thank you as well.

Phil Giroux. Skateboarding and hanging out together in those important formative years was hilarious. I remember those days fondly and miss them every day. I'm sure you'll keep being crazy.

When we started the show it wouldn't have been possible without all the hard work of Trevor Cavanaugh and Darcy Detoni. Volunteering hundreds of hours at community television isn't always fun. Thanks for everything, guys.

Ray Hagel, for being a great producer, a great videographer, and a great friend. You really understand your craft. Your camera has captured more of our insanity better than anyone else's possibly could have.

Ray Skaff, Karen Pickles, and everyone at Rogers Community 22. Thanks for facilitating a place that gives so many people such a priceless learning experience.

Howie Wagman at the Ottawa Yuk Yuk's comedy club, for encouraging me at such a young age and providing a place for so many to get on stage. Also to the many local comics who coached me when I was just a dumb fifteen-year-old kid trying to get a laugh. Denis Grignon, Luigi Sarcino, Harland Williams, and many more, thanks for the help and advice.

Everyone at CHUO 89.1 FM. Especially Karen McHarg and Bob McArthy. For keeping me on the air for all those years.

Ivan Berry and the Dream Warriors. Thanks for everything with Organized Rhyme. I still want to go to St. Kitts and shoot that video!

Chris Mullington. When I was a goofy kid you showed me how to edit video, and I'm not even sure why. Perhaps you saw my enthusiasm in your art, and I thank you for giving me your time.

All of my teachers at Algonquin College in the TV Broadcasting Department, especially Michel Barrette, Ron Cormack, Donna Leon Millen, and Peter Biesterfield. You guys created a fun environment that worked. And I still remember what a "cardoid pattern" is!!! Pretty cool, huh?! Merilyn Reid, thanks for helping us make the step from volunteering at the community cable station to semi-professional Canadian broadcasting.

Alan Pressman at CBC Ottawa and Ed Robinson at the Canadian Comedy Network. Thanks for putting us on the air when nobody else would. Also to the many local Ottawa journalists who supported our little show when we were starting, specifically Ken Rockburn, Tony Atherton, and Traylee Pierce, as well as everybody at the *Ottawa Citizen* and *Ottawa Sun* newspapers.

Obviously I have talked about Howard Lapides in the book, but thanks again, Howard. You have gone above and beyond the call of duty in your "job" as personal manager over the years. Jackie Stern, thanks for putting up with my insanity and keeping me and Howard semi-organized.

John Ferriter, thanks for being a great agent and a great friend. Thanks for sticking with this crazy idea of me being on television. I know how hard you work and I appreciate it. Jim Wiatt and everybody else at William Morris, Theresa Peters, John Fogelman, Rob Carlson, Mark Itkin, and Sam Haskell, thanks! Also, thank you to Stuart Rosenthal for your legal expertise.

Marleah Leslie and Ann Gurrola. Thanks for being great publicists, but just as important, for getting me all the free lipstick and bath products.

Everybody at MTV. Thanks for believing in our crazy idea and putting it on the air. It was a lot of fun. Special thanks to Brian Graden, Van Toffler, Tom

Freston, Judy McGrath, Carol Eng, Bobby Maurer, Don Jaimeson, Chris Brown, Jeff Boggs, Jim Biederman, Tripp Taylor, Andrew Siegal, John Miller, and everybody else who worked so hard during those crazy couple of years.

Burt Dubrow, thank you for showing me more black-and-white television than I ever thought I would care to see. By the way, the fake Rolex you got me isn't winding.

Everybody who worked on and helped to make *Freddy Got Fingered*. Arnon Milchan, David Matalon, Sanford Panitch, and Peter Cramer, thanks for believing in our crazy movie. Mark Irwin, Mark Fischer, Garrett Grant, Larry Brezner, and Lauren Lloyd, thanks.

Todd Phillips, Ivan Reitman, and Tom Pollock, thanks for everything. *Road Trip* was a blast, except for the mousy aftertaste. Todd, keep turning out those funny movies!

Bruce Lagnese and Karen Lalaian, thanks for making sure I don't spend all my money. . . . I haven't, have I? I think I'll call you tomorrow. . . .

Jennifer Rudolph Walsh at William Morris, thanks for the great sandwich at the Carnegie Deli. . . . Oh yeah, and for selling this book. Thanks.

Kristin Kiser and everyone else at Crown Publishers, including Ellen Rubinstein, Trisha Howell, and Lindsey Moore. This has been fun. Sorry about all the spelling mistakes. If this works out, I have another book idea for you. . . . It's about a war in outer space. . . . Between good and evil. . . . There's lasers and spaceships and weird aliens and a cute little robot that beeps and makes funny sounds!

Allen Rucker, thanks for working so hard with me in putting this book together. I really enjoyed the process—maybe you can help me with my *Space Wars* idea. That is, if you can bear to spend another six months listening to me ramble into a tape recorder.

And last but not least, everybody who has let me be a goofball on television, especially Jay Leno, David Letterman, Lorne Michaels, Craig Kilborn, Conan O'Brien, and Mike Bullard. Thanks for letting me be silly on your shows. I'm sorry if I've broken anything expensive. . . .

To anyone I forgot: Sorry. I owe you a beer.

CONTENTS

Hollywood
Causes Cancer

INTRODUCTION

"I think you either really like Tom or you don't. I think he gets a lot of strong reactions one way or the other."

—Mary Jane Green, Tom's mother

SEVEN YEARS AGO I WAS STUCK LIVING IN MY parents' basement in Ottawa, Canada, waiting for something—anything—to occur. Today I own a nice house in Los Angeles. I live in that house with my two dogs, Steve and Annie. Not a day goes by when I don't wake up and think, just for a second, usually between taking a leak and brushing my teeth, What the hell happened?

They say that there is no entrance exam for show business. I didn't go to film school or acting school or talk show school. I did go to the Algonquin Community College in my hometown for two years, where I learned how to shoot and edit video. It was a trade school, kind of like a Devry Institute of Technology. I could have taken nursing, welding, or dental hygiene. I chose the "broadcasting arts."

The reality of it is that all I've ever wanted to do is work in television. I have never seriously entertained any other career objective, if you can call it that. When I was in high school, I ran for student council so I could stand on stage and host assemblies. I once hosted a Christmas concert from behind a desk. I even arranged for my own house band with my own Paul Shaffer, a guy playing a Hammond organ with a Leslie amp.

I began doing stand-up at a local comedy club when I was fifteen; had my own rap group, Organized Rhyme, at sixteen; then, a campus radio show for three years; then, a no-budget community cable TV show for another three and a half years. This is not the conventional route to Hollywood for a comedian. I kind of made it up as I went along.

In the Martin Scorsese film *The King of Comedy*, Robert DeNiro plays a pathetic loser whose only dream in life is to host a talk show. Looking back, I think I was a version of that character in real life. I was a demented talk-show-host-wannabe. I was basically Rupert Pupkin.

Rupert Pupkin had to kidnap a famous talk show host played by Jerry Lewis to escape his own basement and make his sad fantasy come true, if only for a minute. I didn't have to commit any felonies, but I did some pretty bizarre things and also had some pretty bizarre things done to me. And that's what this book is all about.

When you finish reading this book, assuming you get all the way to the end, I hope you come away with perhaps a different impression of me than you may already have. Unless, of course, you already had a good impression of me, in which case I'd almost rather you didn't read the book at all. You might get a bad impression. And we wouldn't want that.

Everyone wants either advice on how to get to Hollywood or more ammunition to trash the place. This book offers a little of both. And if you're a person like I was just five years ago, on the verge of being sucked into the Hollywood machine, then maybe this can help you from getting stuck in the gears.

Up to around the age of twenty-five, everything in my life happened very, very slowly. Beginning in my teens, it took my friends and me ten to twelve years to come up with our own style of video comedy. I learned to edit so I could edit pieces myself. Along with my friends, I developed a free cable show so we could pursue our own ideas and not answer to a "pro" who probably wouldn't see it the same way we did. Because there was no money, everything took twice as long and was twice as frustrating. To most people outside of our small group of co-conspirators—most certainly my parents—what we were doing did not seem like work, let alone a life's work. They just thought we were wasting our time.

Not only was I living in my parents' basement and driving them nuts by my mere presence, I was also using them as video fodder. The first time was on a typical Wednesday night doing the cable show. As usual, we didn't have enough material for that week's show. After shooting all night, my cameraman was dropping me off at my parents' home at three in the morning when I suddenly had a notion. "Why don't we go into their bedroom, tape rolling, wake them up, and see what happens?"

As they sat there staring into the blinding glare of our camera and lights, looking like two raccoons about to become roadkill, we couldn't believe we were doing this. That's what made it so exciting. At the time it seemed like one of the funniest things we had ever seen, and it was the beginning of my complicated on-camera relationship with my parents that continues to this day. Let's put it this way: even though my parents love me, they've threatened legal action more than once.

Eventually our little public-access show got picked up by a Canadian comedy channel and then MTV, and all of a sudden everything in my life began to happen very, very fast. I had been slugging it out in Canada for years. But moving to America was like opening a new door; on the other side was a completely different world I had never known. I walked through it, and before I could catch a breath, I had a hit TV show; starred in four movies; wrote, directed, and produced one of them; got testicular cancer; got married to a movie star; got divorced from a movie star; had a house burn down; and went from media darling to media punching bag. It was a wild ride—much crazier than any stunt I've ever come up with, much more intricate and erratic and ruthless than anything I had ever dreamed of or certainly wanted. In just a few short years I have celebrated tremendous highs and suffered implausible lows. I'm glad I'm still here to talk about it.

The cancer was the real capper, of course, but I think that surviving cancer, more than anything, has helped me renew my focus. On the other hand, it helped me lose my focus, too. Cancer at age twenty-nine will do that.

In preparation for my latest talk show, I watched some of my earlier efforts from ten years ago. As I was watching, I realized I had no ability to relate to anyone over the age of thirty because back then, I had done nothing. I couldn't even carry on a conversation with an older person. I got nervous and tongue-tied. I had nothing to say.

Now, only a few years later, I've been married, bought a house, seen the world, and had cancer. Now I can talk to almost anyone—exasperated husbands, homeowners, jet-setters, divorcées, and certainly potential cancer victims. Like males between fifteen and twenty-five, the prime age group for the kind of cancer I had . . . I can talk to them. "Go see a doctor, kids! Feel your balls! Don't be ashamed! IT'S YOUR LIFE!"

And this is mine. So far.

1.

BELOW C LEVEL

—

"**A** true highlight of this term was Tommy's speech on humor, which he carried off with the aplomb of a stage professional. Tommy is a great study in contrasts. The art he submits is superb, but he misses half of his assignments, so his mark is necessarily low. . . . Try to watch the "talking out," Tommy. It is not appreciated."

—Report card comments
of Shirley Gaudreau,
Tom's sixth-grade teacher

I SEE MY LIFE IN TWO MAJOR PARTS. PART ONE: my birth to living in my parents' basement with no money at age twenty-five. Part Two: getting out of my parents' basement until today. Let's start in the middle.

MY PARENTS' BASEMENT

THE YEAR IS 1996. AT THIS POINT IN TIME I AM STILL financially dependent on my parents. I am at a stage in life where this is beginning to be painstakingly abnormal, much to my embarrassment. I am a generational statistic, a twenty-five-year-old college graduate who has recently returned to living in his parents' basement. I have done this as a way of saving money while I wait for my dream job to materialize. Also my on-and-off girlfriend of five years, who I have recently been living with, has thrown all my stuff out of her house. This most likely happened at a good time since I could no longer afford to pay rent anyway.

It is probably never a good idea to return to the nest. Once you flap your wings and leap from the tree, it is best to migrate somewhere else. If you're really lucky, you might get lost and not be able to return, so go someplace warm. I think returning to live with parents, especially if they are my parents, can be a little bit defeating. So take that as advice and don't move into my house. The place is small enough already.

For the previous three years I had, for free, produced and hosted my own comedy talk show on the local community television station, Rogers Community 22. Over that three-year period the show became reasonably popular in my hometown of Ottawa, the capital of Canada. In fact the show had become so well known that I now had a realistic shot at going network. That would be a real job! Over the past six months my friends and I had been working on a pilot episode of *The Tom Green Show* for the Canadian Broadcasting Corporation, a national network. Producing this single episode had utterly consumed my life for half a year, as producing the cable show on Rogers Community 22 had done for three and a half years before that. But now, we had completed the pilot and it had just aired on the CBC, so for the first time in three years, I had time on my hands. All the time in the world.

This show was the reason why I did not have a job and lived in my parents' basement. Because I was interested only in producing the program, I didn't allocate much time to finding other paid employment. I was motivated only by the television show; it was my only real goal. Unfortunately it was not paying any money yet, and in the faint hope that it might, my friends and I sat around for a year and waited.

How, I wondered, did I end up in this seemingly rock-bottom predicament?

"THERE WAS A YOUNG FELLOW FROM WHEELING . . ."

WHEN I WAS IN GRADE SIX I WON THE PUBLIC-speaking contest for my school. I remember at that time it seemed like the most important thing in the world. In grade school they didn't have talent shows or anything like that, so this was really the only opportunity to see other students on stage. First you would compete against your class. The English teacher would watch everybody's speech and choose a winner. Then you would compete against the other three classes in your section of the school. After that competition they would send three finalists to perform their speeches in front of the entire school.

I had won for my class three years in a row. In grade four I did my speech on rocks. It was pretty dry stuff but contained a few cool words like *igneous, metamorphic,* and *sedimentary.* I won for my class but then lost to Darryl Page in the semifinals. I didn't get to compete in front of the school.

In grade five I tried loosening it up a little bit. I wrote a speech on how I would change the school if I had power. Unfortunately I can't remember any of it. I think there was a joke about a mousetrap in a lunch box, but I'm not sure. That year I also won for my class but then lost again in the semifinals to Darryl Page and a girl named Elizabeth Pang. I felt extremely deflated by the rejection. I was a show business failure at ten.

I was never a great student. I was usually more interested in cracking jokes and falling off my chair. The public speech contest would save my English mark every year. Winning for the class, the teacher would always give me a 98 percent. I don't know where the other 2 percent went—they probably got taken away for losing to Elizabeth Pang.

The sixth-grade competition was my last chance. I was going to be switching to a middle school the next year—this was it for Robert Hopkins P.S. At the front of the school there was a plaque, and they would engrave the names of the public speech winners for the school in that plaque. The prestigious title was usually won by somebody in grade six, although the year before it had been won by a grade-five student, the infamous Darryl Page. I wanted to take his title away. I wanted my name on that plaque.

For my final assault on the title I decided to do my speech on humor. I competed and won first place in my class as usual, and then I competed against the rest of my grade. There were five other students in the semifinals; only two would get to compete in front of the school. I don't remember now what his speech was about, but Darryl Page won hands down. Elizabeth Pang and I tied

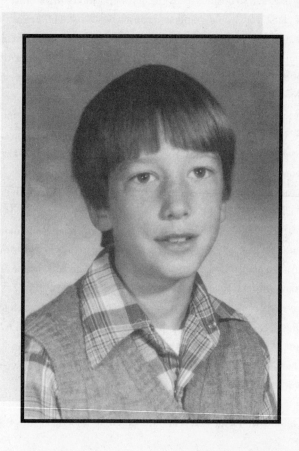

for second place. My teacher couldn't decide who should go to the finals in the school gym, so in an unprecedented move, and much to the surprise of everyone, she asked Elizabeth Pang and me to do our speeches again. She brought in another teacher to help her decide the winner.

The excitement was riveting. Everyone in grade six was caught up in the tension. Elizabeth and I performed our speeches again in the library. When we finished, the teachers sent all of the students to the school yard while they deliberated on the winner.

Elizabeth Pang was a brain who always was at the top of the class. I think people kind of resented her for that. So out in the school yard a lot of the kids were siding with me: "Hey, Tom . . . I hope you win the speech!" "Hey, man, you were way better than Pang!"

I remember that, for the first time in my life, I felt slightly popular. I was always the skinny nerd who cracked jokes in class but got beat up during recess. But now some of the most popular and coolest kids in the school were coming up to me and wishing me luck. They wanted me over Pang!

When we came back from the break, the teacher stood up and announced that I had won the competition. The class erupted into a cheer. They were cheering for me, and I liked the way it felt. But there was no time to rejoice. The next day it was me vs. the formidable Darryl Page in front of the whole school.

My mother actually kept the cue cards from that speech and was able to dig them out years later from deep in her filing cabinet. Here's how I rehearsed it dozens of times in front of the mirror the night before the Big Speech-Off.

"Today I am going to explain the complex theory of relativity. This important law of physics, discovered by Albert Einstein, proves that mass and energy are equivalent.

"I will now refer to a few notes." (I take out an enormous stack of computer paper and clumsily drop it on the floor . . . it unfolds into a banner that reads in large letters E equals M C squared.)

"I hope I made all of you laugh because that was supposed to be funny.

"No one really knows why people laugh or what causes them to make such a strange noise when something is funny.

"Babies learn early to laugh when they are tickled. But as we grow older we learn to laugh at the humorous things we see and hear.

"Humorous stories and jokes are funny because of the element of surprise. The audience is taken off guard by something unexpected.

"There are many different types of humor. For example, I opened my speech with slapstick humor. This is a silly form of humor depending on exaggerated movements, pratfalls, or pie throwing. It was popular in Greece or Rome as long ago as 300 BC. Slapstick referred to the hits a master gave his slave who talked too cleverly.

"Comedians like Groucho Marx and the Three Stooges were masters of slapstick.

"Another form of humor depends on the use of the pun—in which one word is said when another is meant. For instance, one day my teacher decided to visit my parents. She knocked on the door and asked 'Are your mother and father in?' 'They was in, but they's out now.' 'Good grief!' said my teacher, 'Where's your grammar?!' 'Oh, she's out in the kitchen making cookies.' The punch line at the end of the joke uses a pun and surprises the listener.

"Sarcasm is another type of humor in which a remark or situation means the opposite of what it appears to mean. Teachers are particularly good at sarcasm. I once told a teacher that I didn't think I deserved a zero on my test. She said, 'Neither do I, but it's the lowest mark I can give you.'

"Some comedians, such as Rich Little, depend on mimicry and impersonation to make people laugh. They usually choose famous people as subjects, copy their voice and gestures, and place them in humorous situations.

"Most humor is told rather than seen. Limericks are nonsense verse, usually five lines long. As in most humour, there is an unexpected twist at the end. For example:

There was a young fellow from Wheeling
Who had such a delicate feeling,
When he read on the door,

'Don't spit on the floor!'
He jumped up and spat on the ceiling!

"Some humor is told in stories rather than verse. Tall tales use exaggeration to create a humorous situation.

"Grandfathers really like to tell tall tales. My grandfather told us about the time a bear chased him through a field. The bear was right behind him, twelve feet tall, with paws twelve inches wide, saliva dripping from its mouth. 'What happened?' we asked. 'Well, I ran to the one tree that was in the field. Only problem was, the nearest branch was twenty feet above my head.' 'What did you do?' we asked. 'Well, there was nothing I could do. I had to jump for that branch.' 'Did you make it, Grandpa?' 'Well, no, not going up. But I caught it coming down.'

"I've found it helps to have a sense of humor, especially at report card time. If I'm lucky, my parents see the humor in the situation, too.

"Now that we have finished our little chat on humor, I will get back to my main topic of Einstein's theory of relativity. Oh, looks like I'm out of time. I guess I will have to continue next year."

So that was the big speech. The next day I felt like I was going to puke. I had to stand up in front of the whole school, so I was a wreck. But this was the big time. I had dreamed of one day making it to the school finals, and now, here I was. They made such a big deal out of these finals that they even brought in judges from the school board. There were five judges in all. They would pick a winner for the school and send him to compete against all the other elementary schools in the region.

Darryl Page got up and did his speech. Like I said, I can't remember what his speech was about, but I know it was good. He had won the prize last year, so he didn't seem a bit nervous. He looked totally relaxed as he delivered his lines from the stage.

Then I went up to do my speech. I remember them calling my name, and from that point on everything felt like it moved in slow motion. I walked up to the front of the small stage in the gym and stared out at my peers. I was either going to suck or I would do okay. By now none of the jokes in my speech seemed funny to me, as I had rehearsed it at least a hundred times.

I did my speech pretty well, with no big screwups. All of the little jokes got laughs from the crowd. I remember being surprised at how loud the laughs seemed in the large gymnasium. I had never stood in front of this many people before in my life.

After you finished your speech you would stay on the stage for a moment. One of the judges would stand and ask you a question. You had to deliver a good response, to prove your knowledge on the topic. The school-board trustee stood up at the back of the gym. She was a blond woman, probably in her midthirties.

"Very good, Tom, now I have a question. You said in your speech that it helps having a sense of humor, especially at report card time. Can you give me an example of how you would use humor to get out of a tricky situation with your parents?"

It was obvious she was trying to burn me. For about a nanosecond I panicked, but then for some reason, something clicked. I had something to say. I had been reading joke books for weeks researching this speech, and I remembered a silly joke that would be the perfect response to the judge's surprise question.

"Well, I can tell you about the time I brought my report card home to my father. I was a little worried about my poor grades, so I used humor to help the situation. Before I gave my report card to Dad I told him that my marks were underwater. (LONG PAUSE) When he asked me what that meant, I said, 'Well . . . they're below C level.' " (Sea level . . . get it?)

I responded with this joke so quickly that I even shocked myself. When I delivered the punch line, it killed. The entire school, including the adult judges and teachers, were on the floor. The sound was so loud, and the laugh lasted so long, that I vividly remember the moment to this day. I think everyone was just relieved that I had an answer, any answer, to the judge's impossible question. I was standing there and looking at my entire school, which was sitting crosslegged on the floor, laughing with me—not *at* me. I remember looking against the back wall and seeing the pretty girl who I had a crush on, Lesley Dewsnap. Even she was laughing. And although the joke today doesn't seem like "A" material, at the time, coming out of the mouth of a ten-year-old in response to that kind of question from that kind of adult, it made me appear like a real wit. I won the competition and got my name on the plaque. (Unfortunately, Lesley Dewsnap continued to think of me as an idiot.)

That grade-six gymnasium laugh stays with me. To this day it is one of the best feelings I have ever felt in my life, and I am constantly trying to replicate it.

"I WAS A SKATEBOARDER"

I WAS A SKATEBOARDER. THAT WAS, I THINK, A BIG part of where a lot of the video comedy that I do came from—skateboarding culture. It was as big an influence as doing stand-up or watching *Monty Python*. I grew up watching skateboard videos—raw videos of skateboarders skating through the streets of San Francisco and razzing people and stuff like that.

Tony Hawk and me the day we met in NYC. Then we went skating.
I felt like I was in *Future Primitive*. Rad!

Tony Hawk was my hero, and he was in a lot of these classic early videos like *The Search for Animal Chin* or *The Bones Brigade—Future Primitive*.

Skateboarding was far from mainstream back then. It was not cool like it is now. I was the only kid in my school who was a skateboarder, and everyone thought it was kind of weird. It was big in California, but it wasn't something that people did in high school in Ottawa, Canada. Skateboard culture—the music, the clothing, the videos—was unknown to the masses. You could only find any of this stuff at one underground skate shop in the entire city. And that wasn't until skateboarding was relatively popular in the late eighties. Before that you couldn't get a brand new professional skateboard anywhere. I got my first skateboard at a garage sale, and I think I got the next five after that at a garage sale. Then the movie *Back to the Future* came out. I had never seen a skateboard like that before. It was this new style of skateboard—a wide wooden board with thick urethane wheels, nothing like the tiny little plastic boards we had been riding. The way Michael J. Fox rode that board to school in the morning was unlike anything you could do on the crappy little things we scooted around on. I wanted one desperately, but you couldn't get them in Canada.

One day I was at school, and this punk rock kid flew by me on one of them. I was in awe, and even though he was a few years older, I ran after him and asked him where he had found it. He told me about this tiny bicycle shop downtown called Foster's Sports. If you went to the back, they had two more of them, imported no doubt from America. My neighborhood friends and I all bought boards and started skating every day. These were friends I played hockey with from age six to sixteen. We went from hockey to skateboarding. And we got really into it. We'd go to the construction site near the house, steal wood, and come back and build elaborate skateboard ramps. In the middle of the night we'd hop fences into a sewage treatment plant under construction and carry away tons of wood, miles back to the house, through people's back-yards, huge eight-by-four sheets of thick plywood. We were young and skinny. This wood was heavy and it would cut into our hands and make them bleed, but we didn't care. We just wanted to skate.

Eventually my two hockey friends quit skateboarding, but not me. One day this guy Phil—Phil Giroux, the guy who sat in the back and drank coffee

Phil Giroux and me chillin' at a skateboard contest. Cool hat, eh?

on the original *Tom Green Show* on MTV—skated by my house and saw my ramp. Basically that was the beginning of a lifelong friendship. We would skateboard together constantly; together we became part of this new subculture of skateboarding. After a couple of years, the popularity of skating grew somewhat. It was nowhere as big as it has become today, but at the time it seemed huge. There were now two skate shops in the city that specialized exclusively in skateboarding, not just a section in the back of the bike store.

But skateboarding was still a subculture, a deviance like punk rock or rap music or crack cocaine. A skateboard was no longer just a toy that you would ride like a bike. A skateboarder was what you were—it was how you defined your life and a world that none of the "jocks" at school understood. Just because we weren't the most popular kids in our class, it didn't matter anymore. Now we had a reason to not want to conform. Those people just didn't understand us, and we didn't want them to. We had found our own world that was far more stirring and creative and unique. We were skateboarders.

At the time skateboarders were into punk and early rap. You'd pick up a

**Leaning on my skateboard launch ramp
on the street in front of my house.**

copy of *Thrasher Magazine* and they would be reviewing the Beastie Boys, who were not yet a huge group. They'd talk up Run DMC, Public Enemy, and Boogie Down Productions, underground groups who weren't close to mainstream recognition. At the same time we'd be out on our skateboards on the street with this sort of anti-authoritarian attitude. We'd always be getting kicked out of parking lots and malls by security guards. Our whole life outside of school was basically running from security guards because you weren't allowed to skate-board anywhere but on city streets and in your own backyard. And in Canada, in the wintertime, if you were a hard-core skateboarder, you'd have to skate-board inside, in underground parking garages and in the tunnels at Carlton University, where there were security guards in golf carts who would literally chase you around for miles.

Big air!

It was our first brush with messing with authority figures, something that became a running theme on the public access show.

Phil and I started taking the bus downtown every time we wanted to go skateboarding. We'd be on the bus with our skateboards and feel like a couple of badasses. We watched these homemade skate videos and listened to our "underground" music, and though skateboarding wasn't a crime, we felt like criminals, like we were part of a defiant subculture. We felt like we didn't really fit in with the society that was on the bus. There were all these normal-looking citizens reading their papers and doing the crossword puzzle, and we'd be sitting there dripping in sweat with a bloody bandanna and our boards and looking like a couple of punks. It was on these boring bus rides where we began to do what we called razzing.

"WEIRD AND INAPPROPRIATE . . ."

HALF THE FUN OF SKATEBOARDING WAS THAT TRIP downtown. People just sat quietly, staring into space, like the polite Canadians they were. This is probably true of public transportation in general—people sit there, you're crowded in, and you don't say anything for fear of offending someone. Offending people was not our problem. We started to work up a little routine of ridiculous conversations at a slightly too loud level. One of us would say something like, "So we'll meet at the rendezvous point at midnight, then we'll do the job. . . ." Then the other, in a slightly lower but still clearly audible voice, "Does Jimmy have the gun and the masks? . . ." "Of course he does! Now keep it down, I think that lady over there is listening to us. . . ." We'd keep up this conversation that not so subtly implied that we, along with "Jimmy," were in the midst of planning a robbery. Other passengers would start to sit up and eavesdrop. Sometimes they'd get angry and tell us to stop or report us to the driver. "Hey, there are a couple of kids back there up to no good, don't you know . . ." It wasn't uncommon for us to get kicked off the bus. But it was fun, usually more fun than where we were actually going. And we began to change. We didn't even need anything to *do* anymore for entertainment other than be ourselves. We could just go out, be weird, and get reactions from people.

There would always be people on the bus who would get what we were doing—usually young people—and then there was always some stuck-up older person who didn't get it and would get mad and make the whole silly thing worthwhile.

You can see how this was really good training for what I would do later. When we began to shoot video, the idea of getting chased by a security guard or keeping a straight face while having a ridiculous conversation was not new. Bus razzing was a good way to practice deadpan delivery, to play it like "this is not a joke." The first time we shot stuff for the show, I would crack up in the middle and ruin everything. I could do it with Phil on the bus, but on camera, I had to work to not laugh. When you laugh on camera, it's a sure sign of failure. You have just trashed the whole bit.

When we went razzing on the bus, or in the shopping mall, or at the museum, we were never mean-spirited. It was just weird, never mean. It was just fun to do things that were inappropriate. For instance, when you would get off the bus, you'd step down and the bus door would open. If you're standing on that bottom step, the door won't close. Anybody with any sense in their brain could figure this out. And, of course, if the door didn't close, the bus couldn't leave, and this obnoxious buzzer would go "Bing-Bing-Bing" and drive everyone crazy.

On a really crowded bus, I'd wear my Walkman and just stand on that step, acting like I had no idea what was going on. The buzzer would start ringing, and people would be yelling, "Hey, you gotta get off the step!" Oblivious, I'd just crank my music up another notch. And then three more riders would join in. "Hey, hey! You gotta get off the step!"

Soon everybody on the entire bus would be fuming until someone finally ripped the headphones off my head and try to jerk me off the bottom step. I'd turn and look at them like "Hey, what's your problem?" Meanwhile, my friends would be off to the side keeled over with laughter. Forty-five people on the bus would be fuming and screaming at me. "What are you, a fucking idiot? You got to get off the fucking step." It upset their routine and probably gave them something to talk about the rest of the day—that stupid kid who didn't know how the door worked.

That was the kind of stuff we did. It wasn't mean, but it was annoying. And stupid. And to us and our sensibility, it was a lot more fun than going to football games. It was risky, and you had no idea what might happen. It was fucking with reality. And it all grew out of skateboarding and the culture of skateboarding.

A couple of weeks after my show premiered on MTV I got an e-mail from skateboarding legend Tony Hawk. I was blown away. When I was seventeen years old, I had grown my hair like his, with bangs hanging over my face completely covering my eye. When he dyed his hair blond, so did I. And strangely I looked enough like him that on several occasions I was able to fool people into thinking I was indeed him. In those early skateboard years, Tony had come to Ottawa to skate in a demo. I waited in line for hours with about a thousand other kids to get his autograph. Now he was e-mailing me personally telling me how much he liked my show. Later he came to New York and did a bit with us, and we became friends. Today I'm an honorary member of his Birdhouse skateboarding team. How did this all happen? It still seems crazy to this day.

Me and Tony in Las Vegas.

"WOULD YOU BE OPEN TO YOUR DAUGHTER GOING OUT WITH AN AMPUTEE?"

THE ONLY REASON I WANTED TO GO TO SCHOOL WAS to get laughs. I realized early on that a great way to get attention was to run for student council. Student council wasn't about power—it had no power—but about the perks. Basically it gave me the opportunity to produce, write, and perform in every school assembly. Most of the other members of student council thought this was the worst part of the job, but that was the only reason I was there. I loved it, and ultimately I ended up controlling the assemblies. It was kind of weird being in grade ten and hosting assemblies in front of the older students. I was constantly shocked when I would see older students with beards. I was afraid of them.

No one really took student council seriously, except the other people running, of course, who were usually at the top of their class and desperately wanted to get into University and desperately wanted to do anything to make themselves stand out. There was always a "candidates' forum," where each candidate would give a little speech about what they were going to do about a student trip or new band uniforms or something.

One year I showed up at the forum with a big briefcase and took my place on the podium with the other candidates. As they each stood and pontificated on the issues of the day, I quietly opened my briefcase and took out a cutting board, four heads of lettuce, some carrots, a nice tomato, Newman's Own salad dressing, and a big butcher knife. Without looking at anyone or indicating in any way that this was weird, I proceeded to make myself a nice tossed salad. I was slow and methodical about it. I certainly didn't want to disturb the speakers.

Immediately everybody in the auditorium was watching me and not listening to my competitors, to whom they, of course, weren't listening anyway. Even the speakers had to somehow acknowledge my presence. The entire school was laughing through the other speakers' speeches. I never said a word. I quietly enjoyed my salad, put everything back in the briefcase, and when it was my turn to speak, I just rose and waved to the crowd.

I won by a landslide.

I was elected into student council every year for the rest of high school. I realized pretty quickly that people kept re-electing me because they knew I would make the assemblies funny. Organizing these assemblies became a passion. My marks suffered because of it. I started spending a lot of my time preparing the next assembly instead of studying.

Things got real serious when I started hosting the Christmas talent show. It was called the Christmas concert, and all the bands from the school would play. I changed the whole event around, setting up the stage like David Letterman's television set. I sat at a desk on the stage and arranged to have a house band play between acts. I remember some really great bits that happened in those shows.

One year I got the audio-video teacher, Mr. McKinnon, to hook up a cordless telephone to the speaker system. It was quite the elaborate system—he needed to rig some weird descrambler—and it took me about a month of negotiating with him to make it happen. But when I got it set up for the show, it was a wonderful electronic, as well as comic, device. Before the show I got access to a school list, which included the phone numbers of all the students. From the stage I would walk up to pretty girls in the audience and ask them their names. Then I immediately looked up their phone number in my list and called their house. The girl would just be squirming in her chair with me standing right beside her, a hand on her shoulder, in the middle of the crowd. I would usually get her mother or father on the line, with the entire school listening in:

DAD: **Hello?**

TOM: **Hello, is Bridgette in?**

DAD: **No, she's at school. (Big laugh from crowd) Could I ask who's calling?**

TOM: **Yeah, my name is Tom. I go to school with Bridgette. I really like her. (Huge laughs)**

DAD: **That's nice, Tom. Well, she's not home now.**

TOM: **Does she have a boyfriend?**

DAD: I don't think so . . . not right now . . . hey, who is this?

TOM: My name is Tom, and I think that Bridgette is really pretty. Do you think she's pretty?

DAD: Yes I do, Tom. Now, listen, I'll tell Bridgette you called, okay?

TOM: Okay, but do you like me?

DAD: What?!

TOM: I just want you to like me because if Bridgette is ever my girlfriend, I want her father to like me a lot. . . .

DAD: Sure, okay, well maybe I'll meet you someday.

TOM: I'm an amputee. . . .

DAD: What?!

TOM: Would you be open to you daughter going out with an amputee?

DAD: Of course, I would, Tom, but I have to go . . . good-bye . . . (click)

This bit with the phone just killed all night. I even started calling the homes of teachers who were present in the auditorium. I would get their husbands or wives on the phone. It was crazy! The whole school would swivel in their chairs to stare at the teacher while I razzed the hell out of their spouse.

I don't think there was really anything negative about my student council antics. I never got suspended or anything. (Well, maybe once for a couple of days for swearing in a routine.) In fact, every year I won the Spirit Award for the whole school. I'm not even sure what that means, but there's a plaque with my name on it at the school. There's also a forty-by-forty-five-foot mural of rock star Bryan Adams in my school, but nothing like that for me. Wait. He went to the school for one fucking year and then moved to Vancouver, and he gets a forty-foot mural. Just because he's had, like, the biggest number one hit song in the history of music? I don't get it.

In my final year of high school we got a new principal. His name was Mr. Pinard and he had absolutely no sense of humor. He banned me from hosting the assemblies because, as he put it, he didn't want them "turning into rock concerts." I still to this day don't understand what that means. But assembly hosting was good training and preparatory for the real world out there. If you plan to do any kind of comedy, you have to get used to people like Mr. Pinard. Unfortunately, they are usually in charge.

MY GRADES IN HIGH SCHOOL weren't good enough to get into University. This was a serious source of conflict with my parents, but I also think they realized, to a certain extent, that I wasn't a screwup, I wasn't into drugs, that I actually had something that I wanted to do. I wasn't stupid—I had just made a conscious decision to pursue something else. I didn't know exactly what that was, and I didn't know how to do it, but I think I believed there was a real possibility of making that sixth-grade speech into a life.

2.

COMMUNITY 22

"I think it's addictive—that feedback—especially if you get that kind of feedback when you were young. . . . I think it's like a drug, almost."

—Mary Jane Green

KINDA FUNNY . . .

WHEN I WAS FIFTEEN, MY FRIENDS AND I STARTED going down to the local comedy club, Yuk-Yuk's, and heckling. The way we heckled was kind of weird. For example, we'd all sit in the front row with our hands on our right cheek and every time the comedian would tell a punch line we'd switch our hands to our left cheek at exactly the same moment, without laughing. It was like three completely bored people moving in unison. It would, of course, drive the comedian nuts. It wasn't long before we got kicked out of the club and not allowed back.

Then one day we found out there was an amateur night at the club, so we called in our names and got on the line-up. When we got to the club, the manager, Howie Wagman, recognized us as the troublemakers, and he wouldn't let us in. Then the bouncer, his name was Teebor, the guy who had actually kicked us out of the club, went up to the manager and whispered, "You know, when I kicked these guys out last week, they were, you know, kinda funny." So the manager relented and said we could go on.

I was fifteen years old, and Yuk-Yuk's was the first bar I'd ever entered. I guess there must have been a loophole—the club probably had a restaurant license, but it felt like a bar. My friends Derek and Phil and I all blended into the shadows of the back of the club. We were afraid, no, we were scared shitless of the crowd. Not only was it intimidating to be going onstage in a professional club, but it would be in front of a crowd of drunken college students much older than us.

So I went on and did great (my two friends bombed and left stand-up soon after). I'm sure I scored because I was fifteen and looked nervous and people felt sorry for me. And the material was bad, along the lines of "Have you seen the commercial . . . ?" There is a cereal called Trix, and its symbol is a cartoon rabbit. And the commercial says, "Silly rabbit, Trix are for kids." My joke was, "What? You need an ID to buy this stuff?"

Still, they let me come back, once a week, and it took four months or so before I was even close to reaching the level of that first performance. After six or seven months, I started getting opening spots for the pros who came through Ottawa on the weekends. I was paid twenty dollars per performance. They wrote an article about me in a tiny local paper called *The Star*, and someone pinned it up at school. There was something about being at the comedy club that made me feel like I was a part of something real. For the first time I was surrounded by other people who actually believed that being funny could be a career. And for the first time I was able to put a label on what had until then been just stupidity. I was no longer just an idiot—I was now a *comedian*. One day I was doing silly stuff at home to annoy my parents. The next I was getting paid to do it on stage. It was an exhilarating transition.

Around the same time I was becoming a local fixture at Yuk-Yuk's, I began experimenting with music and in turn found a new comedic outlet. In many of the assemblies up to this point, I had often performed these funny rap songs that I had written. By grade eleven I decided that I wanted to actually start a band and take this rapping medium a little bit more seriously. I bought a keyboard for five hundred dollars—it was one of those ones that had drums and electronic instruments, as well as a sequencer built in to compose songs. I hooked up with my friend Greg, this guy who I skateboarded with during lunch hour, and we started writing music.

Out of this came the rap group Organized Rhyme (OR), something I stuck with for a good five years. The group, at one point or another, consisted of Greg Campbell (aka MC Pin), Geordie Ferguson (aka DJ Signal), Bryan Boswell (aka DJ Law), and me, otherwise known as MC Bones. We were a funny white rap group from Ottawa, not exactly the prerequisite for show biz immortality. We were kind of like the Beastie Boys without the Brooklyn accents. We would go on stage and throw pita bread at the audience, string Christmas lights around the hall, and put laundry baskets on our heads. It was as much an absurd stage show as a music show, if not more.

But we did have songs. They contained extremely thought-out and calibrated rap lyrics like:

I lay more chicks than Mother Goose
Pass the O.J. cause I got juice

This was the late eighties, when rap was slowly moving from the fringe to the mainstream, and we started getting regular bookings. A guy from Atlanta came to hear us rap and wanted to record us. So our parents let us take off for New York to live in this guy's brother's studio and record songs for one summer. By doing so, I interrupted my so-called stand-up career and didn't go back to a comedy club for two or three years. Looking back, it wasn't a bad decision. With Organized Rhyme, there were no rules. In the comedy club world, there are people who think they know what they are doing or at least think they can tell you what to do. If I'd stayed in stand-up, I probably would have gotten better and better at telling jokes about breakfast cereal. I probably would not have gotten better at talking to people with meat on my head.

In any case, we went to New York, recorded songs, and nothing happened. No record deal, no stardom. We came back to Ottawa, kept doing shows, and finally did get a record deal with A&M Records in Canada. We had one Top Ten hit: "Check the OR." In case you missed it, it went like this:

MY VERSE FROM "CHECK THE O.R."

Check the O.R. Ya like it so far?

Smack ya back and ya deal with a deep scar

I will test ya from the west of ya

Now ya know that I'm better than the best of ya

I remove you, quicker than a Band-Aid, paid backstage

Then I'm gone like a renegade

And I don't delay, want the replay,

Like Sinatra, I got ya my way

I feel lowly, so I lay low

Never lonely, now that I clock dough

Receive honors, make ya goners

Break the deuce like Jimmy Connors

I make light of everyday establishment

With content, stickin' like Polident

But I paid my dues

I lay more chicks than Mother Goose

Pass the O.J. cause I got juice

Break the silence, and make the truce.

Yes, Yes, Ya'll . . . and ya don't stop

To the beat Ya'll . . . and ya don't dare stop

To the hip, hop, hibbe, hibbe dibbe hip hip hop

And ya don't dare stop—go off like a Canon

You're a copier, much sloppier so I'm gonna drop ya

Ya got a demo well I guess I'm gonna shop ya

Take a risk, like a disk, you're floppier

You misfit, meet the better man

I'm gonna razz you just like Letterman

Hip hop, not a weasel going pop, you don't stop

Check the O.R.

Check the O.R! Ya like it so far!

Check the O.R! Ya like it so far!

So that was our big single. The lyrics for most of the album were comprised of nonsensical metaphors and bizarre hip-hop references. Even so, we actually got nominated for a Juno Award (the Canadian equivalent of a Grammy), we did a few videos, we made the Top 10 Countdown in Canada, and everybody who cared about such stuff knew who we were. In case you don't know, a lot of Canadian music gets played in Canada but never makes it to the States. That's because of something called The Canadian Content Requirement: 33 percent of all music on Canadian radio must be Canadian in origin. We became big in Canada precisely because we were *from* Canada.

We were a white rap group from Ottawa, and we got a record deal, and all of a sudden we were hanging out in the black urban Toronto hip-hop scene. There was one time when we did a show at an underground Toronto club. We were the only white guys in there. We walked into this narrow, underground warehouse. People entered at one end, and the stage was at the opposite end. There was only one way out through the crowd, which wasn't a big deal going

MC Pin and MC Bones (that's Greg Campbell and me) posing in our fancy jackets with some cops. This was years before our record deal. We had jackets made and when we wore them we felt like a bad ass gang!

in because no one knew we were there yet. The Toronto rap scene took a little bit of offense to the fact that the first group who got a major label deal in Canada in years was a white rap group who wasn't even from Toronto. If you know anything about Canada, you know that people from Toronto think they are the center of Canada, when really they're a little bit off to the east.

The Toronto crowd knew us because our video had just been released and was in rotation on MuchMusic, Canada's version of MTV. There was a group that opened for us, and they actually went up on stage and did a song—an improvised free-style rap basically—which they called "Fuck the O.R." Our song, remember, was called "Check the O.R." Their point was obvious—the rap was full of salacious comments about our poseur status.

When that group finished, we came on. While we were doing our abbreviated show—maybe four songs, along with dancing around and making silly sounds—I looked out in the audience and saw something I had never seen before. There was a guy pointing a gun at me! It was like a shitty gun; it had tape on the handle and looked well used. This guy was dancing with the gun in one hand, raised in the air and pointed at me in sort of nonchalant fashion.

I had a decision to make. Keep rapping and pretend that I didn't care even though I was scared shitless or jump off the stage and walk through the entire audience. So we kept rapping. Fortunately, the guy decided not to shoot me. At

This was the CD jacket for our Organized Rhyme album on A&M Records in 1992.

one point someone grabbed the hood of my sweatshirt, pulled me into the audience, and pounded me a few times in the back of the head in the middle of the show. Then I got pulled back onstage by someone in my group, and we kept rapping.

At the end of the show, we walked through the crowd, and a good 50 percent of the people moved toward us. As we got hustled along, everybody wanted to get in a few swipes. We started running for the door, getting a healthy pummeling along the way. We took this send-off as a general statement about how our group was appreciated in the hardcore hip-hop community.

"SMALL TOWN BOY"

ONE DAY, IN THE HEYDAY OF "O.R."—I WAS MAYBE seventeen—we got a call from the University of Ottawa college radio station to come down and appear on their middle-of-the-night hip-hop music show. The station didn't even have a real FM license, just a "cable TV" hookup, which meant it reached about six people who knew what that meant. Anyway, after we did this show, the man in charge of the station, Bob McCarthy, asked us if we'd like to help out around the station. I jumped at the chance—it seemed like a cool place to work.

I kept bugging Bob McCarthy about filling in on one of their shows, and a few months later, he had an opening—2 a.m. until 6 a.m. on Christmas Eve. One show. Audience for time slot: zero. I got excited. I checked out a lot of books from the library—books on the history of cheese, the art of bass fishing, whatever sounded stupid and obscure—and read passages on the air. I played music, took phone calls, and generally just acted like an idiot. I had a great time, essentially doing a four-hour radio show for the three or four friends who promised to tune in.

As luck would have it, shortly thereafter, the host of the hip-hop show got fired, and given my recent success with fishing and cheese, I was asked to take over, along with another guy from the rap group. So all of a sudden I had my own show, Fridays, midnight till 2 a.m. The station even got an FM license, going from five to twenty-five listeners.

The show was billed as an underground rap music show, but I kept interrupting the latest N.W.A. release to talk nonsense. My friend soon got bored and decided he'd rather spend his Friday nights partying, so I had the mike to myself. I started playing fewer and fewer songs and taking more calls and talking more until one Friday night I played no music at all. Bob McCarthy, of course, noticed this and thought it was fine as long as I changed the name of the show. So I changed it to "The Midnight Caller."

Besides giving me my first "broadcast exposure," the radio show was life changing in one other way. It's where I met Glenn Humplik, my future co-host—the man we now refer to as "Hollywood Humplik." He hosted the 2 a.m. till 6 a.m. Friday night show, playing a weird mix of experimental and electronic music. He'd take three or four CDs like Kraftwerk and Brian Eno and a bunch of sound effects CDs and play them at the same time. I started to stick around and see what he was up to, and he started to come in early to help me out. A lifelong friendship was born.

The thing about the radio show was that there were no rules. There was no manager of the comedy club telling me how to write a joke. There was no comedy workshop. It was me at a radio station making up shit and then, later on, doing the same thing at a community TV station. It's the very opposite of going to school or learning at the feet of a master. You are the sole judge of what's funny and what sucks. We had no comedy authority coming in and saying, "No, you don't do it like that. You do it like this." And I think ultimately we ended up creating something that was more original than I could have done otherwise.

Given free reign, it wasn't long before we were putting drunk people on the air, calling up people selling dough-makers or snowmobiles on a feature called "Crazy, Crazy Classifieds," and pontificating about hamsters for an hour. One night I decided to fuck with the few rap listeners still tuning in and played one song, "Small Town Boy" by a group called Bronski Beat, for two hours straight. If you remember the song, you know it's the kind of fey, heartsick, hook-heavy ballad that would drive a hardcore rapper up the wall. That was the idea.

I would play the song, then come on and say, "That was Big Daddy Kane and now here's Public Enemy with 'Don't Believe the Hype,' " and play "Small Town Boy" again. Some suburban white kid feigning a really bad Compton accent would call up and say, "This is for real, yo, someone is messin' with your signal, ya know what I'm sayin? 'Cuz they keep playing this same shit over and over G . . . youknowwhatImsayin'?" I'd promise to get right on it and then play the same shit again.

We started fooling around with cell phones, which were then brand new. I'd leave the station, Glenn would run the board, and I'd drive around Ottawa taking calls and hosting the show. I'd say, "Hey, I'm at the corner of Bank and Lisgar right now, come and follow me." One night we had a snake of twenty-five cars roaming the city. We'd drive by the house of the Prime Minister of Canada and honk our horns. A caller would say, "Hey, come by my house," and twenty-five cars would pull up in front of the guy's house, horns a'blazing, and wake up the whole block.

It sounds silly, and easy. But here's something to consider, and as I write this it amazes me how quickly the world changes. Back in those days, nobody had a cell phone. When I say nobody, I mean NOBODY! We had access to one because we worked at a radio station and they kept it locked up in a cabinet, in a locked office. It was literally about the size of two VHS videocassettes, not including the two-foot-long antennae. What made these live segments so innovative at the time was that people listening could hardly understand how we were doing it. How were we in a car and talking on the radio? How was this possible? They would tune in on their car radios and drive around the city trying to find us, somewhat confused, but laughing at the ridiculousness of the whole thing. It sounds silly because now every twelve-year-old girl has a cell phone. But I can actually remember the time when I would take this phone out of the station and call my friends from a restaurant, or the bus, just because it was weird and amazing that I could! "Hey, guys, you won't believe where I am right now! I'm calling from my car! I actually have a cell-u-lar tel-e-phone!"

Sometimes on the radio we would play on-the-air hide-and-seek with the big cell phone. I would don a leprechaun outfit and hide in a particular forest and do the whole show under a bush. Fifty kids with headsets and flashlights would be wandering around these woods, trying to locate the leprechaun. I'd whisper into the cell phone clues like "You are about fourteen, have a backpack and a brown hat, and are about four feet from me. I'm behind the bush." That one kid would recognize himself being described on the air, turn, make eye contact, and then I'd scamper off.

On a whim one night, I invited anyone listening to join me in a game of soccer in front of the Parliament Buildings at 2 a.m. This is the equivalent of the Capital Building in Washington, D.C., as Ottawa is the capital of Canada. Thirty or forty kids showed up, and we played until five in the morning. Indicative of how ridiculously sane everything is in Canada, the police not only let us play on the front lawn of our national government, they actually turned on the lights.

Eventually I started doing prerecorded bits for the show and editing them into actual material. I'd call up a shipping company and ask about shipping my dead brother to Saskatchewan or do man-on-the-street interviews with a hand-held mike and tape recorder. I did the radio show for almost eight years, and in every way it was the precursor and testing ground for the original cable television show.

THE PINEAPPLE PITCH

WHILE I WAS STUDYING TELEVISION BROADCASTING at Algonquin Community College, I had to learn how to write a pitch for selling an idea for a TV show. Two friends from school, Darcy Datoni and Trevor Cavanaugh, and I decided to write up a pitch for a TV version of my radio show, which everyone in Ottawa listened to. Okay, not everyone, but everyone I knew.

We sent the "pitch" to the three head honchos of Rogers Cable, the local cable outlet, to get on their public access channel, Community 22. Public access in Canada at the time was an all-volunteer affair, but there were staff producers to help you, and the equipment was pretty good. Until we came along, the big community access shows were along the lines of *Portuguese Connection, The Mayor's Hotline,* and, for the German-speaking community, *Deutsches Panorama.* There was no real entertainment programming, unless, of course, you were Portuguese or Deutsch.

I wanted our proposal to stand out, so I sent each of the Rogers executives—Ray Scaff, Collette Watson, and Karen Pickles—a pineapple with my picture pinned to it and a note that said, "Hope you enjoy your pineapple. Please let me do this show!" They must have liked pineapple because they called back and said we could do four episodes. The rap group and the radio show helped, but I think the real reason we got the nod was because we were TV students and probably wouldn't break the equipment.

11 P.M., THURSDAY NIGHT

ONE OF THE FIRST THINGS I DID WAS CONTACT GLENN. We were getting pizza one night, and I said, "Listen, man,"—this is kind of a sappy moment—I said, "Listen, man, I'd like you to be my Ed McMahon guy on the show." It was a major turning point in our relationship. Up to then we weren't really a team. He helped on my radio show, but he had his own radio show, too. I wasn't really sure he would do it, but he said, "Yeah, yeah, that sounds like fun."

Later on, after we had shot a bunch of street segments but hadn't gone on

Trevor Cavanaugh and Darcy Datoni, wiped out
after working all week on the cable show.

the air yet, Glenn and I were sitting having a beer, and he got serious with me for I think the first time. He sort of looked at me and said, "You know, man, I think this is going to be something." It was a big moment, actually. Someone else believed in the thing. Until then it was just me and a couple of friends from high school. Glenn was the first person to think that this could potentially turn into something bigger than Rogers Community 22.

That first show was formatted pretty much like many of the later Tom Green shows. The audience was a lot smaller (maybe fifty kids who were fans of the radio show), there was a desk, and there was Glenn Humplik sitting beside me. We would have self-contained field bits, interview people, and mess with the audience. The big difference between now and then is that even more so than now, we had no idea what we were doing.

Being in Ottawa, there were no celebrities to interview, so we would book people off the street and out of the phone book. Some genuinely unbalanced homeless guy would come on and talk about his life as a vampire. Or we would book a ceiling-fan salesman, and I would ask him ridiculously overly researched questions like "So the cylindrical magnetic head on that ceiling fan, is that made by seven or eight quanders?" He would be completely confused by my arcane knowledge of his business, and that was the laugh.

One of the first bits we did on that first show was shot in the goofy little studio we built. We got our tiny production budget and went to the lumberyard and bought some stucco-looking wood, painted it green, and built in a window. We had stuff hanging upside down from the ceiling, like an upside-down lamp and a goldfish bowl with actual fish. This was extremely creative for public access television. *Portuguese Connection* had a pole lamp and a blank wall.

Here's the bit: I sat at a dinner table with a big chunk of raw pork chops in front of me. I had rigged a pulley system so that there were different pieces of chicken and beef that would lower behind my head and then raise up again. The table had a quaint French-restaurant look with a tablecloth and candlestick holders, loaned to the show by Darcy's wife. Basically the bit was that I would start to eat the raw meat, then go into a bit of a seizure, then slam my fist into the meat and scream "MEAT!!!!" at the top of my lungs. And as I am doing this, the chicken lowers behind me, and then I flip the table over and make some silly faces in the camera. That was the bit. Me screaming about meat.

Preparing for a show on the set for Rogers Community 22.

The only problem was, I went a little too crazy and broke the candlestick holders, and both Darcy and his wife got really mad. Other than that, it was pretty funny. It wasn't really clever storytelling. It was more like a shocking bumper. It was a thirty-second bumper of me screaming about meat with chicken and beef being lowered behind me.

For some reason we were on this meat kick. In the next bit we shot that day, I took some pork chops and taped them to my head, and we called this "character" Meat Head. I went to downtown Ottawa, in the same way that Phil and I used to go with our skateboards, and walked around and asked mundane questions about average man-on-the-street subjects without acknowledging the meat on my head. No one knew who I was, and I never broke a smile. People would laugh, some would say something, some would just look at me with a weird look, and some would walk away. So that was the first real bit we shot where we got strange reactions from people.

On that same day we paid a visit to the Carlton University swimming pool, which had a high diving board. We did a bit called "Hockey Guy," where I put on full hockey equipment, including skates, and I just walked into the Carlton University pool and went up to the high diving board while there was a preschool swimming class going on and jumped in with full hockey equipment and skates. That was Hockey Guy.

One of the more popular bits we came up with that first show was called "Rooftop Sing-Songs." I would climb up to the roof of this five-story parking garage downtown. I would spot people on the street below and start shouting at them with a megaphone, but I wouldn't really shout—I would sing an improvised song about what they were wearing or what they were doing. If a girl, say, was walking down the street in white pants, I would embarrass her by singing, "White pants, white pants, I am wearing white pants." Everyone would hear the goofy little song, look at her, and laugh. It could be anything: "I've got a plastic bag in my hand, I've got a plastic bag, plastic bag, plastic bag." Or if a couple walked by: "We're holding hands, we're holding hands!"

Basically, we were just razzing people for a laugh. It was definitely inspired by Letterman yelling out of 30 Rockefeller Center with a megaphone. Our twist is that I would only sing, which made it sillier, and I was doing it in Ottawa. Ottawa is actually a small city by American standards, and very staid, and there aren't a lot of places where people walk, so the downtown area became our stalking ground. We were essentially stalking people in downtown Ottawa three or four times a week. There were local shop owners who got sick of us fast. "Oh, there's that goof again with his megaphone and his meat on his head." But for a long time we could always find someone who didn't know who we were or what we were up to. Being recognized was not a problem for years.

"IT WAS SORT OF A EUREKA MOMENT"

WE WERE DOING AN HOUR SHOW EVERY WEEK, AND a lot of it consisted of field pieces like "Meat Head," "Hockey Guy," and "Rooftop Sing-Songs." We knew we needed something else, something that didn't involve putting tinfoil on my head or taping baguettes to my ears. And what that something was was sort of a Eureka moment. It came about almost by accident, like bumping into someone on the street, and getting a little bit of your chocolate in that person's curiously opened jar of peanut butter and instantly hitting upon the Reese's Peanut Butter Cup revolution.

It was three o'clock in the morning on a Wednesday night, the night before the show aired. We had nothing to put on the show the next night. We had just finished shooting a bit downtown, probably just me running around screaming at people and making silly faces at the side of the road or something like that. We were packing up, and I was getting dropped off at my house by my friend and cameraman Darcy, when I thought, Hey, why don't we go wake up my parents? And he said that seemed kind of crazy, given that they had to go to work the next morning. And I said true, but then again it might be kind of funny to see what happens, to see what they might do.

Darcy just so happened to have in his car—and I don't want this to be a reflection of the type of people I hung out with—a *Bon Jovi Live from New Jersey* videocassette. I suggested, "Hey, wouldn't it be funny to go and try to get my parents to come downstairs and watch *Bon Jovi Live from New Jersey* with me at three in the morning?" So that was the premise of our bit. It wasn't really thought out, but then again, neither was me slamming my fist into a side of beef on stage and yelling "MEAT!" And by this point we were starting to learn that some of the best video was the stuff that hadn't been overly planned.

We wandered into the house with our camera and a big sun gun, which is an extremely bright light that was necessary for shooting video in the dark at that time. We walked into the bedroom, flipped on the sun gun, and woke up the folks for a little Bon Jovi. They were in shock. My mother said, "Oh, Tom, turn the camera off and get out of here." My dad made a couple of jokes. Under no circumstances would they get out of bed to watch a Bon Jovi video. Basically the tape was my mother looking very tired with a sun gun shining in her face.

We played it on the show the next night, and it got a huge laugh. It got the strongest reaction of any bit on the show and almost any bit on any show up to then. It was a different type of reaction, one that went beyond a joke. People would come up to us on the street and say stuff like, "If I ever did that to my parents, they would kill me," or, conversely, "I'd kill my kid if he ever did that to me." We had hit upon something that crossed generational lines—razzing your parents.

"MAYBE IT'S AN EGGBEATER"

THE STUFF WE WERE DOING ON ROGERS CABLE, including busting into my parents' bedroom, was far more conservative than anything we ever did later on the Canadian Comedy Network or MTV. When we finally got our shot on the Canadian Comedy Network, we had complete creative control, for possibly the only time, and that's when the more shocking stuff started popping up. We did few things on Community 22 that were truly controversial except for one bit involving my grandmother and a briefcase full of vibrators. We consider this one of our classics. It was probably the first time we ever experimented with doing anything phallic or sexual on the show. Over the years we would "advance" to things like interviewing people with dildo microphones or painting lesbian love scenes on the hood of my parents' car. But early on, we thought that was out of bounds. Until we thought of my grandma.

The joke starts with Derek and I standing in the front doorway of my house with my grandmother. Derek, in a rare on-camera appearance, has a briefcase called The Briefcase. He sets it down to shake my grandmother's hand and leaves, forgetting to retrieve the briefcase. And then I say, "Oh, look, Grandma, Derek forgot his briefcase." We take it out into the kitchen, and all the vibrators inside are on and purring. There are about six of them in there, and you can hear them rattling away. I say, "Oh, it sounds like there is something in there." Then my grandmother says, "Oh, maybe we should open it and see what it is." She is kind of performing a little for the camera, but in a cute, grandmotherly sort of way. We open it up, and I say, "Well, what are those things, Grandma?" Her reply, now completely genuine: "Oh, I don't quite know what those are."

And the bit is on.

Next, I would say, "Well, maybe it is an eggbeater." So we cut to us using a vibrator to beat some eggs. "Nope, it's not an eggbeater; maybe they are earrings." We'd then cut to my grandmother trying them on as earrings. They are vibrating and attached to my grandmother's ears with some tape or something like that. "Nope, they're not earrings, that's for sure."

"Okay," I go on, "so maybe it's a nice set of bread rollers." So you'd see us trying to knead dough with them. "No, not bread rollers." And then there's this candy called Fun Dip. It's basically little packets of sugar you dip a candy stick into and lick. So everyone watching knew what was coming when I said, "Well, maybe it is for eating Fun Dip." Cut to a shot of my grandmother dipping a vibrator into a packet of Fun Dip sugar and then sticking it into her mouth.

As you're watching it, you're thinking, "No, surely they aren't going there," and we do. It was crazy enough with the eggbeater, now the thing is going into her mouth. Being that it was on and vibrating, my grandmother got worried. "Oh, I might get electrocuted," she said, and turned it off. The bit ended with her genuinely never knowing what these things were, and in a cute sort of way, that made the whole sick joke all right.

We were clearly entering new territory here.

As I said, this was the first time we ever did vibrator humor. It killed for the audience, and we started to realize that playing with some of the social taboos of sex was just another way to get a laugh. This of course has been going on forever in the annals of humor, but we were amateurs and just developing the nerve to push things to, or beyond, the limits of conventional taste.

The night "Granny & The Vibrators" aired on Rogers Cable, we knew my parents would definitely not appreciate the joke and we would have a serious problem. At this point, my parents, despite the fact we were waking them up in the middle of the night, were very supportive of what I was doing. They didn't like me doing it to them, but they liked the show. They got it. They tuned in every week, Thursday night, eleven until midnight, or they would tape it and watch it the next day after work.

In this instance, they didn't watch the show the night it aired but planned to watch it on tape the day after. Before they got to the tape, I got to it and futzed it so it looked like the tape malfunctioned and didn't record the show. They were disappointed. I was elated. This is great, I thought. Now they are never going to catch Granny sticking that vibrator in her mouth. Of course I knew that when we went into our next down period, we would rerun all of the shows, but I figured I'd worry about that when the time came.

One night during the hiatus I got a call from Ray Hagel, the community producer of the Rogers show and a longtime friend, cameraman, and associate.

He had just found out that the vibrator show was rerunning that night! This was about an hour or so before it would hit the air, and of course I freaked. It seemed my parents had some time off and they weren't working the next day. Under the circumstances, they would undoubtedly stay up to watch the show and see my mother's mother handling a briefcase full of sexual aids. They would kill me the moment they did.

Eleven o'clock rolled around, and there they were, watching the beginning of the show in their bedroom. There was nothing I could do about that. I called up Ray and got the rundown of the show. I found out exactly the minute that the offending piece aired and then went downstairs. It turned out the vibrator piece came on the show at around eleven-fifteen, and about a minute before the piece came on, I was watching on the TV downstairs. Just as I was about to introduce the piece on the show, I ran into the laundry room and shut the power off to the entire house.

Our house wasn't enormous. I could hear the sound of the power shutting down and the TV going off. My brother was in his room upstairs already asleep. I wondered if my parents would react. They were in bed, assuming, I desperately hoped, that this was just a regular power outage. I waited three minutes, listening. There wasn't a sound. I felt like I was in a submarine movie, sitting in the dark in silence, crouched in the basement by the laundry machine, waiting quietly for a depth charge to explode around me. More silence, and I waited, and then turned the power back on.

When I crept back up the stairs, my parents were asleep. The power had failed and they just went to bed. They weren't watching the show anymore. They hadn't seen the bit. I was safe.

Cut to three years later, after we'd been on free cable for years and were finally picked up by the national Comedy Network. We picked some of our favorite bits from the Rogers shows to air nationally. These included the time I painted my parents' house plaid, a couple of late-night attacks on my parents' bedroom, and "Granny & The Vibrators." At this point it had been three years since we had done it, and I felt like the sting of it was gone and so I wasn't afraid of my parents' response. We had done some shocking things to my parents in the interim. So, we put it on the air nationally, and not only did my parents see it for the first time, but my grandmother saw it with my mother's sister

On an early field shoot for Rogers 22 with Darcy Datoni (behind me, to the left) and Ray Hagel (right up front).

and family in small-town Barrie, Ontario. All hell broke loose. My grand-mother genuinely did not know what the vibrators were when she was doing the bit. She found out that night.

Once my mom's sister filled her in, she was livid. I believe that my eighty-year-old grandmother may have contacted a lawyer. It was one of maybe three moments in the history of the show where I actually felt that we had gone a lit-tle too far. My mother, in particular, was really, really upset. It is a funny energy that gets created when you do something like that because, despite the hard feelings, it was an objectively funny bit. We aired it again on MTV, so we really didn't learn a lesson from it. Because it was a great bit. It was one of those things that had to air, and no one really did get hurt by it or anything like that. Or so I told myself.

That was the only time we seriously pranked my grandmother. But with my parents, we were just getting started.

3.

RICHARD AND MARY JANE

—

"**I** mean, how do you stop it? What do you do? Change the locks? This wouldn't have stopped Tom. He just knew he could get away with it because we're his parents and we love him and what can you do? Call the police? Have you ever tried to stop Tom from doing something he wants to do? It's impossible."

—Mary Jane Green

FOR THE ALMOST FOUR YEARS WE DID THE ORIGINAL *Tom Green Show* on Rogers Community Cable in Ottawa, we did literally thousands of bits both inside and outside the studio. We had an hour to fill every week and virtually no money to do anything extravagant, so we had to improvise. In a way it was like rap music—we had to work with very little equipment or other resources to make something distinctive. Early rappers did it with just two turntables and a microphone. We did it with a video camera, a few cheap props, and the reality around us. And given this opportunity to try things and fail, over and over again, and not have to conform to someone else's idea of what's funny or what's inside or outside the bounds of taste, we eventually figured out what we were doing and discovered bits that worked.

We learned, for instance, that it wasn't the prank that was most important—it was the way people *reacted* to the prank. What I was doing, whether it was walking around the street with meat on my head or shouting at people from a rooftop, was premeditated—how regular people responded to these antics was spontaneous and unpredictable. If their reactions seemed canned or pro forma, the bit was a failure, no matter how funny we thought the action itself was. If we couldn't do something to jar people out of their routine and do or say something real and unexpected, then we weren't doing our job.

Which is why waking up my parents became such a staple in our comedy arsenal. When you wake someone up from a dead sleep, they are disoriented, dazed, and surprised. They are not necessarily firing on all cylinders and are prone to say what they really feel, without censoring themselves. And everyone can relate to the experience. We all hate to get woken up, especially by our son and his video camera.

But I think there was something bigger going on with what we were doing. I felt that we were on the cusp of something and would constantly annoy anyone who would listen to my theories. We were young and at the beginning of a new generation—the Internet generation, or Generation Y, or whatever you want to call it. We were growing up in a much different world than our parents. The world had changed, but TV hadn't.

When we turned on television, which was as common as breathing, it all looked the same. Sitcoms were still shot in the same format as *The Honeymooners* and *I Love Lucy*. Talk shows looked exactly like the original *Steve Allen Tonight Show*. All of these shows had originally been shot this way because of the limits of technology. All they had were huge cameras that needed massive lighting and cumbersome boom mikes for sound. Sitcoms became what television was—a silly little play on a couch in a living room in front of a studio audience. That's all they could do.

But that's not all *we* could do. Things had changed. We had tiny, handheld video cameras that almost anyone could both use and afford, something unimaginable to my parent's generation. While we were using this new, highly accessible hardware to run around shooting our little cable show on the streets of Ottawa, we'd often wonder why other shows, real shows, weren't doing the same. Why didn't they ever walk out of the studio on *Saturday Night Live*? As cutting edge as that show had been in the seventies, why were they still shooting it in exactly the same way that they always had?

Surrounded by all these new consumer electronics, our generation was naturally more technically astute than the previous one. While our parents were taking typing courses in school, we were learning computers. We were surfing the Internet. We were comfortable with technology. We'd watched many of the current shows, and, subliminally at least, we saw something that felt antiquated. We loved them when the jokes and storytelling were good, but we were aware of technical, and creative, possibilities that they didn't exploit. When kids began to see us running around on the street shooting with what appeared to be a simple home camera, they immediately got it. In fact, they could see themselves doing it, with their own video equipment. It was both new and accessible. They would watch the show, and it made the hurdles of making television shrink dramatically. They could relate to someone their age using video to skateboard, poke it in people's faces, and goof on their parents. This had the stamp of their generation's television—their reality, their humor, their style—and it was the technology that made it possible. Now, of course, television is full of "reality" TV, whatever that means. The beast is out of the bag.

From almost the very beginning, our little cable show got noticed not just by kids, but also by the local press. This really helped us survive. In fact a local CBC entertainer reporter named Ken Rockburn just happened to catch our very first show and literally called the next day to do a piece on us for his show, *Rockburn and Company*. This was unheard of for a public access cable show. *Portuguese Connection*, eat your heart out. This kind of publicity was a big reason, maybe the biggest reason, why Rogers Cable allowed us to keep doing the show.

> *"Bizarre Green comedy grabs late-night cable slot."*
> —ALGONQUIN TIMES

> *"He's crazy, kooky, catchy and very, very giddy.*
> *He's Ottawa's very own TV oddball."*
> —OTTAWA CITIZEN

*"Tom Green is: a) deranged; b) funny;
c) agitated by car horns; d) all of the above."*

—OTTAWA X PRESS

Every time an article would appear about the show, maybe every three or four months, it always featured the stuff I did to my parents. It struck a nerve and crossed generations. It was never salacious, at least not during this free-cable period, or mean, or even embarrassing. The bits played with that love-hate relationship we all have with our parents. "How far will he go?" "How far will they let him go?" The parents in the audience were laughing and saying to their kids, "Don't even think about it!" while their own kids were laughing and mumbling, "Go further, go further."

"MOM, YOU DON'T LIKE FRENCH PEOPLE, DO YOU?"

MY TV ENCOUNTERS WITH MY PARENTS WERE REALLY just a continuation of my earliest inclinations. As I mentioned, for whatever reason, mental or genetic, I was a hyped-up prankster since the age of six. And since they were the first people I knew, they were the first people I annoyed. I still annoy them. Now I just do it professionally.

My father, Richard, was a tank commander in the Canadian military. He was in charge of the tank. (Bada bing!) Actually he saw duty in Germany and Vietnam, and when I was a kid, we moved to a new army base every six or seven months. My father's father was also a career colonel in the military, so you can see what an initial disappointment I was. They fought wars so that I could invade their bedroom with, for example, Highland dancers at three in the morning.

The truth is, my father was a bit of a card himself. Once while stationed in Germany, he got hit by a tank in his MG while driving home from a late night of gallivanting, and there was rumor that he once threw a kind of dummy hand grenade, called a flash bomb, into a mess hall just to watch his comrades run for their lives.

Dad and me.

My mother, Mary Jane, was a schoolteacher from Barrie, Ontario, when she met her husband, the soldier. When he retired from commanding tanks, we moved to Ottawa, where they both worked, and I became a chronically poor student. My so-called academic record was a huge concern to both of them. In fact, I think it became the main objective in my father's life to discipline me into getting good grades and develop a respectable work ethic. Every 56 on a biology exam would send him into orbit. His explanation was a time-honored one: I was lazy. Every summer he would wake me up at six in the morning and drop me off at the student employment center to get a job. I got the jobs—landscaping, telemarketing, carpenter's helper, you name it—but I never got the point. I'd quit out of boredom after two weeks, and the routine would start all over again—my dad rousting me out of bed at dawn, me fighting him all the way, down to the student employment center, bad job, back to bed.

As much as I frustrated my parents with my lousy schoolwork and annoyed them with my constant urge to act up, they came to realize by the time I was in high school that I wasn't a complete write-off. It was unsettling to them that I spent virtually all of my waking time going down to Yuk-Yuk's or making up silly rap songs, but I wasn't getting high on drugs or knocking over candy stores. They could see I was motivated to do something that vaguely had something to do with entertainment. Actually, I was more than motivated. I was obsessed.

By the time I started waking them up to listen to *Bon Jovi Live*, they were shocked but not surprised. The truth is, my relationship with my parents had always been about pushing buttons. Long before the TV show, for instance, I had a girlfriend over for a very special Christmas dinner, the kind my mom loved—candles, china, and plum pudding. My impulse was to upset this idyllic tableau, not in a mean way, just in a

Me and Mom.

conversationally inappropriate way. So, knowing my girlfriend was French Canadian, and her parents were ardent Quebec separatists, I broke the ice with, "Mom, you don't like French people, do you?" My girlfriend knew I was joking, but my mom wasn't sure, so she'd say, "Oh, that's not true, Tom." Back I came, "But you said the other day," and would make up some anti-French dig she hadn't made, and the verbal jousting would begin. Or I would say something like "Dad, why did you pour water on me at six this morning?" in front of my friends, and my mom would deny it, then my dad would admit it, and it would be both funny and embarrassing at the same time.

So putting my parents on TV in unrehearsed and inappropriate situations was just a heightening of our button-pushing dynamic. But it came with a twist, a catch-22. They were on TV, they were often funny in their response, and then they'd turn around and there would be an article in the local newspaper about them. I'd say, "Hey, look at this article and the show's really working and one day I'll get a network show and you're a big part of it."

I think I infected them with my insane passion for this silliness. They didn't think there was any realistic possibility that barging into their bedroom would turn into a career, and they hated every minute of the actual stunt, but they knew they were helping me out in some way, and there was the nice piece in the newspaper. They were probably largely bewildered. And probably still are.

This is a good point to mention my younger brother, Joe. People often ask me why my brother has hardly appeared on the show. He has, by happenstance, but he is rarely featured. My brother was born with a disability. Early on doctors thought that he might never walk. At the age of four he had to undergo major surgery and have a shunt inserted in his head to drain a buildup of excess fluids from his brain. The result is that he has a learning disability that is quite serious and was always of major concern to my parents. Joe was very slow to develop, and I never felt comfortable playing jokes on him.

On the other hand, my brother gets the jokes. He is a funny guy who now works at a hardware store in Canada. He lives alone in an apartment in Ottawa and supports himself through his work and with government assistance. I think my parents are very relieved, and proud, that he has learned to function on his own.

This year, in a bizarre incident, my brother saw smoke coming from a house on his delivery route. He and his coworker pulled over and alerted the occupants who were downstairs. The house completely burned, and amazingly they saved these people's lives. He was granted a Governor General's award at City Hall, the Canadian equivalent of a presidential citation, complete with a speech by the mayor in front of the entire city council. Good going, Joe!

My younger brother, Joe, my dad, and me.

As I was growing up, the cause of my brother's disability was a big mystery.
My parents only recently determined its origin. As I mentioned, my father was
a captain in the Canadian military. A short time after I was born, in February
1973, my father was deployed, with the Canadian Military, as part of the ICCS
(International Commission of Control and Supervision). Its job was to monitor
the compliance of four parties (North Vietnamese Army, South Vietnamese
Army, the Viet Cong, and the Americans) to the cease-fire agreement that
ended U.S. involvement in the Vietnamese war. He was there to observe and report on violations of that agreement. My dad was deployed with another Canadian captain to a provincial capital called Tam Ky, situated about an hour's
drive south of Da Nang. His team consisted of Polish, Hungarian, Indonesian,
and Canadian representatives. When a violation took place, such as a mortar
attack on a South Vietnamese position, they would all go to the site and inves-
tigate. Normally the Communists from Poland and Hungry saw things differ-
ently from the Canadians and the Indonesians, so agreement was next to

impossible. Nevertheless, they did their best to keep the warring parties apart, although two years later the North Vietnamese invaded again and took over the whole country.

While my father was in Tam Ky, he was lodged in a small fort and ate Vietnamese food and drank the local water and beer. His Vietnamese friends were impressed that my father, unlike most foreigners, would eat anything they provided. If they served boiled duck eggs, complete with a partially developed baby duck and a fishy liquid, he'd eat it with gusto. Little did he know that he was probably ingesting Agent Orange, which would later lead to birth defects in my brother, Joe.

My dad returned to Canada, and Joe was born in May 1974. At about six months of age, my parents discovered that Joe had developmental difficulties. Later, doctors pinpointed a mild form of hydrocephalus and other problems that caused him to have motor and developmental delays. It was through the Internet that they more recently learned that a high percentage of Vietnamese children, as well as the children of U.S. Vietnam veterans, were born with similar neural tube difficulties.

I think that in many ways my brother's situation may have had an impact on who I've become. I'm sure that my parents' constant concern about him inspired me to act out at a young age. When I watch my two dogs, Annie and Steve, I see a comparison. Whenever Annie gets a little too much attention, Steve starts to act out and misbehave. Perhaps that was me. I was Steve trying to get my parents' attention when so much of it was focused on my brother. With this happening in my house for as long as I can remember, it eventually shaped me into an attention-seeking nut! But, seriously, it may be true or it may have had no impact on me whatsoever. Who can really say for sure?

UPPING THE ANTE

BACK TO RICHARD AND MARY JANE—THE SECOND parent bit we came up with involved just my dad. While my mother was out of town, we woke up my dad with a roomful of beautiful models dancing around his bed. It was funny—my dad got right into it—but we learned a few things. One, don't give people lines to say in these situations—it always comes out looking wooden or staged and detracts from the moment. Two, we realized that my dad was less embarrassed or annoyed when my mother wasn't around. He was more prone to play to the camera. Together, they tended to act more naturally, which often meant getting upset or acting rashly.

My friend and long-time creative collaborator Derek Harvie had a lot to do with expanding the parent bits. Derek is my oldest friend—we've known each other since grade three. He was off at college in another city when the cable show began. When he came back to Ottawa to work with us, suddenly the show got a little darker. I supplied the silly, absurd factor, and Derek brought a more cynical and at times grosser edge to the comedy. He still does. Along with Glenn, Derek has been along for the whole ride, right up to the latest talk show.

It was Derek who thought up the idea of busting in on my parents with a Highland dancer and a bagpiper. The Highland dancer was actually Derek's sister, Amber. My mother did not react by getting up and dancing a jig with Amber. Instead she got into a shoving match with the bagpiper. She was on one side of the door, trying to keep him out, and he was on the other side, piping and pushing at the same time. The noise of the bagpipes made it seem like something out of a Marx Brothers movie.

With Derek around, the ante kept going up. One night I woke up my parents with fire extinguishers screaming that the house was on fire. On another occasion, I placed a bloody cow's head between them and roused them to tell them that they just got a message from Don Corleone. My mother really hated that one. At first she laughed, thinking the blood was fake, but when she realized that it wasn't, she freaked.

Of course they wanted me to stop and I would, for a week or two, then they would let down their guard, and I'd hit them with the next prank. It got to the point where one day they said, "Listen, we are going to do something like sue you if you don't stop this nonsense," and then I pleaded with them, "But, Mommmm, you can't. This is the best part of the show. Everybody loves you guys. This is what I want to do with my life. I want to be a talk show host. I want to sell this stuff, and this is the best stuff. I'm not going to come in and burn the house down. People love you, you're great on camera, Dad is hilarious, he always throws something back at me. I know it's a little uncomfortable, but it's great—come on. . . ."

The upshot was, they didn't sue and I didn't stop.

Those were very exciting times working at Rogers Cable 22. It was the beginning, so there were no rules and no structure. I was figuring out the comedy as I was making it. At college I had learned to edit video, so that's what I did. Every day after school I would drive out to Rogers Cable and begin the nightly process of editing. I was usually there in the station alone until two or three in the morning. This went on for three or four years. I think the fact that I was editing the pieces myself actually helped with the process of understanding. Sitting in an editing room, staring at countless hours of footage looking for the right shot, helped me hone my ideas of what we were getting and not getting in the field.

Everyone working on the show was a volunteer. There were no professionals there to guide us and tell us how TV was typically made. Floundering around on our own, we'd come up with some strange stuff. One bit, for instance, was called "Wooden Boys." I painted pictures of small cartoon boys on a piece of thin plywood. Then with a skill saw I cut out each of these colorful boys and nailed them to a stick. We then walked around downtown and creepily asked people if they would like to "touch my boys." That was basically the bit. It was weird.

Another character we invented was called "The Architect." This had nothing to do with architecture per se: I just happened to be wearing a construction hat in these pieces. The Architect had a surreal, glazed-over look and talked in a monotone voice. I would walk around in this "costume" (a hat) and talk about random things, like snakes, or UFOs, or pay phones, or lamp posts. Some of these pieces were funny, some were not, but they were always bizarre. I think in some ways we were mocking the conventions of typical TV storytelling by telling no story at all. Rambling on about nothing was our own subliminal "fuck you" to the media establishment. Not everybody would get it, but we did, and we didn't always care about anybody else.

We had regular bits that were more accessible to the average viewer, like a recurring piece called Celebrity Watching. Being that it was bitter cold in Canada in the winter, Trevor and I found a heated entrance to the Rideau Center Shopping Mall. Because we couldn't shoot inside the mall, we would wait like hunters in a duck blind and approach people walking past who looked in some way similar to a celebrity. We would accost them like eager fans, but not say their names. As we smothered these baffled pedestrians with leading yet stalkerlike questions, the audience would try to guess along as to who these people were supposed to be. It was kind of a game. In the end, the name of the celebrity would get keyed up on the screen. Some of our favorite "celebrities" we encountered: Charles Manson, The Menendez Brothers, Phil Donohue, Lou Reed, Tonya Harding, Bill Gates, Burt Reynolds, Juan Valdez, and, in an eerily prophetic moment in 1994, Drew Barrymore.

"THE CAR IS GONE, THE CAR IS *GONE*"

THE SINGLE MOST TALKED-ABOUT SEGMENT I EVER did with my parents occurred about three years into the community cable show. During a summer hiatus from the show, I pitched the idea of a national version to the CBC, one of Canada's largest TV networks, and they offered me five thousand dollars to write up a detailed treatment. I approached a friend of mine to help, and he convinced me to spend the money to actually make a pilot show. He would throw in the camera and editing equipment and help run interference with the network. I jumped at the chance.

I knew I had to do something extravagant for this one shot at the network. My parents were about to go away for an extended canoe trip to Algonquin Park in northern Ontario, and I knew we'd have the whole house at our disposal. My thought was, Hey, why don't I paint the whole house while they're gone, like the thoughtful son I am, and see the look on their faces when they come home?

This was a big event by our standards. We wanted to cover it from beginning to end and edit it into a real story. I began by interviewing my parents before they left about watering the plants, etc. When they left, I went down to the Canadian Tire hardware store, bought a bunch of cheap paint, and painted their entire house plaid. I just used little paint rollers and made a series of stripe patterns with different colors. I was quite proud of it. Someone said it looked almost "Mondrian-esque."

During the actual painting my brother, Joe, came home from school and asked what the hell I was doing. I said I was painting the house as a present for

Mom and Dad. His reply: "Well, when they get home, you're fucking dead, Tom." That got a big laugh on tape.

We shot the neighbors' reactions, and then we waited. We knew the day my parents were coming back but not the exact time, so we sat in lawn chairs in the front yard and waited for a good ten hours. Finally they pulled up, and it was perfect. My father had this huge growth of beard, because he'd been on a long canoe trip, and his glasses were broken, so they were kind of tilted to the side. There was this look of bewilderment and confusion on both of their faces. You can see in the piece—the shot is just us walking right up to their car with the camera rolling, the window rolls down, and they both look completely amazed and confused. They didn't have time to think up the "right" way to react. I mean, they were looking at a plaid house.

The first thing my mother said was, "You painted the house?" They didn't seem to realize that it was real paint. My dad said, "Oh, it'll come off," and he gets out of the car and he stands there with his arms crossed, then his hands on his hips and he just starts repeating, "Your car is gone, the car is gone . . . my car." At the time I was driving a 1986 Toyota Camry that my father had bought for me for about five thousand dollars. In his mind, at that moment, that car was the only weapon in his armory.

The infamous plaid house.

While he kept repeating, "Your car is gone," I walked beside him, trying to contain my laughter and saying, "But, Dad, I did this for you, this is a present for both of you, don't you like it?" Upon realizing that this wasn't a mirage she was looking at, my mother started to lose it. She marched into the house and locked herself in the bathroom. On the tape there's a succession of shots of her slamming the bathroom door right in my face . . . for real.

The segment ends with me painting the house white again and lamenting my parents' misguided reaction. There is a sad, lonely voice-over . . . "Well, they didn't like the house—they didn't like my surprise gift—but since I agreed to paint it white again, at least I got my car back."

Anyway, that's what we shot and later edited, but it didn't end up on the CBC pilot. The pilot never got made. The man who agreed to help me with the pilot, Chris, had all the right equipment, but he also had his own view of what the pilot should be. Chris, being older than me, thought he had an obligation to the CBC to deliver something that had "substance." I thought he was just lending me his equipment. He thought he was crafting the show.

I edited my first piece for the show, and he announced, "I don't like it." Encouraged to elaborate, he said he thought I should do something of a more universal theme, something that had real social value. His idea? Go off and write a piece about love, or a piece about hate, or greed, or envy. I said, "Hey, I just want to go out on the street, do something crazy, and watch people react to it."

As they say in Hollywood, we had "creative differences."

It was a good lesson. It is very easy, especially when there is money involved, to trust someone else's instincts more than your own, and almost every time that happens, you end up kicking yourself for doing it. We ended up giving the money back to the CBC, and I went back to public access, where no one was interested in a video essay on The Human Condition. (Although I should add that my friend Chris is a genius at what he does and we are still friends and have also worked together since.) After a few months, I realized I had all this footage lying around and I should try to make something of it for the cable show. That's how the "Plaid House" piece finally got finished and seen.

The bit was an instant hit. Every time someone wrote a story on the show, they would focus on that bit, and every time someone would encounter me on the street, they'd inevitably ask, "Hey, man, did you really paint your parents' house plaid? I mean, come on, really?" For three solid years I got a constant earful about that plaid house and "How crazy is that?" and "Man, your parents must still be pissed," yada, yada. It actually became a bit frustrating because we were still doing the show every week and would have enjoyed a little feedback on the other fifty-plus hours of material. "Listen," I felt like saying, "we've been doing ten to fifteen bits a week for the last three years, can't we talk about something else?"

In any case, it struck a definite nerve with people, probably because of the scale of the prank. If you were sixteen and had a party in your parents' house and broke a lamp or stained the rug, imagine the trouble you'd get into. Now take that to the level of fucking up the whole house. It's kind of a grand gesture of youthful disregard for personal property.

After three and a half years of doing the cable show, basically for free, we finally got a real shot at a network show. I got a call one day from a local producer named Merilyn Read who I had been told had "worked with Disney." In Ottawa, "working with Disney" either meant you had sold Mickey glasses at one of the amusement parks or actually met someone who really did "work with Disney." In any case, Merilyn and I decided to pitch the show to the CBC, again, and this time they were more receptive, maybe because Merilyn, an actual adult, was involved. The CBC would pay for the facilities and crew, we would make a new pilot—for free. With some coaxing, Panasonic even threw in a five-thousand-dollar digital video camera that, at the time, was state of the art. We were stoked.

To prod the CBC a little, we had already hustled up some production money from one of the biggest of Canadian sponsors, Molson beer. I remember a meeting at Molson where they asked me to sign their "celebrity wall." The year was 1995, but I signed the wall, "Tom Green 1992." "Why'd you sign '1992'?" they asked. "Because," I said, "it makes it look like I've been around the scene a little longer." It got a big laugh. And to this day if you see my autograph, it usually reads, "Tom Green 1992."

The CBC show went well, though it was the first time I had ever had to deal with network executives who would insist, from their official perch, that I had to change something. For instance, we did a field piece called "The Mustard Inspector." I'd walk into a convenience store in a white lab coat with a clipboard and announce I was there to inspect the mustard. I would find

Glenn, Merilyn, and me on the set of the CBC pilot in 1996.

the mustard section, grab a jar, open the top, pour it all over my face and mouth, and start screaming. The shopkeepers would freak, which of course was the reaction we were looking for. Why else would you impersonate a mustard-eating maniac?

The CBC people instinctively thought we should edit out the part where the store people looked uncomfortable. I instinctively thought that was exactly what should be left in—that unrehearsed reaction *was* the comedy. We went around and around about such issues and usually met somewhere in the middle. Looking back, the CBC, a hidebound conservative public Canadian broadcaster, was much easier to deal with than the oh-so-hip MTV.

Another highlight of that show was a bit I had done early in the public-access show. On this occasion, we went to the Toronto offices of MuchMusic, the Canadian cable-music show, and found a lamp post right outside their on-the-street windowed studio. I then climbed a ladder and my cameraman climbed another ladder and duct-taped me to the lamp post with twenty-five rolls of duct tape. They removed the ladders and there I hung, ten feet in the air.

Phil, Glenn, and me on the CBC pilot set in 1996.

It was aesthetically weird. I looked like a lamp post crucifixion, right down to the scruffy goatee.

Dangling on the lamp post, I began to loudly profess my love for one of MuchMusic's most popular on-camera deejays, Monica Diol, and announced that I wasn't coming down until she came out of the studio and kissed me on the cheek. After I created a serious traffic problem, the cops arrived and cut me down. Monica finally came out and gave me a big kiss. Like many of our pieces at the time, this one had a sweet ending.

This pilot was full of winning elements—SCTV legend Joe Flaherty; Canada's answer to Carson Daly, Monica Diol; a cute old man named Dan The Man, whom I picked up at a bus stop and drove home as he dripped yogurt on his crotch; and, of course, my parents. It was a hot show, in our minds, anyway. Now all we had to do was wait on the geniuses at the CBC to commission a series, and we'd be on our way.

We thought the wait would be two or three weeks. It turned out to be nine excruciating months.

4.

MY PARENTS' BASEMENT

—

"**H**e really is resilient. . . . I still don't quite know the source of this obsession. . . . That's his mystery, I guess."

—**Richard Green**

WHEN I RETURNED HOME FOR THAT YEAR OF waiting, my parents were a bit rusty in dealing with my presence. I had been out of the house for years, living in various crack-infested neighborhoods, plying my so-called trade as a budding TV personality. They were in fact fans of the community cable show, hoping against hope that it would lead to a "real" job like prop assistant or children's show joke writer. Their way of support and encouragement was to put up with my many intrusions into their life. But this was different. When I moved back in, penniless, my hype of impending stardom was wearing thin. I was back in the basement, under their parental thumb.

What I'm about to tell you will probably meet with a stiff denial from my parents. They will say I was the one who was (and is) weird and that they are in every way normal. I can tell you now in all honesty they'd be lying. And if they told you they were not lying, then they'd be lying about that, too.

My parents had long ago decided that the role God had handed to them was that of disciplinarians. They saw themselves as teachers with no other purpose but to keep me on the moral high ground. This all sounded fine, but there was a problem. First, I was twenty-five, commonly considered beyond the age of discipline training, and second, I was a pretty good person already. I didn't have any big problems. I wasn't on crack or in heavy debt to the mob. I spent most of my days working on my little TV show, giving me direction in life and no time to act out. In fact, I didn't really do anything wrong at all.

This left my parents confused. They were like a pair of salmon swimming upstream to spawn only to find the government has dammed up the river. They had two choices—turn around and go back to the ocean or bang their slimy heads against the wall of the dam. Like the mighty salmon, they had been programmed by nature to go only in that one direction. They've been doing it for eons. So they instinctively slammed their slimy heads against the dam until eventually they'd get caught in a turbine. (This is the reason I secretly removed all the electric fans from our home.)

Of course my parents didn't literally bang their heads into a dam all day (that would be crazy). Here's the truth: because they were confused, genetically programmed disciplinarians with nowhere to go and nobody to discipline, they had no choice but to evolve. They did this by creating new rules.

These new, unconventional rules of conduct made it impossible for a once-normal twenty-five-year-old human being like me to exist in peace. There were rules so irrational I was unable to obey them. This of course gave Richard and Mary Jane the opportunity to do what they do best: discipline.

All the rules seemed to have one underlying purpose: to deny anyone in the house, other than Richard or Mary Jane, the right of privacy.

The basement where I now lived had a bathroom with a shower, a family or TV room, where I slept on a fold-out couch, and a large laundry room. Mysteriously, my parents had the ability to be in all of these rooms at the same time. No matter which room I happened to be in, one of my parents could find some reason to also be there. When I went to the computer room upstairs to write, my father would realize that he needed some computer books from that very room. He'd walk in and out of the room constantly until eventually my concentration was destroyed and I'd have to stop writing.

My parents never watched much television before I moved into the TV room. I couldn't lie down on my couch-bed and relax with my mother sitting on it. Soon after I moved in, she discovered a newfound fondness for Andy Rooney. I had my own phone line down in the TV room, so when the phone rang I'd have to talk in front of eavesdropping pundits commenting on my every word. This was just dandy if and when a girl might call—there's no way to have a flirtatious chat with your parents listening. Usually, I'd ask to call her back. But by the time my parents had finished *Sixty Minutes* and discussed the stories in depth, the girl had gone out or decided to avoid me by not picking up her phone. I learned to turn off the ring and let the answering machine talk for me. I came to think that *Sixty Minutes* was on a twenty-four-hour-a-day programming loop—it was always on.

Plus, my father had a strange attitude about the phone. He hated it. What was it, he wondered, that made others so cheery when they used it? Could they not see the real things in life? Could they not smell the air, or see the trees, or rake the leaves, or shovel the snow, or mow the lawn? Could these people not find joy unless it came coldly to their ears through miles of copper wire? How did this machine cast such a strange magic spell over its victims? Sometimes Richard wondered about why he even owned one.

I—Tom—of course had my own line and talked all the time during all *Sixty Minutes* down periods. Richard would often peer into Tom's room and watch as his son entered mysterious codes into its interface. Who was he talking to? For what reason? More important, why was Tom having fun?

This was not appropriate behavior for an unemployed, seemingly rudderless twenty-five-year-old man. As a strong disciplinarian, Richard felt it was his duty to ensure that his son did not become a "Chatty Cathy." So he took action. Whenever Tom was privately in his room speaking on the phone, Richard would make life very difficult for the boy. One simple tactic was to sing loudly while walking in and out of Tom's room, but this method quickly became too obvious. Richard had to crank it up a notch. His favorite trick was to always have dinner ready. Twenty-four hours a day, somewhere in the house, Richard and his wife, Mary Jane, would have a dinner prepared in waiting. A complete meal, with roast beef, rolls, vegetables, and rice. As soon as Tom appeared to be on an important phone call, Richard would pounce into the room shouting at the top of his lungs: "Dinner is served, son! Come upstairs, your mother and I have made a wonderful meal! ROAST BEEF!!!! C'MON TOM, UPSTAIRS FOR ROAST BEEF!!!"

It was baffling to me that this was always the case. Was there a secret pantry hidden somewhere in the home where preprepared roast beef dinners were stored? Or was this repetition simply part of Richard's torturous strategy? Perhaps the roast served no purpose other than creating excitement. Richard always seemed more excited about a meal when a roast was being served. Begging the question, what was the big deal with roast beef? Had there been a loathsome shortage at some point in Richard's early years? Did an epidemic of anthrax or mad cow disease destroy cattle on his grandfather's farm?

In any case, Richard had more phone games in his repertoire than just "Singing While Tom Talks" and "Roast Beef Tonight!" There was "I'm Not Answering That." This game was more subtle, as it involved Richard doing basically nothing at all. For example, let's say Richard was sitting at the kitchen table on a Sunday night, perhaps paying bills. There is nobody in the house except himself and Tom. The family phone sits two feet from Richard on the kitchen counter, and it starts to ring . . . and ring . . . and ring.

"Dad!! Are you gonna get that!" Tom shouts from the hallway.

"Dad!! Hey, are you gonna get that!" Tom repeats two or three times.

In this scenario Richard has the clear advantage and will always emerge the victor—he places significantly less importance on the telephone than his son does. On top of that, he rarely receives important calls at home. Unlike Tom, who has no office to receive critical calls, Richard isn't worried about missing a call. This makes it easy for him to soak in the annoying rings while his son stews in the computer room down the hall. The game usually ends with Tom running into the kitchen and leaping past his father for a phone on its final ring. Inevitably the caller wants to speak to Richard, and the winner is declared.

"NO LONG SHOWERS"

EARLY ON IN MY STAY I FOUND A PRIVACY LOOPHOLE.
My parents could wander into any room where I was talking, sleeping, or just avoiding them, but they couldn't follow me into the shower. So I began taking showers whenever I needed to spend some time by myself. I must have been the cleanest twenty-five-year-old man in the Western world. I would always smell like Irish Spring. The chicks were gonna love this! But then my parents made a rule.

No long showers. According to them, the steam generated by the hot water during a long shower was bad for the walls of the house. I would get out of the shower and my mother would instantly come storming down the hall. I'd open the door wrapped in a towel and have to stare this crazed angry woman in the face as she spewed forth her irrational fears about overshowering.

"You are gonna rot the walls in here. Look at all the steam! You are gonna rot the walls and ruin my bathroom! Open the window and let the steam out of here! Are you trying to wreck this house? Open the window and let the steam out of here, now!"

As soon as they had developed a rationale for the short-shower rule, my private spot was ruined. I just didn't realize it right away. I still thought I had them beat. I figured, Hey, there was a lock on the bathroom door, and when I was showering, the noise of the water made it almost impossible for me to hear their angry, steam-hating rants. This was perfect: I would keep showering, steam or no steam.

This drove my parents nuts. I would go into the shower, and within thirty seconds there would be incessant banging on the door telling me to get out. The banging would get louder and more frequent, but I just sucked it in and kept on showering. This was my private spot to relax, and I was not about to cave.

Faced with such resistance, the salmon began to evolve.

They soon learned that by going to the other shower in the house, they could play with the cold and hot water knobs and disturb the temperature of the water coming into my shower. One second the water would be scalding hot,

Proud parents!

the next second freezing cold. Clearly, this made showering extremely unpleas-
ant. The weird part was that they didn't tell me they were doing it. I think even
they were embarrassed that their insanity had sunk them to such a low. It was
obvious they were doing it because I could hear the taps shutting off and on
with loud clunks through the ceiling. The upstairs bathroom was right over
me, and every time I heard a clunk, my shower would go freezing cold or scalding hot. My parents were trying to scald me to death! This was shower warfare,
and I wasn't prepared to lose.

The next day I put on my coat and shoes and went into the bathroom
downstairs. I locked the door, turned on the shower, and just waited. I didn't
actually get in the shower, I just let the water run while I sat there on the toilet
reading an old copy of *Time* magazine. About thirty seconds later the knocking
began. It was my father, and he was yelling through the door about conserving
hot water. I just waited. They usually didn't start playing with the water temperature for a few minutes after the initial door pounding.

Three minutes into my fake shower I started to hear the clunking sound from upstairs. As usual, he was working the taps with furious abandon. I stuck my hand into the stream of the shower and felt the freezing water, and then the scalding water, then the freezing water again. I just sat reading my *Time*.

After about six minutes I heard him coming down the stairs. He was walking fast. There was a hinge-jarring knock on the door.

"You're gonna rot the walls in this house! You're gonna rot the walls, so get out of the shower!" he yelled.

"Just a second alright!" I screamed right back from my nest on the toilet.

I heard him storming back up the stairs. Seconds later I could hear him back at the tap. Now was the chance to make my move. I quietly opened the bathroom door, stepped out, and locked the door shut with the shower still running inside. Then quietly I tiptoed upstairs. I wanted to see the insanity. I peeked around the corner between the kitchen and the hallway. There he was at the end of the hall, running the water in the bathroom with a maniacal look on his face. He was nuts!! This is nuts!! This was my father, a fifty-four-year-old retired tank commander, playing shower tricks on his son, the twenty-five-year-old would-be-media-figure who lived in his basement.

I didn't want to ruin his fun, so I slipped out the back door, jumped in my car, and drove up to McDonald's for a hamburger. Knowing my father, he probably ended the ordeal by kicking down the bathroom door. To explain my absence on the other side, I later told him that the long shower had caused me to melt. I was lucky enough to be washed down the drain.

THE MASTER PLAN

THE TROUBLE WITH ALL THE RULES AND GAMES IS that they produced only sporadic victories. Richard and Mary Jane needed a bigger plan—a master plan—to drive Tom either (a) into an institution where the government would pay his keep or (b) into the real world and a real job.

They called a late-night clandestine motel meeting to hatch this plan. They were willing to spend money to rid this hapless parasite from their lives. If they just gave him money to move out, that wouldn't solve anything. He would just peter it away waiting for his show-biz life to begin, and when the money was gone, he'd be back in the basement, yearning for a three-hour shower. The money would have to be spent to not just change his living quarters, but to change his whole mind-set about the real world. This was psychological warfare.

The hardest part about waging war against your own son is to make it appear as if a war is not really being fought. My parents did not wish to disown me or create a hateful emotional estrangement. They just wanted to drive me crackers so I would "come to my senses." This meant subtler means than disconnecting the phone service or bricking in the downstairs shower.

Mary Jane was the brilliant mind who realized her son's weak link, the gash in his armour—privacy. The family home was already too small for Tom to have a private life, but with the right plan, it could be made even smaller, giving the rat even less room to hide. The house shrinking had to be done with an alternate reason, one that Tom would buy. The solution, in the end, was simple: remove the entire upstairs of the home.

By totally renovating the upstairs kitchen and living room area, this would condense the group living quarters for months. The entire family would have to cram into Tom's room in the basement, which of course would be renamed The Family Room. And this major renovation would never be suspected for anything more than a mom's desire for a bigger, more efficient kitchen.

Immediately after the plan was conceived, Steve became a new member of the family. Steve was the carpenter who began working on the kitchen upstairs. Steve would rip down walls, sand floors, and run up and down the stairs to and from the basement to get more supplies. All of this activity began about seven-thirty every weekday while Tom's parents were at work. And all of this early-morning activity and noise inflicted immediate damage on Tom. He had to wake up like normal people.

Within a week from the eve of construction, I began to crack. My sleep patterns of going to bed late and getting up late were horribly disrupted. I was used to a quiet and private daytime while my parents were at work making money. My evenings became even worse, with the entire family piling around my fold-out bed to watch TV. My mother was impressed with her cunning. She stared across the family room at me, the degenerate dupe. I was miserable.

JUNKIE

I HAD TO GET AWAY FROM THE HOUSE AFTER THE construction began, and when it was time to dither away the hours, my friend Derek was indispensable. As I said, Derek had been my friend forever. He worked on the show and though he appeared on camera much less than Phil Giroux or Glenn Humplik, he was still nuts. His role on the show was writer, i.e., concocter of pranks and schemes, a role he has continued to fill on every incarnation of the *Tom Green Show*. At the time, Derek, unlike me, had a part-time job as a building superintendent, but he didn't have much money and did have a lot of free time. And we were most alike in one respect: neither of us had found a real-world niche to fill. We were both "in transition."

We often spent this prolonged downtime wandering around in the woods. This was both a good way of avoiding responsibility and reminded us of happier days when doing nothing wasn't considered a moral failing. For instance, every year from ages fifteen to twenty-five, we dreamed up a ridiculous adventure and took pride in its accomplishment. While other people our age were off to medical school, we were running around the woods pretending to be Davy Crockett. One year the dream was to float down the Mississippi like Huckleberry Finn, but we picked the wrong year—a flood year. We had already announced our riverboat excursion to all of our friends, so to avoid public humiliation, we had to come up with a quick Plan B. We could only think of one thing—riding the rails. You couldn't get more romantic than that—a free ride across Canada, dodging the railroad cops, the open sky, trading stories with real hobos. We were gone.

We took off at midnight. We had everything you'd need: coffee, Kit-Kat bars, cigarettes, Band-Aids. Derek's girlfriend dropped us off at the switching yard, and we immediately spotted a long train of flatcars. All we had to do was jump on one car and wait. Piece of cake.

That was the longest night of our lives. The train we "hopped" didn't move. Every minute or so it would make a sound as if it were preparing to leave, but motionless it remained. Anticipating the final take-off, coupled with the wide-eyed excitement of embarking on this exercise in ridiculousness, made sleeping impossible. And it was cold, and damp. By 2 a.m., we were ready to head home.

As morning approached, the train started making a loud noise. It had begun to get light, and the train seemed to awake, fueled by the energy of the sun. This was it! We had waited all night, and now the adventure was about to begin. Suddenly the train began to move . . . bang, bang, bang, bang. The iron connection between each car was pulled tight, causing a loud metallic bang to fill the air. We began to slowly pass men working on the tracks. If we weren't moving away from the station, we'd be caught for sure.

But, finally, we were on our way! Riding the rails to some unknown destination, much like Huckleberry Finn rode the Mississippi! Just as we began to rejoice, though, something unexpected happened. The train slowed down, then stopped, and then eerily began to back up. It was headed back to the loading dock, back to the waiting arms of the railroad police. Huck and Jim were going nowhere.

That was day one. It got better, sort of. We did finally hop a train and came back with a few good stories. One was about Junkie.

It was the second night. We had made a short hop to a small town in rural Ontario and were starving. We loaded up on peanut butter, brownies, and bread at a local grocery and sat down by the tracks to eat. Bored to death, we tossed some bread crumbs to nearby seagulls. This resulted in a seagull feeding frenzy. Then I reached into my pocket and pulled out a bottle of Tylenol 3. Tylenol 3 contains codeine and is a fairly powerful painkiller. At the time I suffered from intense headaches due to allergies.

"Hey Derek," I said, "you think the seagulls like Tylenol 3s?"

"Only one way to find out," Derek responded.

So we crushed a couple of the pills into a powder and wrapped it into a small piece of bread. I tossed the drugged morsel on the ground where it was instantly snatched up by one of the birds. This was the entertainment we had longed for.

The seagull that grabbed the slice of bread was smaller than the other birds. It also had a strange dark strip of feathers along its back, so it was easy to keep track of among the large group of gulls. After a few minutes it began acting silly, squawking louder than it had before, and stumbling around awkwardly. We decided to name him Junkie.

Junkie became friendlier than the other birds. He was much more confident now and stood much closer to us. But Derek was no longer impressed with Junkie. Both of us had grown up deploring drugs and staying away from them. We'd even avoided pot. Now that Junkie was in fact a junkie, Derek could no longer consider him a friend, even if I was the bird's narcotic supplier. This pathetic little creature now symbolized to Derek what was wrong with the world today.

DEREK: Look at that thing, it's disgusting! He's standing way closer than any other bird! It's making loud sounds. None of the other birds are making those sounds. It can't even walk straight.

TOM: That doesn't mean it wants more drugs.

DEREK: Of course it does! You wanna hang out with a junkie?

TOM: It's a bird, Derek.

DEREK: It's a junkie bird! Look at it. Look how much it wants the drugs. I'm not impressed. See, that's the problem with society today. It's not that there are too many drugs on the streets; it's that there are too many junkies on the streets! People aren't raised with enough moral fiber anymore, so they take drugs, they don't care!

TOM: Derek, it's a bird. And besides, we tricked it into taking the drugs—we wrapped the drugs in bread. The bird just thought it was eating bread, it didn't know it was taking drugs. If it had known that there were drugs in the bread, it probably wouldn't have eaten it.

DEREK: Tom, get real! It was right beside you when you put the drugs in the bread! It saw you put the drugs in the bread!

TOM: Maybe it didn't know they were drugs.

DEREK: That's not an excuse in my family, I don't know

about yours. If I got hooked on drugs for whatever
reason, whether it was from eating bread or not,
I'd be out on the street on my ass.

TOM: Yeah, but do you think drug dealers are going to get
people hooked on crack by stuffing it in their bread?

DEREK: It's possible.

TOM: Well, that's crazy. Who the hell are we supposed to
trust, Derek, if we can't trust our fucking bakers
anymore?

DEREK: You can't trust anyone, Tom. You're in this life for
the long haul, and the only person you've got is you.

TOM: Well, that sucks.

We would go off on these nonsense conversations just to entertain ourselves. Even though nobody was around, Derek and I could spend days together just being ridiculous and cracking each other up. In addition to Junkie,
we did encounter one real hobo on that trip. He had just gotten off a train we
had missed, one of many, and was setting up camp. We were in awe. This man
was basically God at this moment to us, two wide-eyed travelers. This would
be the perfect moment to learn about train hopping from a real pro.

The first thing we learned is that real hobos, at least this one, didn't ride on
some grimy flatcar. He rode in the engine, one of the extra ones.

"You look for a train with three engines," he said. "You get in the third one;
there's no engineer in that one. You got a nice chair, you can even have a sleep.
In fact I'm gonna sleep right here, right now in the grass. Okay, boys." The man
wanted to be left alone.

As we walked away, we didn't get five feet before I was stopped cold. I had
almost stepped right in it. On the ground in front of me lay the largest, freshest,
wettest piece of crap I had ever seen. It just lay there in the grass like an enormous brown oyster glistening in the sunlight. It was obviously the work of the
hobo, as it was so fresh and so close to him. In fact it seemed strange that somebody would have excreted in a field and then lay down for a sleep so near to the
vile creation. We decided to have some fun. Again, this spelled entertainment.

TOM (loudly):	Look at the size of this crap!
DEREK:	Wow! That's insane.
TOM:	It must be from a bear or something. Excuse me, sir, are there bears in these parts?
HOBO:	Yes there are, lots of 'em. (He was clearly embarrassed by our discovery.)
TOM:	Wow, Derek, we must have just missed the bear, look how fresh it is!
DEREK:	And it's insanely enormous! Wow, bears must have gigantic assholes! Let's pick through the crap and try to figure out what the bear ate today.
TOM:	Excuse me, sir, do you know what bears eat?
HOBO:	No, not really.
TOM:	We're trying to figure out what bears eat by picking through this gigantic piece of shit.
HOBO:	That kind of stuff doesn't really interest me that much.
TOM:	Well, you're lucky you didn't step in it. If you had of stepped in it, I'm sure it would have interested you then.

Of course this kind of excitement could last only so long. It was time to catch the train home. Waiting by the tracks, we finally spotted the perfect train. Unlike the first one we hopped in Ottawa, this train had box cars. Although they were not ideal for a sophisticated hobo like our big-crap buddy, the walled cars allowed us to hide among the cargo inside.

We waited patiently in the hot sun for hours. When the train began to leave we had already chosen the car we would get on as we ran from the hillside toward it. I grabbed hold of the ladder on the side of the car and ran with the moving train. Jumping, I was able to catch my foot on the bottom rung of the ladder and climb aboard.

But the train was quickly picking up speed, and Derek had not yet gotten in. For some reason, Derek decided to grab onto another ladder between the cars rather than the one on the side of the train. This was extremely dangerous. Now if Derek was to lose his footing, rather than tumbling harmlessly beside the train to the gravel, he would go right under the wheels. But Derek wasn't thinking, and I screamed with fear from my perch on top of the car.

"Grab the ladder on the side! Fuck off, Derek, you're crazy!"

Me and my buddy Derek at Lake Louise in Alberta.

For the first time I saw real fear in the eyes of my friend and companion. As the train sped up, Derek bounced along like a pogo between the cars. He knew the heavy iron wheels spun only inches from his feet. If he was to let go of the ladder now, he would be dead, or at least lose an important body part. Even in that scenario, he would still probably bleed to death beside the isolated tracks.

It took far too long for Derek to get on the train, and it was far too close for comfort. Even Derek, who is uncanny at playing down dangerous situations, was breathless. Even Derek admitted that he had not thought out his approach, he had been stupid, and he had nearly died. The only thing that had saved him had been luck.

SOUTHPOLE SHIRTS

I ALSO ENJOYED WASTING TIME WITH MY FRIEND Phil during this period, as I still do. One Saturday afternoon I met him downtown at the mall. We walked around for a while, but with absolutely nothing to do, we did the first thing that came to mind: We bought shirts.

We dropped by Stitches on Rideau Street, a clearinghouse that specialized in what you might call wack dance-music apparel. One can easily walk into Stitches as a normal human being and emerge moments later as a Backstreet Boy or a New Kid on the Block. We had been in the store only a few minutes when I instantly realized what must be done: we must buy matching shirts.

I searched for the most ridiculous shirt in the store, a shirt that neither Phil nor I would ever wear. My eyes fell upon a rack of pull-over, long-sleeved, multi-colored soccer shirts in extra-extra-large only. They had gigantic lettering: SOUTHPOLE. And like everything in Stitches, they were dirt cheap.

Phil and I wore our matching shirts out of the store, and every human we passed was forced to stare. It was, in retrospect, an enlightening razz. We didn't *want* to be walking down Rideau Street in these hideous boneheaded SOUTHPOLE jerseys. It was uncomfortable, embarrassing, awkward, disturbing, and tense. But for all of these reasons it became an exercise worth doing. It was training.

What I realized then and there was that if my true goal in life was to be paid for being an idiot on TV, I must do a better job of behaving like an idiot in real life. It was important to maximize my skills at behaving like an idiot. I had to become that idiot as often as I could. For being this idiot is what I wanted to do, and I wanted to be this idiot in complete comfort. Buying those stupid shirts and wearing them with pride was just another way I could truly become that person.

We then took it a step further. We bought a couple more SOUTHPOLE shirts for our friends Glenn and Derek and took off for our favorite bar, The Cave. Strutting down Bank Street, we looked like a break dance crew, or an Asian gang, or a soccer team, or Russian tourists. But even more important, we looked extremely confident. It is amazing what confidence a uniform brings. There definitely was a feeling of strength in numbers. We had those numbers now. We were the Southpole Crew, and nobody was going to mess with us.

It was a dead Monday night at The Cave, and as luck would have it, the deejay was spinning really obscure Old School hip-hop. It was perfect break dancing music. The floor was empty, and though none of us had any break dancing experience, that didn't stop us. We were the Southpole crew, and we were going to rip it up. Through the spirit of Southpole, we invented moves like the Wet Banana Belly Slide (one dancer slides on his belly through the legs of another) and the Step Step (stepping on metal stairs to the beat of the music). Buy matching shirts with your friends and make up your own moves. Team Break Dancing is both fun and a great way to exercise.

The secret, we found, to successful Team Break Dancing in Matching Soccer Shirts is to always insinuate seriousness. The dancers must never crack a smile. This is unlike synchronized swimming, or cheerleading, where the athletes are encouraged to always have bright smiles plastered on their faces. Silly Break Dance Crews in matching shirts must appear stoic at all times. The goal is to make the audience feel that you are very serious about your craft. It is much better for all involved if the stoic stance can be maintained, underscoring the impression of clinical insanity.

Actually, given my impossible living situation and the increase of impulsive acts like the Southpole Crew, I began to feel that I was indeed slipping into the netherworld of insanity. I don't believe these blue, black, and white-lettered shirts were the cause of the slide, only a barometer of my mental state. I wasn't sure at the time that it was such a bad thing to be going insane. It seemed to help me deal with this horrible predicament of waiting on a show that might never happen. Sure, wasting time was profitable. Otherwise, I would have never met Junkie nor experienced the pleasure of sliding between Glenn's legs on a dance floor. But I didn't know where the increasing insanity was leading. I didn't know where anything was leading.

SUICIDE

DEEP INTO THIS HELLISH YEAR, I BEGAN TO CONSIDER jumping off the Ottawa Hilton if the show was rejected. It even became something of a running gag. "Hey Tom, you want to go snowboarding tomorrow?" Phil or Derek would ask.

"I'm not sure if I can," I'd reply, "I might be diving off the Hilton."

The idea of suicide can at times seem easy. It really doesn't require that much work to put together a good suicide. If you're committing suicide for any reason whatsoever, when you've finished the act, that reason will quickly become irrelevant. Any problem that previously existed in your life that drove you to your death is immediately eradicated. That's a pretty efficient exercise in problem solving. And if you find that you don't really enjoy your suicide, it doesn't matter; you won't have to do it again. Realistically, the only way suicide can be a drag is when it doesn't work, when you survive. But what's the big deal? If you don't properly execute it, you get to live. And that's a pretty good consolation prize, isn't it?

I often joked about suicide back then. It's not that I really ever had any true intentions of pulling it off. But occasionally my random thoughts on the matter came dangerously close to a plan of action. I had a specific way of thinking how I'd off myself. First of all, I wouldn't use a gun. A gun would be way too quick. You want to be able to savor your death, and blowing off your head would be so fast you wouldn't even know what hit you. I didn't understand why anybody would want to shoot themselves in the head. First of all it seemed like it would be extremely painful, and second, it didn't always work.

Drugs were a definite out. They could also fail in their mission, and they seemed scary. Vomiting into a toilet bowl was not exactly a fear-free, fun-filled last moment on earth. Besides, drugs are bad for you, and many are illegal.

Of course, suicide itself is illegal, which is a bit strange. I mean, is that a deterrent? I certainly wouldn't want a suicide conviction winding up on my record. Perhaps many depressed yet law-abiding citizens wouldn't want that black smudge either, even in the Afterlife.

Still, I wouldn't use drugs or a gun to the head, and I didn't think hanging was all that attractive. Neither was jumping into traffic or throwing myself into a thresher. Call me crazy, but in my suicide musings, I leaned toward jumping off a tall building. The Ottawa Four Seasons (now a Sheraton) was perfect. It was tall, the view was nice, and it was easy to get to the top. When I visualized jumping off this building, I didn't see myself doing it out of depression, but rather as a humorous event. In fact if the stunt was performed with imagination it could become "the ultimate razz." Or as I like to refer to it, "The Last Laugh."

Here's how "The Last Laugh" would go: First, you haul a couple of TVs and a VCR to the top of the building, along with a long extension cord. You tape these appliances to your body, on top of the blue and red Superman costume that you are wearing. In the VCR would be placed the third Superman movie, the one with Richard Pryor. The extension cord would be measured to stretch one half of the height of the building. It can be easily plugged in, as there is an outlet on the roof. Also included in the list of equipment are a .45 caliber semi-automatic pistol and a sandwich.

Upon pushing play on the VCR, I would then sit on the building's edge and watch the movie. After getting wrapped up in the exciting plot, I would "mistakenly" tumble from my perch. This is where the .45 comes in. As I am falling from the building, laughing at Richard Pryor's humor and marveling at Superman's ability to make diamonds from coal, I'd reach for the weapon. Continuing to fall, the extension cord would reach its length and become unplugged, as if to suggest a failed bungee experiment. No longer able to enjoy the movie, I'm forced to find other ways of entertaining myself—namely, unloading the ten-round clip of bullets from the gun into my foot.

Shooting your foot while falling is actually a game I hope to perfect one day. It has two goals: one, blow off the entire foot, like you have to do with one of those paper targets at the BB-gun range at the county fair, and two, unload the entire clip before hitting the ground. If you do both, you receive extra points. And if somehow you do miraculously survive, you get to eat the sandwich. Hurray!!!

Here's the note that goes with this particular form of suicide:

A Message from the Dead Body

Upon reading this note, I want you, the reader, to know that this was not a suicide. It was an unfortunate accident. By no means did I intentionally fall from this building, since that would be breaking the law. I apologize to anyone who may have been caught by a stray bullet, my body, or worse, a chunk of my foot. Although I am aware it is illegal to discharge a firearm within city limits, I had no other way to remove my toes. Plus, there are no tall buildings outside of city limits, making it difficult to blow off my foot while falling.

Could you please inform my next of kin that there is an egg salad sandwich in my costume pocket? I would request that you get this sandwich to them quickly. Also, could you find my pen? I dropped it when I was writing this note. I'm a fast writer.

In finishing this letter, I request that you copy it out, word for word, by hand, ten times. Then send it to ten people whom you know. If this chain letter works, then together we may be able to end human life on this planet. And perhaps dolphins and monkeys, too, should they learn to read, though dolphins live in water and have nothing to hurl themselves from. Oh well. . . . Thanks for helping.

The Dead Body

5.

THE OTTAWA STALLION

—

"He always got plenty of action, don't let him fool you. He'll say that he's had a hard time, as a kind of defense, but that's not true. . . . I know, I was there."

—Phil Giroux

MACHINE GUN MACK DADDY

Since I couldn't spend that entire year at home contemplating suicide, I had to come up with another critical self-defense mechanism to avoid having a nervous breakdown and all the hospital time that would require. I had to come up with distractions that were challenging enough to take my mind off the TV show that might never happen. I can describe the principal distraction or challenge as two-pronged: one, picking up chicks to escape my parents' basement, and two, picking up chicks when you're a twenty-five-year-old man who lives in his parents' basement.

I've always liked to talk to people, especially, you know, cute mamas. Occasionally, in my Ottawa days, I'd be lucky enough to trick one of these mamas into going out with me. The ritual that followed became quite standardized. Maybe we'd see a movie or try to get to know each other over a cup of coffee. Usually we'd meet in a bar, and I'd somehow manage to score her phone number. Then I'd call her the next day and desperately plead with her to go out with me. If she agreed, we'd go out on a date and spend about seven hours together. It usually took about one hour for the girl to realize I was a moron. The remaining six hours of our date became the longest nightmare of her entire life. I'd drop her off, she'd change her phone number, and I'd never see her again.

For years I tried the "sniper approach" to successful dating. I would try to find and focus on one love interest at a time. It usually went like this: If I entered a room filled with one hundred beautiful, available women, thirty of those women would think I was an idiot before I ever opened my mouth. Approximately sixty of them would talk to me for a couple of minutes, and if they didn't use the word "idiot" to describe me to the next person, they'd use the word "nice," which is even deadlier. Maybe five of the remaining women in the room of one hundred would think I was irresistibly sexy, funny, and fun to be with. These five women would call me day and night, constantly craving my time and affection. I'd pursue them, one at a time.

Unfortunately, after a couple of months of serious dating, I would realize that all five of these women were mentally unstable. I would then spend the following six months to a year in an emotional hurricane, a psycho-romantic tsunami. When I finally get back to the room of one hundred, there are only five possibilities left. The problem is obvious. I now have a twenty-to-one chance for one woman who is willing to kiss me in public and not be clinically insane.

Who wouldn't want to date this guy?

That's not a good ratio. Given my poor sniper instincts, the chances are I would never come across that woman-in-a-haystack.

I know this to be true because that's how I lived my life at the time, and I was a failure at it. I set my sights on many an individual target, got my hopes up, pulled the trigger, and missed. I put too much importance on each target and choked when pulling the trigger. After a while it got to be a little discouraging. So I decided one day, in a fit of munitions analogies, that I was going to drop the sniper approach and try my hand at the "machine-gun approach," i.e., just blast away and see what happened.

I was going to become . . . Machine Gun Mack Daddy.

My first victim of this new, devil-may-care persona was a woman who worked at the local skateboard shop named Sonya. As I was explaining machine-gunning to a friend at a bar one day, she came up and said, "Hey, Tom, how you doing? You should drop by the store more often. . . ." My first thought was professional—I skated, I had a semipopular cable show, etc., but my friend wouldn't buy it. "No way, Tom, she wants you, man, she wants you."

She stopped by twice more to ask me down to the store, then a member of the band playing at the bar came over and said, "Hey, Tom, Sonya really wants you to go down to the store tomorrow." I said, "What is this, a Sweet Valley High novel? What is going on here?"

Then Mack Daddy clicked in. The next morning, I got up, jumped into the car, and drove to the skate store. I wasn't kidding around anymore—I was going down there, machine gun ablazing, to get that girl's number, and we were going on a date!

I walked into that store with the confidence of a porn star selling fifty-cent carpentry books at a builders' convention. Sonya greeted me with open arms. She handed me a free T-shirt and pointed out all the renovations they were making. It never occurred to me that hyping the store on my show might have been her motive for inviting me down. Mack Daddies don't think like that. They just shoot.

I closed my eyes and asked for her number. They were closed so tightly that I didn't notice the glance that Justin, the store owner, gave Sonya. Sonya nervously looked around for a piece of paper to write her number on. At this very moment her mind was racing. She realized that I thought she liked me when really she thought I was a skinny moron who did a shitty show on the community channel. I mistook this nervousness for the look a middle-aged woman gets at a Fabio book signing just after he's rubbed a felt-tipped marker all over her breast. Strangely, the two looks are very similar in appearance.

As she nervously wrote down her phone number, she looked at me and said, "I hope you're not looking for a date."

I suddenly felt my entire body get really tingly and cold. It was as if all the blood in my body had rushed instantly to my head. I must have looked like a strawberry ice-cream cone. Or maybe a boiling kettle sitting on top of a pile of tooth picks.

"Uh . . . lookin' for a date . . . why not?" I sheepishly replied.

"Well, because everyone around here knows I'm married," she said.

I picked my embarrassed, blushing, steaming Mack Daddy head up off the toothpick-covered floor and drove home to read a book.

"THE FIRST-DATE RAMMER DOESN'T KNOW THAT I'M NOT AN IDIOT"

Phil Giroux and I had an important conversation about Mack Daddying shortly thereafter while riding a ski lift to the top of Camp Fortune in Quebec. We were both snowboarding and shooting for philosophical clarity on that day. It went like this:

PHIL: There are seven really important characteristics that a girl can have that will directly affect how we get along with them. Most girls score about four on seven, but fail in about three on seven. She can be amazing in four of those seven categories, but it's those three that always mess everything up.

TOM: What are the seven categories?

PHIL: Well, let's see . . . a girl may never phone you back when you call her, that could be one characteristic that a girl might have.

TOM: That probably means she just doesn't like you.

PHIL: Yeah, okay, so let's factor that in: she doesn't call you back because she doesn't like you. Then maybe you have a girl who does call you back, she does like you, but when you go out, she's not fun to be with.

TOM: Yeah, that's exactly what it was like with my ex-girlfriend. All we really liked to do together was have sex and fight. We got pretty good at doing both those things together.

PHIL: I'd say in the seven characteristics that a girl has to have or not have, liking to have sex a lot is probably worth about two points.

TOM: So what you are saying is there are only six factors, or categories.

PHIL: I'm saying that there are seven, but sex makes up about two.

TOM: I don't understand.

PHIL: Let's review. One, you have to be able to have fun with the girl when you go out, that's one. She has to like you, and call you back, and not keep you guessing all the time, so . . . no head games . . . that's two. And she has to like having sex all the time.

TOM: All the time?

PHIL: Well, as much as her partner does.

TOM: Okay, all the time. What about looks?

PHIL: Totally . . . being cute is a major factor. So that's four, and I'm not sure what the other three are.

TOM: Well, remember Smoochy? She was fun to be with, she always called, she was cute, and loved sex. But she was always going out with other guys while we were dating.

PHIL: I guess that's a factor, too, going out with other guys. If she doesn't want to take the relationship seriously and you do, then that's a factor.

TOM: So what are we up to then, five? What about like, porn stars? Is that a factor?

PHIL: Porn stars?

TOM: Like girls who are too fast, you know, like porn stars. And they seem a little bit too crazy, and speedy . . . you know like . . . first date, "Do you want to come back to my place for a chocolate milk" and then ramming you on the first date.

PHIL: Totally . . . that's another factor.

TOM: I mean if a girl is willing to have sex with *me* on the first date, she must be jumping into bed with just about anything that moves! I mean, look at me! I want at least two weeks. I want to have to work a little bit. I don't want to be having sex with a girl who has sex with idiots!

PHIL: But you're not an idiot.

TOM: But she doesn't know that!

PHIL: Why not?

TOM: Because she doesn't! The first-date rammer doesn't know that I'm not an idiot! It's the first date!

PHIL: Maybe she doesn't think you're an idiot!

TOM: I AM AN IDIOT! I AM A TOTAL IDIOT, ALRIGHT! IF I WAS FEMALE, I WOULD NOT HAVE SEX WITH ME! AND ANYBODY WHO HAS SEX WITH ME IS AN IDIOT!!! I AM AN IDIOT!!! I AM AN IDIOT!!!

PHIL: Tom, lift the bar.

TOM: What!

PHIL: Lift the chair-lift bar, we're at the top of the hill.

TOM: Oh, Okay. I think that's six factors, eh?

"I LOVE A GIRL WHO MAKES
GOOD CHOCOLATE MILK"

IKNEW WHAT I WAS TALKING ABOUT. ONLY A COUPLE
of nights before this philosophical exchange took place, I had some first-date
sex. It wasn't completely 100 percent sex, but I guess you could say it was sex—
I'll get to that in a minute. I was a little bit disturbed by the whole experience.
It's not that I wasn't happy to have had the sex. I was a man who didn't have a
lot of sex in those days, and men tend to like having sex, I think. It's just that I
was a little disappointed at the way the whole deal went down. It wasn't the
most romantic first-date sex I could have imagined, assuming any first-date sex
can be romantic. This was not normal, picture-perfect sex. In fact, if it was any
kind of picture, it was a pornographic picture.

Glenn, Phil, Ray, and I went out to this show in a club. This girl started
talking to me; Glenn thought she looked like Rosanna Arquette from the David
Cronenberg film *Crash*. Little did we know at the time that she would act a little bit like her, as well. I ended up getting the girl's phone number, and we decided we would go to a movie.

About a week or so later I called the girl up, and we go see *The People Vs.
Larry Flynt*. It was her choice, a movie about the early history of *Hustler* magazine. Here we are on a first date, in a movie theater, watching a movie about
porn. Call it weird real-life foreshadowing if you want.

Normally, on a first date, I consider myself lucky if I get a kiss at the end of
the night. And I mean, that's like . . . really lucky! About halfway through the
movie, this girl turns into a cat. She grabs my arm, and puts her head on my
shoulder, even starts rubbing my chest and body with her free hand. And she's
purring! This is in the movie theater! Here I was thinking about taking the bold
step of reaching for her hand, and all of a sudden this girl is all over me! This
kept up for the whole movie. All I can say is this, if you have to have a girl rubbing your chest in a movie, *The People Vs. Larry Flynt* is a pretty good one for it
to happen at. (I'm just glad we didn't go see *101 Dalmatians*.)

When the movie ended, I suggested that we go get a drink. We go to this
cool little piano bar that I like a lot. It's called Fridays, and it's in a 180-year-old

house downtown. If you go upstairs, there are soft chairs, fireplaces, and a live piano player. It's really warm and cozy on a cold winter night.

We sat and talked for about two hours. The girl was really nice, she laughed at my jokes, and made a few of her own. We even seemed to share a lot of the same interests about comedy, and movies, and even politics. The more I was with her, the more I liked her. But remember the factors that Phil and I discussed on the ski lift. Check out this factor.

All of a sudden the girl starts talking about her work. It turns out she works at a strip club. Now that's an out of nowhere . . . like, what? At first she tells me that she doesn't actually strip, but rather works as a secretary booking girls at local clubs. But then after talking about it for a while she casually says, "Yeah, well, I strip sometimes, but not that much." I was too afraid of even getting into what "not that much" meant. To me, if I was to have stripped once in my life in front of a crowd, that would be "way too much." Probably wouldn't be that great for business at the strip club, either. But what did "not that much" mean to this girl? Did it mean once a week, once a year, or twice a day? I still don't know exactly. I didn't want to know at the time either, I just wanted to curl up into a ball and pretend I hadn't heard her. (Keep in mind, this was before I moved to L.A., where being a stripper is no big deal. In fact, once you realize that it's no big deal, you quickly determine that it's a pretty good deal.) Shortly after she dropped the stripper bombshell, she dropped another. Kind of like Hiroshima and then Nagasaki.

"So Tom, do you want to go back to my place for a nightcap?" she asks me.

I'm thinking, What the hell is going on here? I'm an idiot, you're a stripper, you got a great ass. I'm a skinny moron, you don't want to have a nightcap with me! What are you thinking!

"What exactly do you have in mind, like . . . a glass of milk or something . . . I love chocolate milk, can you make chocolate milk . . . I love a girl who makes good chocolate milk." I was rambling.

I figured if I rambled for a few seconds, it might get us past the uncomfortable feeling of the old stock line she had just spit into the ether. I paid the bill, we put on our coats, and went to her house. For some reason, now that I knew she was a stripper, or worked at a strip club, or whatever the hell she did, I couldn't stop looking at her body. I was trying to visualize what she would look like stripped of her tight, black spandex pants that she was wearing.

We get to her apartment, she turns on the television, and sits down on the couch beside me. Now, a lot of stuff happens really quickly here, so I want you to pay close attention. The girl pulls a blanket over the both of us and throws her arms around my body. She claims to be cold and says that she wants me to warm her up. Using the cold weather as an excuse, she then straddles my left leg with her legs and begins to softly moan as she rubs her groin against my knee. I wanted to ask her if her groin was cold and if my knee was warm. I decided to save the sarcasm for another day because I didn't want to change the course of this seemingly self-propelled situation. (Just wait, it gets weirder.)

All of a sudden the girl stops, and she looks into my eyes.

"Before I kiss you, I just want to ask you a question," she says matter of factly.

"Sure, uhhh. . . . Okay . . . sure, ask." I was intrigued.

"Am I ever going to see you again?" she asks me.

"Of course, why wouldn't you?" I say.

"It's just something that I've heard about you," she says.

"Well, what did you hear?" I ask.

"I heard that you have a lot of girlfriends," she says.

This was crazy. I'm sitting here on a stripper's couch, she's been moaning and rubbing her groin on my knee, and then she stops and tries to make me feel like I'm about to take advantage of her. Hold up a minute here! She's taking advantage of me! She's in the driver's seat here, I'm just along for the ride! I don't even know where she's heading, and I'm not sure if I even want to go! I would have told her my thoughts, but I guess I really didn't mind being taken advantage of. In fact, I wanted the advantage-taking to continue for a while. So I just told her the truth.

"Lots of girlfriends? That doesn't make any sense. I haven't had a girlfriend in six months." (Maybe, I thought, all my disastrous dates you've heard about count as "lots of girlfriends" in some circles.)

She looked a little bit relieved, then closed her eyes, and started kissing me. It was kind of crazy because all of a sudden I'm kissing this stripper, and I can only think about the fact that somebody told her that I was a male slut. Who the hell told her that? I don't want to kiss the stripper, I want to get to the bottom of this!

"Who told you I have lots of girlfriends?" I ask.

"It doesn't matter, nobody. Just follow me, Tom, this couch is too small."

And without another word, the stripper grabbed my hand and led me like a frightened puppy dog up the stairs to her bedroom.

I want to pause for a second. Before I continue, I need to make one thing clear. I'm not really sure if I should be writing what I'm about to put down on paper. I think if you are Glenn Humplik or Derek, maybe I could be proud of this story. But if you are my mother, or my future wife, or my future son or daughter, or somebody I've never met, I'm probably not so proud.

Unfortunately, with the stripper, I can't just tell you that we had sex and move on. I have to give you the gory details. Otherwise, it wouldn't be fair.

Already we were off to a bad start. As we walked up the stairs toward her room, I knew I was walking into it—first-date sex. My mind wanted to say to the stripper, "I should go, I'll call you tomorrow." But my body just kept on walking. I guess my body wasn't in complete agreement with my mind about the appropriate course of action.

This didn't turn out to be just any ordinary "first-date bang." This stripper girl turned out to be the most forward, foul-mouthed lunatic in the sack that I have ever encountered. Maybe I just haven't been with enough women to see all types, but this was crazy. And it was definitely too much for me. We got to the bedroom, and she pushed me onto the bed, kissing me as we lay back into the pillows. She reached up and turned off the light. I at this point was still quite happy about what was going on. "This is a good date. I'm having fun." Who wouldn't be? Unfortunately the stripper hadn't even started to get weird.

We kept kissing. This was not just happy smooches, this was hardcore, sweaty, violent sucking smooches. It didn't take long for the stripper to strip. She peeled off her spandex pants and her silky blouse thing. I helped her with the removal of her bra, and I was pretty impressed with the way I reached around her back and unbuckled it with one hand. I was smooth. This babe probably thought she was in the hands of a seasoned pro. I reached down to-ward her tiny panties . . . this was it, the excitement was building, Holy Doodle! I can hardly wait!

But the stripper grabbed my hand and pulled it away.

"I can't have sex, I'm having my period," she said.

Strangely, although I hadn't made love to a woman in months, I was relieved. This was a first date. I didn't really want to have sex. I wanted to take it slow. I was glad to hear we weren't about to have sex. I didn't know her that well anyway. If she had wanted to have sex, I would have, just because I am a male, an excited male. But I was glad that it seemed we wouldn't. It meant this girl was constructed of enough moral fiber to know better than to screw on the first date. Or at least she knew not to screw on a first date while having her period. This was excellent. I may have just found me a real winner! That's what I thought for a few seconds, at least until the stripper opened her mouth again.

"YOU WANT TO FUCK ME, DON'T YOU!"

SHE SCREAMED THE WORDS LIKE A JAPANESE KAMIKAZE pilot slamming his Zero into the deck of an American aircraft carrier. It was a raunchy, raspy-throated, gut-wrenching scream. It made the hairs on the back of my neck and various other parts of my body stand on end. As if they instantly stood up at attention, to signal the commander . . . "Yes, Ma'am . . . we heard you loud and clear! You are asking us if we want to fuck you, *Ma'am!*"

And the tone of voice was only the half of it! What the hell was with the choice of words? Was this girl born in a barn? Why not "make love" or "have sex" or even "do the funky monkey"! I was sitting there baffled. "You want to fuck me, don't you!"?!? Does she really want me to reply to that! Was this just a kinky rhetorical question, because I couldn't speak. I was completely silenced and dumbfounded. Suddenly I'm starting to wonder what the hell I've gotten myself into here.

But I didn't have too much time to wonder. As if she were getting points for efficiency, the stripper flipped me onto my back and straddled my pelvis. Keep in mind, I'm still wearing my jeans and a T-shirt, but it didn't seem to matter to her. The girl was crazy. It was high speed pants-on sex like I'd never seen or imagined. She attacked my panted groin with hers and began moaning and screaming so loud that I thought somebody was surely going to come in the room and make her stop. It would probably be someone like God.

The strange thing about it was I was so interested in the comedic aspect of her performance that I really wasn't getting that much enjoyment out of the strange sexual experience. As if she sensed this occurring, she began to liven things up with some more dirty-mouthed gutter talk. She also put her hand in my pants.

> **STRIPPER:** (SCREAMING, AS ALWAYS) **DO YOU LIKE MY BODY!!!!**
>
> **SCARED BOY:** Uhhh . . . sure, yeah . . . looks pretty nice . . . uhh . . .
>
> **STRIPPER:** **YOU'RE MAKING ME SOOOOO HOT!!!!**
>
> **SCARED BOY:** Ohh . . . hmmm . . . well, that's me for ya.
>
> **STRIPPER:** **DO YOU LIKE THE WAY THAT FEELS, BABY!!!!**
>
> **SCARED BOY:** Uhh, what you're doing with your hand there, uhh sure.
>
> **STRIPPER:** **OHHH, BABY, DO YOU WANT ME TO SUCK YOU!!!!**
>
> **SCARED BOY:** Hmmm . . . I dunno, what's your guess?
>
> **STRIPPER:** **YEAH!!! YEAH, BABY!!! DOING THIS MAKES ME WANT TO FUCK!!!**
>
> **SCARED BOY:** Hmmm, well, we wouldn't want that to happen tonight, I mean this is our first date and all.

The insanity went on for way too long. Eventually she stopped, I don't really want to get into the reason that she stopped, but if you think about it, you might figure that one out. I lay there beside her for a few minutes and held her in my arms. I was trying to put together in my mind whether or not I was still having fun. I think I was, but it was a weird kind of fun. The kind of fun that felt wrong.

Wrong or not, I went out with the stripper a few more times. She liked loud sex, but in most other ways she was delightful. She was certainly beautiful. Up to this point, I was starting to believe that for beautiful women, a date with me was very much like a trip to the dentist. It was painful, and the shorter, the better. My confidence around females in recent months had sunk to an all-time low. My TV pilot might get rejected, my whole life plan might get rejected, but at least I wasn't being rejected by the stripper. That was something for the plus column.

On our second date, after a romantic dinner of Chicken McNuggets, the stripper invited me back to her place. She had two roommates, both young and fetching, and as far as they knew, I was a stud. We all watched a bad movie and afterward, the stripper motioned toward the stairs leading to her room. I wasn't at all sure I wanted to go up there, but I did anyway. No sooner was the door closed than she whispered into my ear, "I want you. . . ." Oh, my God, not again—I can't handle this sex talk, I thought. I can't respond to these explicit comments without sounding goofy and rehearsed, as in "Oh, baby, I want you, too." It was embarrassing just to think about.

But the stripper had her way with me anyway, and boy, was she loud and dirty. I have never heard a human being scream so loud in my entire life. Amidst these nonstop, blood-curdling cries of ecstasy, I got worried. The house was full of people. What if they thought I was hurting the stripper? Even worse, what if they thought the stripper was hurting me?

And then, as if struck by a bolt of lightning, the entire situation flipped over in my brain. The sex noise ceased to be unnerving and became funny. The screaming stripper was suddenly hilarious. In fact I decided to make her scream even louder. I wanted to break the stripper's scream record. When I walked out of that house, I wanted to leave with my head held high and the screams still reverberating in the hallways. I wanted the roommates to report all over town, "Tom Green came over last night and you should have heard how loud the stripper screamed! It was, like, crazy!"

That never happened, of course, but the fact that I wanted it to was a sure sign that my sexual depression was lifting.

Preoccupied with the show, I finally decided to cut it off with the stripper; not knowing how to do this smoothly, I simply stopped calling her. She continued to call me for a few more weeks but eventually got the hint and saved face by dumping me on my answering machine. It was a relief that this thing ended so cleanly and with a minimum of mayhem. I had visions, à la *Fatal Attraction*, of a rabbit being boiled on my stovetop, or looking up from a restaurant table years later and seeing her across the room, screaming obscenities at me—"YOU *DON'T* WANT TO FUCK ME, DO YOU?"—in her trademark style.

"WOMEN LOVE BASTARDS"

WAITING FOR THE SHOW TO GET PICKED UP CONTINUED to be a living nightmare. I felt like an eight-year-old waiting for Christmas, except on this occasion, it was Christmas with a nasty twist. This year it was a race.

Santa Claus had a bet with his North Pole neighbor, an axe murderer. Santa bet the axe murderer that this Christmas he could give more kids presents than the axe murderer could decapitate on the same night. The rules were simple: both had to go down the chimney, and once one had entered a certain house, the other couldn't. For a four-year-old, or a twenty-five-year-old, this makes for a pretty scary Christmas. You had a 50/50 chance between present or axe.

So every day I sat all day staring at the telephone. What was it going to be? A jolly red elf with some wonderful news or an axe in the head?

Amidst this heightened state of career anxiety (i.e., the anxiety of having no career), I suddenly realized something. After a year of abysmal failure as a Machine Gun Mack Daddy woman chaser, I had given up the search entirely. I was now content just hanging out with my friends to meet my social needs. Masturbating had become an excellent substitute for my sexual ones. I was happy being girlfriendless. I wasn't just saying it—I was really happy.

Here's where it got interesting. As soon as I realized that I was happy, naturally I began to behave in a happier manner. I also ceased to be the constant stalker of women. When I spoke to a beautiful girl in a social setting, I no longer asked for her phone number or hinted at maybe a coffee date. I decided I no longer wanted to go on all these lame dates. Unfortunately this decision had an adverse affect.

The moment I stopped pursuing, and meant it, I became the "pursuee." I had never been so pursued. I'd never had so many attractive women ask me out in such a short span of time. In one week alone I was asked out by a total of six different ladies. THEY ASKED ME OUT!!! I didn't necessarily understand the reason precisely, but it was happening. And it said something about the female mind, though I wasn't sure what.

Then it hit me: women like bastards.

For most of my teenage and postteenage life I had chased girls like a sad puppy. A lot of guys get into this pattern, usually ones like me who are, ah, slightly insecure about their looks.

So I would counteract this deficiency by being a really nice guy and trying to be funny. Unfortunately, most girls don't like nice guys. I could never understand why so many of my female friends were always going out with people who were, in their words, "jerks." But now it's crystal clear: Women love jerks. Women love bastards. They do not want to be chased around by a sad, insecure, puppy boy. If a woman ever says that she wants to go out with a nice guy, she's lying to both you and herself.

I'm not saying that I wanted to be a bastard. Or that I had become more of a bastard during this period, and that's why all these girls were calling me. But I was displaying all of the characteristics of a bastard without knowing it. With all the shit going on with the TV show, I was stressed and distracted. I put the pursuit of women onto the way-back burner. And, boom, there they were, dozens of them.

I was now fully convinced of the fundamental dynamic of modern romance: Women do not want to be chased by men. Women do not want to be pursued by men. Women do not want to be courted by men. Women do not want to be stalked by men. They want a challenge, just like the man wants a challenge when he is doing all his chasing, pursuing, courting, and stalking. Women want to find a man who they believe is unattainable and test their limits. Women want to be chasing. Women want to be pursuing. They want to be courting. And they want to be stalking. They want to be stalking a difficult and elusive prey.

It is all about the challenge, and the ego. The greater the challenge that is won, the greater the boost to the ego. So immediately after my show, stress kicked in; I indeed became an elusive and difficult challenge. This has made me a trophy catch for the babes!

My looks had not improved. I was still a skinny, sickly, and not all that handsome kind of a guy. I was lean, lanky, spindly, malnourished, and awkward. I lived in my parents' basement. I had no money. I essentially had not much of a life at all. I was what you might well describe as a loser. Yet on the surface, I suddenly appeared to women as a winner, simply because I was no longer in awe of them.

I was so distracted with worry that I paid no attention to even the most spectacular women. While only a few months earlier I had been shaking in my boots in their presence, now I was not fazed. On the outside this was perceived as confidence, sureness, virility, strength, and disinterest. Of course it was none of these things. But because it appeared this way, I, for the moment, had become prey for all females in this city.

I *was* the Ottawa Stallion.

6.

THE SWEET SMELL OF ROTTING FLESH

—

"Tom never fakes it. A lot of times you might think that what he's doing is staged or a prop or not really happening, but everything he's ever done, he never fakes it. It's always real. An example would be, on the Comedy Network in Canada, he did this bit with a piece of real shit . . . it was Phil's shit. The bit was, 'I Don't Have to Do Potty Humor.' And then, to show what real potty humor is, he went to the washroom, pulled a turd out of the toilet, and took it out to the audience. Two guys in the audience thought it was a prop turd, right, and dipped their fingers into it. . . .

"In the end he took the turd, brought it to his desk, and there was a Barbie bed on his desk, so he put the turd in the bed and pulled up the covers. Why did he do it? It keeps it real. Somehow he knew that a real

turd would get a much realer reaction, and that reaction was a big part of the joke. And it's also cheaper.
I mean, how much would a realistic-looking fake turd
cost? The real thing is free."

—Ray Hagel, Tom's first producer
and longtime associate

AFTER WAITING ON AN ANSWER FROM THE CBC
for nine months, the answer finally came: no, thank you. I was devastated. I
had been sitting around my parents' house for nearly a year, fast-talking them
into believing my "career" was about to start any day now. It turned out that
the big decision maker at the CBC, Slawko Klimkew, had watched the show
only a week or so before rejecting it. The reports were that he thought it was
unintelligent, immature, and childish. His response, when I thought about it,
wasn't all that surprising, coming from a humorless bureaucrat at a network
whose idea of good programming was some stirring period drama about God-
fearing Alberta farmers.

Nevertheless, this was not good news. I saw a grim future for myself.
Laughed out of the house by my we-told-you-so parents, I would move to
Toronto and become a waiter. After a couple of years I'd get my big break making a silly face on a Chicklet's billboard. But then, sadly, I'd get hit by a car
whose driver was distracted by the billboard as I crossed the street. I am not
killed, but my left leg has to be amputated. Unable to perform my duties as a
waiter on one leg, I am sentenced to a life on the streets. I am too proud to ask
my parents for help and eventually die of exposure on a cold Toronto night.

As I was practicing "Hi, I'm Tom, your waiter," the local producer who had
joined us during the making of the CBC pilot, Merilyn Read, had some other
cards up her sleeve. Merilyn deserved a great deal of credit for getting the pilot
made in the first place, and she didn't want the show to die. She got a then-
brand-new Canadian cable channel, the Comedy Network, interested in the
show. To make a long story short, when the big boys went south, the Comedy

Network stepped up, and it turned out to be the best thing that could have happened.

For the next two years we let go of any of the restraints we had felt on the G-rated community station and took off. We had creative freedom, and we had a little money to try things more complicated than wrapping my head in meat and stopping people on the street corner. Much of the stuff I became known for—the road trips, the roadkill, the gross, the shocking, and the outrageous—was created for the Comedy Network.

The Comedy Network show changed everything. All of a sudden I was getting paid—$400 a week Canadian, thank you—to do what I had been doing free for years. I immediately moved out of my parents' house and into a cockroach-infested apartment for $550 a month. It was kind of a hole, but no one told me to get up at 7 a.m. or get out of the shower. Then I went out and leased a brand-new Jeep Cherokee. I drove around Ottawa so damn proud of myself. I

Interviewing one of our higher-profile guests, a sock puppet named Ed.

had fucking made it big! A show, a car, a slum apartment—all that wearing of meat and tormenting my parents and staying up every night until 5 a.m. editing had finally paid off. I really was the Ottawa Stallion!

Derek and I were creatively in charge of the show, and we knew this was our big shot. We turned a wall of my apartment into a big segment board for the thirteen shows of the first season. We'd come up with goofy ideas, write them on three-by-five cards, and pin them on the wall. We had to come up with enough material for thirteen twenty-two-minute edited shows, both in-studio pieces and field pieces. It seemed at the time like a ridiculous amount of stuff.

The general setup would be the same as the community access show. I would sit in front of an audience of a hundred or so kids and do something on stage, then throw to a field piece. I would, say, have on a butcher and we would cook some food, but then I would interrupt the demonstration by pulling out a baseball bat and first smashing the raw meat, then smashing the frying pan, and then, for no earthly reason, proceed to smash the whole set into a pathetic pile of plywood. The poor butcher just sat there, not knowing what the hell was going on.

We did that bit, in fact, and Merilyn the producer almost had a nervous breakdown that day. We didn't have enough money in the budget to build a new set, so we just patched together the remains of the old one and kept doing the show.

We also had an in-show bit where, in a fit of self-abuse, I spontaneously shaved my own head and remained completely bald for the next eight shows. The studio material was largely impromptu. When all else failed, I did things like jump on the back of a guest for six or seven minutes and sniff his hair. Because we had the luxury of editing the show, the funny hair-sniffing moments stayed and the boring ones got cut.

A big part of what we ended up doing on stage was razzing the audience. I had never heard of Andy Kaufman in my life at this point, but what we were coming up with on our own seemed, in retrospect, Kaufmanesque. One night it was very cold in Canada, like negative 40 Celsius, and at the end of the show, with no explanation or reason or even prompting, I pulled out a high-pressure hose and doused the entire audience with a powerful spray. Some people were laughing, and some, of course, were pissed. The show ended and 120 kids were dripping wet, so I announced that because it was so cold outside, I was going to drive them all home.

I had a bus waiting and we all piled in. It took like ten hours to get everyone home, since they lived all over town. I would pull up in front of someone's house, go in with them, wake up their parents, and explain why their kid was a wet rag. Unlike Andy Kaufman, we were not trying to turn people against us. We were just trying to get a rise out of them. A few years later I would figure out how to do both.

Another of my favorite in-studio bits didn't involve the audience—it involved Glenn. This was during the time that the Monica Lewinsky scandal was just heating up, so I decided to do a little test. We invited a DNA expert on the show so that he could identify the DNA of some semen on a blue dress. I provided the dress, and my friend Phil, who had always sat in the window behind me on stage, provided the semen. This was like the science portion of the show—the chemical fingerprints of jizz.

The DNA guy came on and I held up the blue dress and a condom full of Phil's genetic excretion. We all knew that it was Phil's real semen, including Glenn. What Glenn didn't know was that I was going to place a large dollop of that semen in a spoon and then flip it all over him. This wasn't about science; this was about me figuring out a tricky way to throw one of my friend's semen all over another one of my friends.

So I carefully cut the condom, poured a healthy dose of the jizz in the spoon, and as I'm about to pour it on the dress . . . Whack! I flick it all over Glenn. He freaks out and jumps up, looking for something to get this horrible sticky stuff off of him. The audience, let alone the DNA man, couldn't believe it because they knew the semen was real and that Glenn had just been genuinely splooged. In effect, the dress and the DNA expert were all irrelevant. This was the *joke*.

Phil got his own share of abuse. On one show we brought in a homeless guy to give Phil a massage. To get the full effect, Phil stretched out nude on a long table, just a towel covering his buttocks. While he was getting this homeless massage, I wandered over to the table to watch. In my hand I had an electric fly swatter/bug zapper. Phil didn't see this device because he was on his stomach facing the opposite direction, plus the lights were low. By the time he noticed what was up, it was too late. I had the zapper ready to strike and had taken away his last line of defense—the towel.

Phil was now lying there naked on the table, and his ass, sans towel, was being broadcast across Canada and to our boys overseas. I started zapping him with the bug zapper. It was not pleasant. Phil had to lift his feet up to try to block me zapping his bare butt and his butt was moving around and Phil was both exposing himself and yelling at the same time. The audience was going crazy, because they knew this guy hadn't intended to get into this situation; he'd just signed on for a massage with a towel and now there was no towel. He was getting mildly shocked but couldn't run because he didn't want to completely expose himself in front of two hundred kids and all the viewers at home. It was a great, hilarious, crazy moment.

"THE DEADLY VACUUM CLEANER SHARK"

WITH THE FIELD PIECES, WE KNEW WE HAD TO DO much more planning and at the same time push ourselves well beyond the community access show. I remember Derek and I sitting down in a restaurant one day and trying to map out exactly what we were going to do. We even went so far as to create general categories for our field pieces. There were at least four of them:

#1 *Story Pieces.* These were the more elaborate events with a beginning, middle, and end, like the "Plaid House" piece. A good nonparent example would be the time we hung our own "modern" painting in the Canadian National Gallery of Art during an exhibition of a painting by the famous abstract artist Mark Rothko. My painting, in faux Rothko style, was a series of red and orange stripes. I called it *Tiger/Zebra*. We walked in the National Gallery, found an empty wall, and hung it up. It had its own little plaque and everything.

We then proceeded to tape people "interpreting" my childish artwork, which, of course, was no less confusing to most of them than the Rothko and many other modernist paintings. A guided tour would pass by and nod in appreciation, at least until the point when I strolled up to the painting with a black Magic Marker and began to improve on it. The crowd's reaction, of course, was the whole story.

#2 *Gross Stuff.* In other words, the kind of stunts we would never try to pull on a public access show, like sucking milk out of a cow's udder or keeping a dead raccoon as a running set piece for the in-studio crowd. The MO of this kind of piece was pretty straightforward—do something distasteful and see what happens.

#3 *Barging Down Main Street.* These pieces involved no dialogue at all. They were just premeditated bits of insanity. For instance, I would don a dress, cover myself completely with skin cream, and barge down Main Street moaning and screaming. Or we did one called "The Canterbury Tales," in which I wore a dress and a blond wig and had a goat's head tied to my body. What did this have to do with Chaucer? Nothing other than the fact that it was about the furthest thing away from *The Canterbury Tales* as you could get. That was the irony.

These pieces were often thought up the same day they were produced. It was like, "Hey, what do you want to do today?" "Oh, I don't know, let's throw some vacuum cleaners in that little pond in the park where the model boat enthusiasts hang out, and I can go fishing for the deadly Vacuum Cleaner Shark." "Sounds like a plan, let's do it." Sometimes it worked—sometimes it was just a waste of a good vacuum cleaner.

#4 *Stumblers.* These were those completely unpredictable moments or characters that we would "stumble" across in the act of doing something else. I might be running around with the goat's head, and some street wretch would come up and start babbling about how he was a vampire while wiggling one of his loose teeth, and we'd just drop what we were doing and follow him for a while. "This is gold!" someone would say. One of the funniest all-time stumblers happened completely by accident. We called it "None of Your Damned Business." One day I was just walking around asking people where they were going. For some reason this sixty-something-year-old fellow didn't appreciate being on camera. "None of your damned business where I'm going!" I started to back away, but he grabbed the microphone and tore the windsock off it, ripping it to shreds. "Where are *you* going?" he screamed in a hilarious, sarcastic warble that was funnier than anything we could have ever planned. He grabbed the microphone again, and suddenly I found myself in an awkwardly twisted wrestling match with an absurdly overreactive senior citizen. The camera just kept rolling.

Of course these categories weren't hard and fast. They would often bleed into one another—there were plenty of gross stumblers, for instance. But breaking them down like this gave us a way to craft and pace the show. We quickly learned, for example, never to put three or four gross segments in one half-hour show, because the audience would be almost numb to numbers three and four. It was always best to set up a really distastefully gross piece with something feel-good, like a cute old lady we met on the street. Then you'd get the much-desired audience whiplash effect.

"I'M CALLING THE POLICE"

THE STORY PIECES, LIKE "PLAID HOUSE" OR "NATIONAL Gallery Painting," were the most difficult to pull off and demanded the most planning. Given that "Plaid House" was the most successful piece we had ever done, we knew we had to top it. We thought of painting my parents' car plaid, but that seemed lame. Then someone said, "Hey, remember those bands in the seventies who would airbrush big-breasted naked ladies on the sides of their vans?" That led directly to the idea of having such a pornographic scene—lesbians lovers, legs spread, tongues a-licking—painted on the hood of my parents' car as a tribute to the fine art of the 1970s. After we stopped laughing, we wondered if we could really pull it off—Richard and Mary Jane's Slutmobile.

We went to the Yellow Pages and found a guy in Greeley, forty-five minutes outside of Ottawa, who still did that style of graphic, Hells Angels–style airbrushing. We drove out and showed him a picture of lesbians in action that we ripped out of an old *Penthouse*. It was going to cost four hundred dollars, which was a lot of money for us at the time. After we talked Merilyn the producer into giving us the money, we had to figure out how to get the hood to the painter. The solution: we went to a salvage yard and bought an identical hood to the one on my parents' 1992 blue Honda Accord. When the time came, we'd just switch out their hood with the lesbian one.

I borrowed my parents' car for an errand and got an extra key made. The night of the big switch, I snuck their car over to a mechanic friend of Derek's, who kindly removed one hood and attached the much more colorful one. With the car back in the driveway, ready to take my parents to work, I got up at five and crawled into a little garbage bin next to the car with a handheld digital camera. I didn't want the presence of the camera to interfere in any way with my parents' spontaneous outburst at seeing their car decorated like the gas tank of a Harley road hog.

My dad comes out, looks at it in awe, tries to rub it off, and then starts cursing . . . "Ho-ly shit. . . ." My mother was equally stunned, but her concern was multiplied by the fact that my grandmother and my aunt were driving down to visit us that very day, and she had no interest in my poor grandmother seeing unclothed lesbians cavorting on the hood of her Honda. She spent the rest of the day leaving messages on my answering service demanding that I fix this abomination. "If you don't," she said, "I'm calling the police." It was the first time, I think, that I'd ever heard the word "police" mentioned in reference to my comedy work. At least from my mother.

My mother ended up not going to work that day, probably because our relatives were coming, and my dad was forced to take the bus. My dad was angry, for sure, but there are moments on tape where you see him start to break up— it was, after all, too ridiculous to take seriously. At this point I realized that my dad was going to be sitting at the bus stop a good fifteen minutes, so why not drive by in the Honda and continue to try to convince him that this was art, a tender act of love between two loving women?

I got to the bus stop, and there were seven or eight neighbors waiting for the bus, as well. In probably the funniest moment of the whole piece, my dad was both laughing and steaming as the neighbors admired our handiwork and no doubt quietly thanked God that He didn't bring them an idiot son like me.

We kept doing razzes with my parents on the show, but they evolved to the point where we realized they weren't having the same impact. No doubt as a survival skill, Richard and Mary Jane were on guard all the time. The one moment this became clear happened later on. The premise of this particular bit was simple: since my parents liked animals so much—I held up a picture of our dog, Sport, and our cat, Dino—I decided to surprise them with a houseful of loveable animals—llamas, donkeys, pigs, and sheep. Because I didn't want to totally ruin my parents' hardwood floors—there were lines I wouldn't cross— we covered them in plastic and moving padding. That took a little bit of the spontaneity out of it.

Nevertheless, the shock still registered when my mother walked in and saw a donkey urinating on her living room floor. Her reaction was, of course, "Oh, my God, Tom!" But when she saw that no permanent damage would occur, the "Oh, my God" came with a smile on her face, not the kind of utter dismay we were looking for. It was a smile that said, in essence, Hey, I can handle this nonsense, my son's an idiot and everyone knows it, it's just farm animals defecating on my floor, Tom will clean it up, and I'll look cool because I'm not screaming and crying like a madwoman. The piece ended with us all sitting on my mother's couch feeding livestock animal crackers.

THE COMEDY NETWORK SHOW created enough buzz, at least in Canada, to get picked up for a second season. Although we still didn't have much money, we wanted to find a whole new slew of material by taking a road trip across Canada. After all, we were a national show and needed to expand beyond the narrow turf of Ottawa.

We couldn't afford to buy a car or a van for the trip, so we went on our Web site and announced that we needed someone to donate a camper van and if they did so, they could come with us for the first week of the trip. Soon after, this kid named Sean stepped up with his beat-up 1980 Ford Econoline van, complete with big foam captain seats and a fold-out bed in back, and off we went. The van was an old junker that Sean's late grandfather had passed along and had been parked in their driveway for a year, unused. We weren't exactly choosy—it was like a brand-new Land Rover to us.

We hung with Sean for the required week, then, cynical pricks that we were, we put him on a bus at North Bay, Ontario, yelling as he rode away, "Thanks for the van, sucker!" It was very generous of Sean to help us out, but we reveled in the faux pas of being "celeb" ingrates. After leaving Sean, we took off for Vancouver. We spent a total of ten weeks on the road, shot tons of video, and tried to figure out how to insert it into the upcoming thirteen shows. It was a massive trip. For you with no sense of geography, Canada is twice the size of the United States. Ontario, the province I'm from, is almost twice the size of Texas and it took us sixteen days solid to get out of it. And since not all that many people live in Canada, you can drive for hours, if not days, without seeing a soul.

We'd drive about fifty miles a day, stopping often to run into some field and get attacked by something. We were like Charles Kuralt on crack. We'd be

Our borrowed Ford Econoline van.

in the middle of the prairie and strange things would happen. One day we were driving somewhere between Swift Current, Saskatchewan, and Medicine Hat, Alberta—look it up on a map—and we saw a herd of deer running through a field. "Hey, let's chase those deer!" someone shouted, and out of the van we bounded. The minute we were outside we realized we were standing in the largest mass of mosquitoes ever gathered at one time in the Western Hemisphere.

It was awful. If you pointed the camera at them, the lense began to darken with mosquito flesh. Derek and Ray immediately hopped back in the van, but I stayed outside. "This is what we should be shooting!" I shouted as I ran after the deer. There were moments where there were so many mosquitoes on my back that you couldn't see my actual back. The buzzing noise was insane. By the time I got back to the van my entire neck was a bloody, bubbly mess. I looked like a smallpox victim.

Once we took off, I went into some kind of mosquito-induced shock. I actually got high on mosquito venom, and if you want my two-word review, "Not bad." I began to play the ukulele and sing at the top of my lungs for an hour. No one recorded this madness. They were pissed. We had been in the van for about six weeks at this point, and some things were no longer funny. A crazed mosquito-pocked uke player was apparently one of them.

Early on we realized we had a real problem. We were three young guys crammed into this junker van. We couldn't afford to pay for a hotel room. We had someone back at the office calling each Travel Lodge along the route to try to get us a comp room in exchange for a mention on the show. Occasionally we'd get lucky and have free lodging for a night. Even then it was three guys in one small room with a cot. If one person snored too loudly, the others might have to evacuate the room and sleep in the van. These were battle-front conditions. It was edgy.

We were young guys, remember, so it took only about three days before I announced I had a comment. They seemed to know what was coming. "We've been on the road for three and a half days now," I said, "and I think that this is the longest I've gone without whacking off in about fifteen years." And everybody just started laughing and realized, "Yeah."

So that became a reality of the road—how long would we go without whacking off and how could it possibly happen since we were never more than four feet away from one another? The only conceivable time would be in the morning in the shower in the hotel room, but out of respect for the next show-erer, that would be wrong. Plus, knowing your unshowered friends hovered just on the other side of a flimsy piece of glass kind of spoiled the mood. We even invented a term for our new mental condition: Whacker's Giddiness. You got this kind of hormonal energy—an altered state of mania—when you abstained for this long. We were hyper and maybe even funnier. "What's wrong with him?" one of us would say at the insane antics of another. Whacker's Giddiness. Next question.

One day we were at one of our freebie hotels, and it was maybe the first time Derek and Ray had gone off by themselves. I said I was going to stay back and sleep, but I knew, and they knew, that I was going to order up a porno movie and . . . amuse myself. Which is exactly what I did. About four and a half seconds after the movie began, I was finished. This is a dilemma that happens to many a young man when he spends twelve bucks to order up a hotel porno movie. You watch maybe fifteen seconds of the damn thing and aren't all that interested in watching the rest of the story, assuming it has a story at all. If you could rent a hotel movie thirty seconds at a time, the movie service would have many more satisfied customers.

I'm sitting in this hotel room with two more hours of porno playing on my television set when I got this brainstorm. I set up our portable video camera in a tripod, stuck in a blank tape, framed the TV screen perfectly, hit RECORD, and pirated the rest of the movie for my friends. Knowing we had a monitor in the van, anyone of us could drop in the porno tape while parked in some woodsy junkyard in Thunder Bay, close the built-in curtains on the Econoline, and have at it. I was doing Derek and Ray a public service.

What I didn't plan to tell them was that two or three minutes into the show—and every two or three minutes after that—I would lean into the shot and say, "Hey, how are you guys doing right now?" I was hoping, of course, that they would be, ah, near completion as they saw my smiling face. One second they would be enjoying some shameless lusty woman egging them on. The next second it would be my friendly greeting, something they surely would find less than arousing.

I sat in the hotel room for the next couple of hours, leaning into the recording every once in a while with "How you enjoying the tape, fellas?" I left the tape in the van with a little note reading, "For your enjoyment. You're my friends." No one announced that they had snuck off with the tape, but I knew

Me and Ray in one of our many cheap motel rooms.

when they did, because they couldn't help but comment on my on-camera shtick. I remember Derek coming back a day or so later and saying, "Okay, that was funny. That was very funny. The timing was a little off, but very funny."

Bit-wise, we were out in the middle of nowhere most of the time, so all we could do was improvise. We had no choice. One night we were driving through the middle of Alberta and we saw this spectacular flame from an oil derrick shooting two hundred feet into the air. We knew we had to stop and shoot, but shoot what? We saw a camper next to the derrick and figured there was a lonely oil worker living in there. So we said, "Hey, let's stop and talk to that guy. In fact, let's audition him for a movie!"

In the last outpost we had passed through, we had picked up a book called *The New Baby Book*, which led us to create a bit called "Audition for a Movie." We went to a local Kinko's-type place and had a sign made up reading "MOVIE AUDITIONS." So we put on our orange oil-field-looking jumpsuits, pulled out our "script," the baby book, and knocked on the camper door, and asked the guy if he was interested in a role in our new film, *The New Baby*.

Of course he was. What else did he have to do? In the middle of this field under this massive flame with a horrendous sound, this gruff, oil-covered oil man read dramatic passages from the baby book. We shot the audition, shook his hand, and told him we'd be in touch with his agent. He may still be waiting for the call.

We felt like we were at war or at least on a high-priority creative mission. We had to get to the other end of the country and shoot everything we saw. In Moosejaw, Saskatchewan, we bumped into this eighty- to one-hundred-year-old native woman who didn't speak a word of English. I was wearing a cowboy hat and speaking through a plastic cone at the time. I walked up to her singing some silly nonsense chat and she immediately responded with a traditional Indian throat-type singing that was much weirder and more mysterious than my inane mutterings. We began this musical duet that lasted five minutes. On some level we were communicating. Years later, after this bit had re-aired on MTV, I got a request from the pop producer, Pharrel Williams, of The Neptunes, for a copy of that duet. He thought it was musically cool. So did I.

Some bits, of course, were more sketched out than singing ancient love songs with a mystical eighty-year-old woman. In Vancouver, very late in the journey, we concocted a set of leg and arm casts that made me look like the last guy pulled from a burning automobile. With my head also wrapped and trying to walk with crutches, I'd stand at an intersection, lock eyes with the man next to me, then fall to the ground, screaming in pain. Of course people jumped to help me, but the more they touched me, the more I screamed, and the more they tried to pull away from touching me, the more I held on for dear life.

Early on in this endless trip we realized that roadkill was high on the order of shooting priorities. At one point we came across a dead eagle, which we quickly transported in the van to the nearest town, where I ran into the local roadside truck stop shouting, "Please help me! My pet eagle is very sick! Please help my dying eagle!" At 6 a.m. one morning, someone woke me up in the back of the van to announce we had come across a major roadkill find: a gigantic dead moose.

For reasons that escape me now, my instinct was to get down and hump this moose. This wasn't easy. A moose is a big animal and a dead one is not exactly conducive to humping, but I did the best I could, given the hour, the location, and the other creative options available to me. This of course became one of those things that continues to haunt me to this day. "Tom Green? Oh, yeah, he's the guy who humped that dead moose, right? Boy, he is one sick son of a bitch. That is fucking weird."

While on the subject of dead animals, I should mention the dead raccoon we later discovered and turned into a member of the family. We found it near Ottawa and I took it home, stuck it in a Tupperware container, and kept it on my balcony for two months in the winter. Despite the cold, it began to ferment. Smitten by this little fellow, we decided to move it to a box and take it back to the studio to have around during tapings. It became the mascot of the show, and we brought it out on the set, thoroughly wrapped up to contain the horrible smell, every time an interview wasn't going well. Old TV shows used to have on-stage pets. Dave Garroway, one of the first hosts of the *Today* show, had a pet chimp named Kokomo, Jr. We were just trying to revive a time-honored TV tradition with our pet raccoon.

During the second season on the Comedy Network, I was invited to appear on a very popular Canadian talk show called *The Mike Bullard Show*, based in Toronto. Mike Bullard is the late-night talk-show star of Canada—the David Letterman of Canada—and also happens to be the brother of comedian Pat

Bullard. Up to this point I was known in Canada but was not a household name. I was well-known in Ottawa, for sure, as a silly guy, a goofy goofball, even a turd and a weirdo. My name was not yet inextricably linked with the words "gross," "shocking," and "a scourge on Western Civilization." I was a silly boy from Ottawa with a silly show on the CBC.

The moose!

Anyway, a lot of things converged around my first appearance on the *Mike Bullard Show*. Knowing I should do something crazy, I walked on stage with a bag of milk and a ten-dollar bill. In Canada, milk comes in bags instead of cartons. They are clear plastic bags sealed at both ends, and you stick the bag into a specially shaped pitcher for pouring. In the middle of the interview I calmly snipped the milk bag open and sprayed it all over me. It was messy and crazy. As I was doing this, I also damaged a very expensive microphone. For weeks after that, Mike kept making reference to the time Tom Green came on and destroyed five thousand dollars' worth of equipment. It became a running joke.

Hollywood manager Howard Lapides happened to be at the show that night. Howard grew up in Buffalo, New York, and for a while in his twenties

We had a fascination with using dead animals in our pieces.
Here's a dead cow in a "Mutilated by Aliens" bit.

lived in Ottawa. He knows the Canadian entertainment scene very well and has been instrumental in bringing a lot of Canadian talent to L.A. He brought, among others, Norm McDonald, Harland Williams, and Mike Bullard's brother, Pat, down to the States. He also happened to represent Mike, which is why he was there that night.

As he was coming to the show, Howard noticed a line of kids standing in the freezing cold, waiting to get in. "Who are they waiting for?" he asked someone. "Tom Green," they said. Howard decided we should talk.

After the milk-spewing bit, Howard came up to me backstage, slipped me a business card, and said, "Hi, I'm Howard, I'm Mike's manager. I live in Los Angeles." To me, this had "big deal" written all over it. This was the first real Hollywood businessman I had ever met. It sounds like a lame scene from a bad Hollywood movie—"Hey, kid, I can make you a star."—but that's pretty much how I saw it.

Howard came into my life when I was very confused about what I was doing and where I was going. I had been to L.A. only once in my life, when we made a trip to Mexico for the Comedy Network show. At the time I had a very low-key meeting with the Fox Family Channel about using some of my bits as interstitial programming. Somehow I didn't see myself fitting in with the whole Fox Family approach to television, but what did I know? After meeting Howard, I knew I could trust his opinion. He knew a lot more about Hollywood deal making than I'd ever know.

I returned to the *Mike Bullard Show* a couple of months later, and it was that second appearance that changed my public profile radically. As a way of topping the milk/microphone mess, I decided to take our pet dead raccoon with me and shave it during the show. Perhaps it would be educational to anyone out there who had a raccoon around the house that needed a shave. Our pet was nicely nestled in four layers of garbage bags in a suitcase. I came out with the suitcase, and Mike, being the polite Canadian that he is, said, "What's in the suitcase, Tom?" So I showed him.

The smell of this horrible little cadaver was gut-wrenching, and that's exactly how Mike reacted. When I threw the raccoon on his desk, he freaked and seemed like he was going to throw up. It wasn't that he was squeamish. It was purely a physical response. Of course I was a little more used to the sweet smell of rotting raccoon flesh, so I tried to keep things going.

Hangin' with Mike Bullard.

They had to stop the taping of the show so that Mike could go outside and actually throw up and the whole studio could be aired out. While Mike was outside, I chased a local soap opera star around the stage with my slimy little pet. It was insane.

The next day this was front-page news in every major paper in Canada. Instantly, the mainstream Canadian media dubbed me a "shock comic." I was the new King of Gross. From then on, if we would do ten bits on a given show, the one that would get noticed and written about was the gross one, i.e., humping a dead moose, sucking a cow's udder, or eating worms. I admit, I often did that stuff to get noticed so that people would pay attention to the other, often much funnier stuff. What started out as merely one element of our humor became, in essence, my brand. Tom "You Know, That Guy Who Humped a Dead Moose" Green.

The very last bit I did on the CBC show involved the raccoon. In the dozens of silly, stupid, inane, and genuinely funny bits we did on that show, it may have been the most bizarre moment of all. After the Mike Bullard appearance, I rewrapped our little friend and brought him back to Ottawa. We invited an actual magician on the show and built a raccoon-sized box with a lid. You could unclip the top, open it up, turn it around on wheels, close it, and place a saw across the top. It was a sawing-the-lady-in-half–style box, only a lot smaller. I think it was one of the more elaborate props we had ever concocted.

So the magician comes on stage and does a couple of tricks involving string and cards. I wanted the audience to firmly believe this guy was for real. Then I said, "Now I have a trick for you." I pulled out the box and, in my best David Copperfield pseudodramatic flair, I showed him the box and announced that I was going to proceed to cut our dead raccoon in half, right there on stage. It was a trick people had seen a thousand times. The audience figured the magician had set this up and was going to pull it off with no damage to the dead coon.

I pulled the raccoon out of his four layers of plastic, and by this point it was a sickening sight and smell. Glenn automatically started gagging, if not vomiting, the magician backed up, and I proceeded with the trick. I put the raccoon in the magic box, spun it around a time or two, and started sawing away. Of course the joke, much to everyone's horror, was that I really did saw the raccoon in half. It was messy. Slime started spewing everywhere, on stage and in the audience, the stench got even more unbearable, and now there were rotting raccoon guts to add to the overall visual impact. The audience was gagging at the sight of these intestines shooting out of the magic box. There were people vomiting under their seats and covering their mouths and pulling their shirts over their faces and screaming in horror. Some of the audience shots were so vile that the Comedy Network asked us to censor them, something they rarely did. It was great.

The audience wasn't just reacting to the sight and smell of a dissected raccoon; they were reacting with astonishment that this was actually happening in front of their eyes on a television show. They couldn't believe what they were seeing. They came out to see a comedy show and all of a sudden there is a guy sawing a dead raccoon in half. Some were squeamish, some were angry, some were laughing, some were upset, some were vomiting, some were out the door before the saw first touched fur.

We didn't analyze this, we just watched in amazement. After having watched literally thousands if not millions of hours of television in our twenty-some years of addiction, we were seeing something we had never seen before—

an entire television audience reacting in an extreme, spontaneous, completely unpremeditated way. It was gross and it was thrilling, simultaneously.

SUPER STAR

WHILE WE WERE ON THAT TEN-WEEK ROAD TRIP to see Canada and bring back enough field material for an entire season of *The Tom Green Show,* I got a phone call that signaled a new phase of my life. Somewhere this side of Vancouver, I heard from the office that Bruce McCullough from *Kids in the Hall* had called and wanted to talk to me. This was a huge deal to us because, first of all, we were from Ottawa, meaning we weren't from Toronto, which is the entertainment capital of Canada. Toronto, not Ottawa, was the home of SCTV, *Kids in the Hall,* and 90 percent of all important entertainment figures north of the border. All the major TV channels are there and most feature films come out of Toronto, so if you were working in entertainment business in Canada, you were in Toronto.

I had never met a famous person at that point in my life, let alone someone whose work I respected. I didn't even know what to think when Bruce McCullough called. It turned out that he was a fan of the cable show, and he was about to direct a *Saturday Night Live* movie in Toronto called *Super Star,* a vehicle especially designed for Molly Shannon and co-starring Will Farrell. He wanted me to come to Toronto the next day to audition for the movie. We had started our trip out in Toronto, because that's where Sean had the van. We'd been driving for eight weeks and were a day away from Vancouver. We had just about completed the mission.

I had zero experience as a professional actor. I had never thought about being in a movie or even wanted to be in a movie. I wanted to do a TV show, a talk show. A MOVIE? I also had never seen or read a movie script before. So Bruce FedExed me the script to *Super Star* the next day. He wanted me to come out and read for this part, Dylan, one of a series of small background characters. Dylan had maybe ten lines in the whole movie. He was Will Farrell's friend, and his job was to stand beside Will Farrell for the entire film.

I didn't have any money to get back to Toronto to audition, so Howard Lapides, my new manager, talked them into paying for a plane ticket to take me back. At the time, I thought this was weird, since I wasn't much more than an extra in the movie. But all of a sudden, I'm on a plane flying to Toronto with this movie script in my hand. I went in, read for the role, and they sent the tape off to Lorne Michaels, the famed *Saturday Night Live* producer, and Paramount Pictures to look at. I didn't know what to do at the audition. I came from the world of going out in the street, going crazy in front of a video camera, and editing it down to something later on. So I did the only thing I knew how to do. I went in to this audition and crawled up the walls for my three lines. I was on top of the chair and then on the ground thrashing around, i.e., a whole bunch of stupid shit. I've never seen the audition tape, but it's no doubt very embarrassing and will probably end up on a Dick Clark "World's Worst Audition Tapes" special some day.

I returned to the van with Derek and Ray to finish my "real business," shooting cross-country field pieces for the TV show, but that *Super Star* audition, though a very minor moment in the scheme of things, was something of a turning point. It was the first time where I could see the potential of what we were doing. One minute I'm doing a cable show, still borrowing vans and scrounging around for weird, impromptu comedy bits, and the next moment Bruce McCullough and Lorne Michaels and Paramount Studios are calling, if only to be Will Farrell's on-camera sidekick.

I got the part, and not only that, I was making more money for ten days as a glorified extra than I made in a whole season of the Comedy Network show. You might have missed me in the movie. I was the one who yelled "You suck" at Molly Shannon and later poured salad all over myself. I had to shave my goatee—that was part of the deal.

The first day of shooting I was dressed in a skin-tight football outfit. Remember, I had never "acted" a day in my life. We were shooting this scene where Molly Shannon was supposed to grab onto Will Farrell, and "Dylan" (me) and this other Will-loving slacker were supposed to pull her off. So the scene started and we pulled her off. Bruce said he wanted us to do it again and this time make it look real. We decided to pull her harder and start a little tug of war. Fine, said Bruce, but it still didn't look real. He told Molly to hang on harder and told me and my partner to really, really pull. So, we did as told, or at least I did, and all of a sudden Molly was screaming. She broke a rib! The first day of shooting her first movie and some lamo from Ottawa broke her rib! She kept her distance for the rest of the shoot. For some reason, even though two people were pulling, she thought I was the rib breaker.

Anyway, broken ribs aside, I was in awe of everyone I met—Will, Molly, Lorne Michaels, and Harland Williams, one of my early comic heroes whom I had last seen when I was fifteen hanging around Yuk-Yuk's in Ottawa. They were in turn probably a little surprised to see this bit player off to the side of the set signing autographs for the neighborhood kids. The cable show, which I returned to and finished after *Super Star* wrapped, had done exactly what Derek and I had hoped when we first started pinning ideas up on the roach-covered wall of my apartment. It had become a hit in Canada and gotten us to the next step—a shot at MTV.

7.

"YOU'RE NOT IN
CANADA ANYMORE"

—

"So we flew out on Boxing Day, with little carry-on bags, thinking we were going down to New York and then they would send us home in a couple of weeks, but after three weeks, I asked Tom, 'When are we going back?' and he said, 'I don't think we are going back to Ottawa. I think this is it. Like I think we've moved to the United States for the rest of our lives—I think that's what's just happened.' "

—Derek Harvie, on Tom
and his first trip
to MTV in New York

"HEY, YOU'RE TOUCHING MY CONDOMS, RIGHT NOW!"

IT WAS JUST CRAZY. EVERYTHING SEEMED TO TAKE off at once. The time between being on the road with Derek and Ray, staying three to a room in a cheesy motel and spending the day looking for roadkill, and the time I walked onto *David Letterman* for the first time seemed like no time at all. Soon after *Super Star* and my return to Ottawa to do the Comedy Network show, the word came from Howard that MTV wanted to talk. It turns out that John Miller, the MTV executive who wanted to meet me, and Howard had another show in common, *Loveline,* with Adam Corolla and Dr. Drew. I'm not sure exactly how it happened, but my name came up and John saw some of our tapes and all of a sudden I had a line of communication to MTV. Like many things in Hollywood, it was part knowing someone and part accident.

I was still editing the second season of the Comedy Network shows, using some of the more-than-eighty bits we shot on our trip, when I found myself flying down to New York to meet the MTV executives. They had seen plenty of our tapes and were ready for me to move to the next crucial stage—the Pitch.

Networks get pitched show ideas every day, most of them unsolicited and unwanted. Writers and producers in Hollywood can spend years pitching one "breakthrough" idea after another before some suit on the other side of the table finally says, "Yeah, we'll develop that." "Develop" usually means commissioning a script that the network nitpicks to death, then rejects anyway. Writing rejected pilot scripts is a whole other business in Hollywood, as is producing rejected pilots. Enough money a year to feed everyone in Liberia is wasted on scripts and pilots that networks just throw in the trashcan.

We were in a slightly different position because we had been doing our show for years and had hours and hours of material to show for it. This was attractive to MTV. It wasn't like starting a show from scratch. If they bought the show, they could repackage the best bits from Canada and it would be brand-new comedy for their voracious American audience.

MTV was in the habit of having a yearly pitch session where they'd fly in talent to talk about their ideas in front of a *Flashdance* type of panel of judges.

Clockwise from lower left: Glenn, Derek, Phil, and me in a bar in NYC.

In this case, the judges are MTV executives whose careers depend on making the right programming decisions. So they flew me to L.A. to pitch my show in the Foundation Room at the House of Blues in West Hollywood, the site of that year's big pitch-off. They put me up at the Mondrian Hotel just down the block, which was like no hotel room I'd ever stayed in. The bed was on the floor, it was all white, and it was just weird. It didn't feel at all like the Econo Lodge I had just stayed in in Medicine Hat or Moosejaw. We were clearly not in Saskatchewan anymore.

John Miller and I talked by phone about a series of particular bits that I should show at the pitch, the ones he thought would win over the *Flashdance* panel. One bit featured a trip to a drugstore where I bought some condoms and got into an uncomfortable discussion about sex with the salespeople. A second bit was the Vancouver setup where I flailed around bandaged up and on crutches. At the last minute, right before I left Ottawa, I decided to throw in something not even John had seen before, let alone okayed—a clip of me dressed as Captain Kirk sucking off a cow's udder. I actually suck the milk right out of the udder—it had a grassy tinge to it, with just a hint of manure. The piece was quite dramatic, and I was, in my perverse way, quite proud of that.

Someone once asked me, in the area of man-animal barnyard activities, if I had ever had intercourse with a sheep. Apparently horny farm boys and banjo players have been doing this for a long time. My reply was no, I have to draw the line somewhere, and I think that line is between sucking a cow's teat and fucking a sheep. I am not exactly sure where that line is, but it's in between those two things.

So here I am in L.A. for only the second time in my entire life. My plan was to walk into the room at the House of Blues, show the tapes as the funny part of me, then explain in a very sane, adult, businesslike way all the practical reasons why they should buy the show: it was cheap to produce, it would appeal to their show-me-something-new demographic, we could hit the ground running, etc. I had been doing this pitch for years, of course, to anyone in Canada who would let me in the door, so I felt like I knew the important talking points.

I sat in the shower of the Mondrian Hotel for four hours before the pitch, literally in the fetal position in the bathtub with the shower blowing in my face. I'm surprised the hotel didn't charge me for extra water. The only time I've ever done that in life, before or after, was about six months later, right before I was a guest on the *Letterman* show for the first time.

As I sat in that shower, I became a little worried that the whole presentation might come off as too dry and rehearsed. At the very last minute, just as I was leaving the hotel room as undoubtedly the squeakiest-clean pitchman MTV had ever seen, I stuck two cans of shaving cream and some hotel towels in my bag.

I was completely intimidated walking into that room. I had never met

John Miller before in person, let alone anyone else sitting there about to decide my show-business fate. I remember I was a bit taken aback when I first saw John. He wasn't the cliché fifty-year-old TV exec. He was young and wore thick, dark-rimmed glasses that made him look a little like Buddy Holly.

I started showing the predetermined tape bits and talking about them, awkwardly. At the time, remember, there was nothing remotely like this on TV—no *Spy TV*, no *Jackass*, no *Punk'd*, no Jamie Kennedy. The closest analogy, at least to some of the surprise pranks, would be the old *Candid Camera* show, without the rigid, camera-in-the-mailbox format and without the hokey tagline, "Smile, you're on *Candid Camera*."

The executives laughed hard at the man-on-crutches bit and I started to relax. Then I switched to the nonphysical humor of the show, i.e., the condom bit, where I chat to the pharmacist about how Al Capone died of syphilis and tell a female cashier, "Hey, you're touching my condoms, right now." More laughs. John Miller thought the presentation was over at that point. He figured I'd jabber on for a few more minutes, answer a few questions, grovel like a dog, and get out. That's the standard-pitch MO.

Instead, I told them I was going to show one more tape, and, tah-da, they found themselves watching a grown man sucking away at a cow's udder. The execs started screaming. They couldn't believe what they were seeing. They were literally crying with laughter. John Miller was covering his face, which I took as a sign of complete surprise and not a sign of a man about to lose his job. My thought at the time was, "God, I am killing here. I am probably going to get picked up on MTV."

Then John Miller blurted out something like, "Hey, you didn't tell me about *that!*" and that got another executive-type laugh. I then talked a few minutes about the practical stuff, the cost, the appeal, the vision, blah, blah, blah. At this point I announced my fear that I was boring them and was coming across like a sedate, stick-in-the-mud kind of guy. And then I sort of went into the zone.

I reached in my bag, pulled out the shaving cream, and started covering myself in shaving cream. I laid down flat on the boardroom table in front of this row of "suits"—of course, at MTV, they don't actually wear suits—and I started thrashing around like a lunatic. I screamed, "I want to be on MTV! I want to be on MTV!" They were laughing. They were no doubt concerned, but they were laughing. This definitely wasn't a hard-pressed, pony-tailed, middle-age producer in the room pitching his "killer" idea about a sexy show about sexy kids set in a sexy locale with, you know, a lot of sex.

I then stopped abruptly and said, "Okay, I'm sorry about that—maybe I carried that way too far." As I started to leave, I wiped a dollop of shaving cream onto the forehead of Brian Graden, who happened to be (and still is) the top executive of MTV. Of course I didn't know that at the time. That got a huge laugh. "Anyway," I said, "thank you very much, I am really sorry about all of this, I don't know what I was thinking," then walked out the door. Everyone behind me clapped. Of course they could have been clapping as if to say, "Thank God that fool's gone."

I got on the elevator with Howard and a colleague named Chip Butterman and for a moment we were completely silent. Then Howard said, quietly, "That was the most insane pitch, the best pitch I have ever seen in my life." I'm sure he says something like that to every client after every pitch, but this time I think he meant it. All I knew is that I had my one big shot at MTV, and I had to leave an impression. I didn't want to leave anything back in the hotel room.

I don't know if it was a week or a month later, but very soon after that I was living in New York City editing an MTV show called, just like all the others, *The Tom Green Show*.

THE TRANSITION FROM CANADA to MTV was a major culture shock. First of all, it was just Derek and I who went to New York to put together the initial shows. I remember, on our initial trip, we were sitting in a microbrewery in Times Square, drinking our beer and staring at a billboard of Marilyn Monroe. We just sat there slightly stunned, watching all the cars and signs and lights, and I said, "What in the hell are we doing here? Are we actually getting picked up by this channel?" Or even stranger . . . "Are we actually living in New York City?"

At that point I had never really seen MTV. Of course I knew about it—Dire Straits had written a song about it—but we didn't get it in Ottawa. I

Yippeeee!

watched it for the first time in the hotel room that MTV had arranged for us. That was right before they sent by a town car to take us to the new *Tom Green Show* offices a few blocks away. The office they gave us was at 1633 Broadway in the Paramount Plaza. It was the same building where they shot *The Jerry Langford Show*, the talk show starring Jerry Lewis, for the Scorsese movie *The King of Comedy*. This is exactly the place where my big-screen alter ego, Rupert Pupkin, played by Robert DeNiro, kidnapped Jerry Lewis from his office so he could have his own talk show. It was a freaky coincidence.

They finally put us up in a place called the Flat Otel (no *H*). I had a suite with a huge living room and bedroom and a bathtub with a whirlpool in it. When I walked into the production, there were all kinds of people running around—producers, writers, editors, assistants—and they all seemed very "big city" cool.

I was intimidated by New York and New Yorkers. Growing up in Canada, the message was that Americans, and especially New York Americans, are rude, obnoxious, and often dangerous. The opposite, of course, proved true. Most people on the staff at MTV were extremely outgoing and hospitable. They went out of their way to make sure we were comfortable in this new world.

Americans in general have the impression that Canadians are really polite, but they actually aren't. They are just really polite to Americans because they are so in awe of them. It's funny to watch people I know in Canada. When there are no Americans around, they like to bag on America in the same way someone from a small town will bag on the big city. It comes from a place of national insecurity. That may be part of the reason so many comedians come from Canada. It's funny to watch the same people who talk down about America change tone when an "actual" American is in their presence. They completely shift gears, so desperately wanting to impress "The American." When you live in a nation that feels it is constantly overlooked, you really try to be on your best behavior when Daddy is in the room.

Anyway, America invited us into the room. It was my first five minutes at MTV and everything was great.

"HEY, EVERYBODY, COOL IS COMING, THIS IS COOL"

MTV HAD A WAY OF APPROACHING *THE TOM GREEN Show* that was so alien to our style of working that Derek and I didn't know how to deal with it. First they brought in producers to shape the show who were certainly experienced, but not in any way experienced with the idea of being subversive. Derek and I had always wanted to make a show like nothing else on TV. These people seemed like they wanted to mold us into something they had seen before. Soon after we arrived, they would hold closed-door production meetings and not let me in. I'd knock on the door and someone would open it a crack and say, "Sorry, you can't come in right now, we're talking about the show. We are mapping out what you are going to do."

Then they brought in some "big comedy writers" to help "punch up" the material and punch up me on stage. We were very much in awe of these people until I started reading what they wanted to put in my mouth. It wasn't that it was bad; it just wasn't what I had been doing for the last nine or ten years and what I was comfortable and obviously successful at doing. Actually, no . . . it was bad.

Of course Derek and I were equally cocky and full of ourselves, if not more so. We decided early on that even though we were in New York, even though we had never eaten matzoh ball soup at the Carnegie Deli or hung out backstage at *Letterman* or *Conan* or done anything else that New York show-biz types take for granted, we weren't going to be treated like a couple of stupid hicks from Ottawa. We went to great, probably boring lengths to "explain" what made our show work, i.e., our "philosophy" of comedy.

I sometimes had a hard time convincing people of the subtler aspects beneath the craziness. I did have one great John Cleese quote that I liked to throw around at parties. It was something I thought really applied to our show. He said, "It's funny to look at somebody acting silly. But it's even funnier to look at somebody who is looking at somebody acting silly." This was very important when editing our pieces. The new editors were trying to tighten up our bits, but in doing so they would usually cut out the reaction shots. We tried to explain that that was essentially the joke. Me dancing around on the street in a silly outfit isn't all that funny. It's the shot of the confused old lady looking that gets the laugh. As obvious as it seems on paper, when egos got involved, people would refuse to understand.

The MTV people were very polite listening to our spiel, but it didn't take us long to realize that they didn't consider us the comic savants that we thought we were. It was starting to become obvious that many of the producers considered us some lucky kids that needed to be taught a lesson in television production. They were going to do us a big favor and step in and "fix" our little Canadian show.

Along with their desire to punch up and smooth out our crude attempts at comedy, they had a style of production that wasn't even in the same ballpark as the approach we had been using for years. Take the guy-on-crutches bit, for instance. It was shot with one video camera manned by Ray. People reacted very naturally to my falling down because I was the focus of the situation and the technical aspects of the shoot were unobtrusive, if not invisible. I did have the problem of Ray laughing every time I fell, but not even that destroyed the reality of the moment.

We had learned early on that it was better if people on the street didn't think we were shooting for TV. It was better if they thought we were just some troublemaking kids with a home video camera. This way they would get mad, or confused, or help out, or run away. Even in a simple interview, this was effective in making people far less intimidated. Any time in the past we had shot with a big Beta Cam camera, people assumed we were from the local news and put on their best behavior. The size of the production completely affected the story. This is why one cannot electronically produce a "pure" documentary. The act of recording an event essentially changes the event itself. We were trying to minimize that and skew it to our advantage.

When we went out on our first MTV shoot, there were four production vans, eight producers with walkie-talkies, and enough equipment to make *Matrix 2*. I felt like I was invading Baghdad or something. Actually, it was like a scene from *The X-Files* when FEMA shows up because there has been a nuclear explosion or a bio-terror scare. There were production assistants with clipboards. In all those years in Canada, we had never used a clipboard. After the shoot, everyone from MTV came up and said they thought it was the best bit they had ever shot. They couldn't wait to edit it.

Now, I tried to explain, I edit this stuff. I've been staying up nights editing this stuff since I was a college student. So they would edit a chunk and it struck me as painfully corny, so I would go back in and reedit it, which didn't make them that happy, and they would look at it and say it was great, then go back in and reedit it again. It was a creative tug-of-war that went on for a month or more. They'd take a joke out, I'd put it back in, they'd take it out again, I'd put it back in again. By the end maybe 65 percent of what should have been included made the cut, which, of course, was much better than the 4 percent that was part of their original cut.

They ended up rejecting a number of our favorite Canadian pieces outright. One was me sucking the cow udder. This completely baffled us. "Hey," I said, "didn't we use that in the pitch? I mean, is this not what sold the frigging show? Was this not the pièce de résistance or whatever of the whole thing?" No, someone decided, it was too gross for America. We brought probably 250 separate pieces down from Canada. In the end, initially at least, MTV selected about thirty to reair.

Plus, they were taking some of the best pieces we had made—"Slutmobile," for instance, or "Plaid House"—and remixing them. That means they would take out the music I had made on my keyboard in Canada—weird, surreal music, sometimes just strange sounds—and replace it with a hip-hop instrumental by Will Smith. The music said, "Hey, everybody, cool is coming, this is cool." It stepped on the joke. They thought it helped the piece, I thought it took the edge off of it. It was "Trust us, we know what we're doing, we're MTV" versus "Trust me, I know what I'm doing, I've been doing this in Canada for years." The problem was, I wasn't in Canada anymore.

It felt to me like a lot of what they wanted to do softened the comedy by overexplaining. Every word of every setup had to be written out and read on a TelePrompTer. Everything had to be *planned* so that everyone from the director to the camera people to lighting people to the censors knew exactly what was coming next. I tried to explain, in my defense, that for the show to work right, you couldn't write what you didn't know was going to happen—it was unwriteable—it was me reacting to the reaction of someone to the reaction of someone else." You couldn't say, "Okay, now I'm going to throw milk all over you or now I'm going to spray the whole audience with a very powerful fire extinguisher." They would have been more comfortable with me telling knock-knock jokes off of cue cards. It was two different world views, or at least comedy views, clashing during those early days, and I was caught right in the middle of it.

On the other hand, while I was in the thick of this creative death match, they were treating me very well. I was making four or five times as much as I was on the Comedy Network, I was about to appear in a full-page ad in *Rolling Stone*, I was making it! Once they even delivered a brand-new Fender guitar and amp to my hotel room because they thought I'd like it. I know only three chords on the guitar, but it was a very cool gift.

The very first field shoot, the one with the four production vans and a crew of thousands, taught me a lot. First of all, it taught me about the power of MTV. Probably the most surprising and shocking thing about going from Canada to MTV was the raw power of the MTV marketing machine. As I said, Derek and I were brought in almost as observers of their version of our show. Of course we didn't see it that way and did everything we could to make our show our show again. Anyway, we had been in New York for no more than a couple of weeks when MTV had decided to take some old footage from the Canadian show and package it as an on-the-air promotion spot. We had nothing to do with this. They chose whatever they wanted and slammed it together as a hit-the-air-quick promo.

A few days after the promos hit the air, we took off to Princeton, New Jersey, for that first field shoot. I was going to do two bits. One had me dressed as a security guard, generally harassing people on the street. The second bit involved yelling at people through a megaphone, something I did quite a bit in Ottawa. I was going to be dressed in camouflage fatigues and yell at people that I was camouflaged and they couldn't see me. I would, for instance, hide in the bushes and as someone walked by shout, "You can't see me, I'm camouflaged!" Low-brow humor for a high-class college town.

Our production battalion pulled into town, and I probably hadn't been out of the truck for eleven seconds when people started screaming my name from the other side of the street. They recognized me not from my show, because it had yet to air. They had never seen one show or even a guest appearance on someone else's show. They hadn't even seen my debut bit acting role yelling "You suck!" in *Super Star*.

They had seen one promo, a thirty-second clip of me humping a dead moose. "Hey, man, we saw you humping a dead moose on MTV. Could we, like, have your autograph, man?" They came running out of coffee shops, hopping off bikes, pulling up on skateboards. Of course, given the nature of TV promos, they had seen me humping that moose carcass a thousand times.

It just kind of hit me as an instant shock when I realized that my show hasn't even aired yet in America and already I am getting barraged with more attention than I ever got after years on the air in Canada. It was virtually instantaneous—on the basis of one promo, I was a celebrity in America. I was "Tom Green." I'd been hammering away for eight largely unpaid years in Canada and no one gave much of a shit. One MTV ad, a month and a half before a show had aired, and I was a twenty-seven-year-old shock-comic boy wonder.

The downside of this circus, of course, was that no one was the least bit confused or surprised by either the camouflage or the security guard bit. They knew who I was. There was a convoy of trucks and dozens of people walking around in MTV jackets trying to get releases signed. In other words, all that production hoopla on top of all the "I know you" media hoopla ruined any chance of getting natural, spontaneous, off-guard reactions. People I was supposed to shock and confuse were running out and trying to get in the shot. Some of them were trying to sign their release forms first. They wanted to be on MTV!

I was concerned at the time, but eventually we figured out a new system of shooting so that the original style and rhythm of the field pieces could be preserved. To me, the shift in scale was just weird. Early on they announced they had some promos they were going to shoot for the show. They had written spots already. All I had to do was show up and do what I was told. So, on the day of the shoot, I showed up at this New York studio. It was bigger than any studio I had ever seen. It was about the size of two Ottawa high school gyms side by side.

Inside the studio was a complete New York street set. Actually there were eight New York street sets. It was like *Sesame Street*. There was a front porch of a brownstone building, the interior of a brownstone building, the alleyway of a brownstone building. It was wild. Instead of just going to a New York street corner and shooting something quick and dirty with a small video camera, they had built it all on a set so they could carefully film a fake setting that matched a real setting that was about a hundred yards away.

And they filled the set with actors. They had kids playing kids. The promos actually turned out fine—the kids were convincing kids—but the whole approach was new and strange to me. They did the same thing with the opening of the show—they built a set. The budget for the MTV opening to *The Tom Green Show* was more than *the entire season's* budget for the show on the Comedy Network in Canada. I repeat: one MTV title sequence = one whole season of thirteen shows. The Canadian title sequence was shot in a local car wash on a Tuesday afternoon.

ONE OF THE MOST outrageous, and perhaps funniest, segments I ever did starring my parents occurred early in the MTV series. It involved a set of

Greek statues I had made and placed on their front lawn. The statues depicted, in tasteful, classical form, my dear parents *in flagrante delicto*. In other words, they were posed for love.

Actually it was two sets of statues with different poses. Being at MTV, we finally had a little money to do things, so we contracted two set designers in Ottawa to create these works of art. They used papier-mâché and plaster and painted them with a texture that looked like granite. At a price of ten thousand dollars, they looked very impressive.

The bit began with a *60 Minutes*–style interview with my parents ostensibly about my childhood. I wore a tie and looked very professional. Of course, two questions in—after "What was I like as a child?" and "How did you feel about my marks in school?"—I turned an embarrassing corner. I abruptly posed the question, "Dad, tell us about the angry dinners . . . you know, the dinners where you would come home from work and get angry with Mom if your dinner wasn't ready?" This never happened, of course, but that was beside the point.

Despite their denials, I pressed on. "Why," I asked, "would you say 'Where's my dinner, bitch!' when dinner wasn't ready?" Or, "Did you ever hit Mom when dinner wasn't on time?" They quickly got furious, pleading "Stop this, Tom, stop it right now."

So I switched to sex. "Mom, did you ever perform oral sex on Dad?" "Stop this." "Anal sex?" "Stop it!" "Dad, did you ever say . . . 'You like it like that, bitch'?" By this point, they were walking up the stairs. The interview was over.

My parents were livid. I had been on MTV for about seven weeks at this point, more or less, i.e., not for long. My parents went so far as to call MTV to have the segment kept off the air. They actually called MTV in New York and left a message on a corporate answering machine. It said, in essence, "This is Richard Green calling, and if you ever come up here again and do anything like that to us again, we are going to sue you bastards for one million dollars."

We played both the interview and the answering machine message in the studio on the show. I then said, in essence, "Well, I guess we did make my parents kind of mad, so we decided to apologize to them. I made them a special gift as a way to apologize." We cut to a clip of me showing up at their house at six in the morning, waking them up in their pajamas, and dragging them out to the front lawn to proudly present my "gift."

The first set of statues had a nice plaque reading, "Where's my dinner, bitch!" One statue had my mother cowering and holding her hands up in fear as the statue of my father was raising a fist and a baton to beat her. Upon seeing this, my mother freaked and ran into the house. My father said, "Oh, get out of here." They were not laughing.

I then ran into the house to calm them down. Meanwhile, a van pulled up, loaded with statues, and replaced the "Where's my dinner, bitch!" ones with a new set, identified, naturally, as the "You like it like that, bitch!" statues. This plaster duet had my mother in the familiar doggy position with my father standing behind her, erect. Water from a garden hose was in fact shooting out of his, ah, nozzle. They looked like they were having a good time.

My parents come out again, see this, and are beyond comforting. My mother dashes back inside, mortified, and my father actually kicks the statues over and smashes them. Back to the studio: MTV refused to let us air the "dinner" statues unless I made a stern on-air disclaimer that MTV and *The Tom Green Show* are opposed to domestic or spousal abuse. So I stood next to the statue of my dad beating my mom, announced that we do not condone violence against women, because "violence is wrong," then proceeded to smash the statue to bits with a baseball bat. This wasn't really violence against women. It was violence against plaster of Paris.

My parents feel to this day that this particular razz crossed every possible line of decency and fairness. They were obviously concerned with what might lie ahead if they didn't do something drastic to make me stop. I had been doing this kind of silly joke at their expense for years, but now I was in New York, with the media power of MTV, big crews, and enough of a budget to commission Greek statues in their likeness. They were no longer helping their goofy son get a leg up in the world. His leg was now way up, and their message was clear: "This better not happen anymore."

Of course I couldn't *not* use the statue segment—it was a huge crowd-pleaser to an audience of MTV watchers, all of whom would rather not think about their parents' sex life. I begged my parents to let me use the piece, and they stood their ground. They really were going to sue everyone involved if those statues saw the light of cable day. I promised never to do any more sexually oriented assaults on their privacy if they just allowed me to show this last one. I probably couldn't top it, anyway, so it was a good negotiating concession on my part. And it was in fact the very last frankly insulting/embarrassing/potentially libelous prank I ever pulled on them.

I probably learned a lot more about my parents through this episode than I had ever learned growing up in their house. Lesson #1: when it comes to discussing their sex life in public, they are very, very conservative.

Anyway, in the middle of this argument, Oprah called. She had seen the MTV show where I painted my parents' house plaid while they were on that canoe trip. She was planning a Mother's Day show where children come on and apologize to their moms for some egregious slight, and she decided she wanted me to come on and apologize for painting the family home like a Scottish tartan, among other things. I was this new goofball guy on MTV and, though most of her audience wouldn't know who I was (and probably still don't), Oprah thought she could have fun with me and my parent pranks.

So I called up my mom and said, "Hey, you guys, Oprah Winfrey wants you guys to go on her show in Chicago," and all of a sudden their whole attitude changed. Of course they *wanted* to go on *Oprah*, statues or no statues, and so we all ended up together on Oprah's stage. Oprah showed three segments—"Plaid House," the animals in the living room, and "Slutmobile." The biggest laugh came with the series of phone messages my mother left after seeing "Slutmobile." She wasn't laughing at the time, but sitting next to Oprah, it was just show business, and all was forgiven.

Then, to ice the cake, I announced that I was giving my long-suffering parents a twelve-day luxury cruise to Tahiti and two new padlocks for the front door. Of course, Oprah was the one giving the cruise, but it still made me look good. "Very funny, Tom," Oprah ended by saying. Just the kind of big-time confirmation both my parents and I had always hoped for. After all, this wasn't a bunch of pimply-faced, gross-loving kids on MTV cheering me on. This was *Oprah*.

8.

SPACE SHUTTLE *COLUMBIA*

—

"It was just like a rocket, you know?"

—Derek Harvie

"READ THE FUCKING TELEPROMPTER!"

THE FIRST MTV SHOW DID NOT GO WELL. IT BEGAN with a "read-through," a practice session the night before where I read all my lines off a TelePrompTer in front of the producers, writers, and MTV executives. I'd never used a TelePrompTer in my life. Nor had I ever done a formal read-through in a boardroom with all these worried faces looking at me. Our MO in Canada was to chose a basic premise, improvise the lines on stage as the show was being taped, then edit out the boring parts later.

Now I was being asked to hit every line exactly, word for word, and to hit particular stage marks as I was saying them. One of the bits on that first show involved a guy from the zoo who would bring on some exotic turtles. I would then dip my hand in a can of mealworms to feed the turtles and, while doing it, pop a couple of mealworms in my own mouth and freak the guy out. The writers had this bit completely written out. I would say my lines, then someone would say the zoo guy's lines. I guess I was supposed to infuse some humor into these scripted lines, but they didn't strike me as funny and it took me a while to show any enthusiasm for the material. They probably just chalked my TelePrompTer stiffness up to lack of training. I chalked it up to apples and oranges. Their script was an apple, and I was an orange.

On the day of the taping, I was nervous as hell. I thought back to the time I was seventeen and in New York for the summer with Organized Rhyme. I got up at four in the morning to stand in line for tickets to the then-NBC version of the *Letterman* show. I remember sitting in the audience when Letterman came out and talked to the crowd for about two minutes before the show started. He had his jacket thrown over his shoulder, and he came out and basically goofed around with a few people. He then turned around and walked around a corner of the set, putting on his jacket as he went. Literally the second he turned that corner, the theme song kicked in and he walked right back out. It was like, "Holy shit, this is cool."

That stuck with me—how well oiled of a machine that show was and how easily Letterman made the transition from guy talking to the audience to star talking to millions of people. So, when my big moment came, my debut in America, I walked out in front of this audience of fifty to sixty kids to do my little Lettermanesque warm-up, and they freaked out. They freaked out for me, and when I introduced Glenn, they freaked out for Glenn, even though they had no idea who Glenn was. Then I said something about Phil sitting in back and they loved that, too. I finished my little chitchat, walked over, and sat down at the desk, fully expecting the theme song to kick in and the show to start. Just at that point: "Can we just hold for a second, Tom? Uh, we just gotta adjust some things here."

So there I sat, after I just did this great little monologue, while they adjusted things for about twenty-five minutes. All the energy was gone. The show finally started, and I was kind of bummed. And we did the show, and I did all the lines with as much enthusiasm as I could muster. When we got to the zoo guy and the worms, I shifted gears. I didn't throw a couple of worms in my mouth—I ate *all* the worms. I grabbed the entire tray of worms, and I ran out into the studio audience like a crazy, worm-eating fool. I crawled around, threw worms on people, you know, the usual stuff. Of course, none of this had been scripted and none of it had been "blocked," meaning the director and the camera people hadn't prearranged each shot. It was unrehearsed like virtually everything else I had ever done in my entire TV existence.

We finished the show and gathered in a room backstage. Glenn was there, along with Phil, Derek, and Howard. The MTV executives came into the room, and they were somber and silent. We knew they were mad, though we had thought the worm bit was pretty funny and were high-fiving ourselves about it. There was one particularly abusive executive who had berated us constantly and decided to use this occasion to reach new heights of vitriol. He made a speech for the whole group, actually more of a rant than a speech.

He yelled, repeatedly, "YOU'RE NOT IN FUCKING CANADA ANYMORE! Read the fucking TelePrompTer!" He screamed, "This is your fucking shot! If you want to fucking ruin your fucking career, then just keep doing that shit! I repeat, you're not in fucking Canada anymore! That was the worst piece

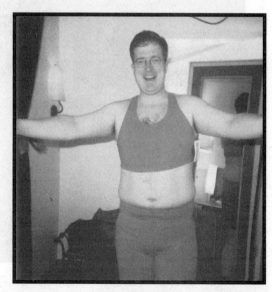

Glenn at MTV.

of shit I've ever seen in my life! That was fucking HORRIBLE!!!" And on and on. Everyone on their side was silent and angry. Everyone on our side was silent and angry, too. These fucking show-biz heavies didn't get it.

The feeling on our side was, Let's just get on a plane and go home and just say "Fuck this." I mean, who gives a fuck. I went in my dressing room, which was about the size of a closet, and I sat there, crushed, surrounded by my complementary "Break a Leg!" MTV bottle of champagne and my MTV fruit basket and flowers. John Miller came in and said, quietly, "Listen, man, this is a big deal. Read the TelePrompTer or you're going to ruin your shot." The MTV plan was to do each show twice and put together the best parts of both. So, more or less beaten down, I did the same show again, leaving out the worm-eating craziness. I read the TelePrompTer and went home. Pissed.

This is how it went for the first six shows. I played ball with the network. I rarely veered from the prepared text. I restrained myself from freaking out. I remember by the third show it got really embarrassing for me. I read something well off the TelePrompTer and an MTV exec ran on stage in front of the whole audience, gave me a hug, and said, "That was great, Tom! Good job! Now let's

do it again." I think the audience expected to see a guy who was in charge of his own ship. What they got was a guy constantly bombarded by a director coming over a speaker and shouting, "Can we try that again, Tom?" or "Let's do a quick pickup on that, Tom." I'd never done pickups before, which is where you repeat part of a sentence or turn your head another direction so the thing looks carefully shot.

I kept fighting for the field pieces to come out right, and the audience seemed to like them. I didn't fight for the stage stuff. Howard's advice was, "Listen, just get the stuff on the air. Don't make a big deal, because the field pieces are what it's all about. It's going to be good." So that's what I did. I put all of my chips on the field pieces and just "acted" the part of the host. We finished up the first six shows, edited them, and they went on the air. It was out there.

We began to prepare the next batch of shows while those six aired, which meant going out and shooting new field pieces. Two weeks after the initial airing, we were on a street in Manhattan and the response was obvious. Kids were freaking out and everybody knew who I was and everybody wanted my autograph. Soon articles were popping up with titles like "Tom Takes Manhattan." *Rolling Stone* weighed in. *Teen People* weighed in. Everybody liked it. It was a hit!

All the people who had been yelling at me for weeks on end were probably surprised, confused, relieved, and elated, all at the same time. We weren't the highest rated show on MTV at that point, but we were soon drawing a couple of million viewers a week, which were big numbers for cable at the time. The show quickly entered the pop culture zeitgeist. I was surprised, confused, relieved, and elated myself. I *wasn't* in Canada anymore.

The thing I realized quickly about MTV—remember, I was from Ottawa, where they don't get MTV—is that they played the show six times a day every day for a week. So the show was literally on thirty times a week. It was crazy! Every time you turned on MTV, our show was on. At the time they really had only five or six nonmusic shows, so they reran them constantly. If you were under thirty and owned a TV with cable, you saw all or part of *The Tom Green Show*. And if you were under thirty and liked the idea of embarrassing your parents in front of millions, you loved *The Tom Green Show*. It was new, it was different, it was gross!

"WHAT WAS THAT, LIKE FORTY BUCKS
AT THE GAP OR SOMETHING?"

ABOUT TWO WEEKS INTO THE SHOW AIRING, WE
got a call from David Letterman. I remember I was out on a field shoot on the
streets of Manhattan, dressed in an Eskimo costume and driving around a
dogsled full of sausages. I had just gotten kicked out of an office tower when
Bobby Maurer, our producer, came up and said, "David Letterman wants to
book you. You're on *David Letterman.* Tomorrow night." Apparently there was
a last-minute cancellation and I was the designated fill-in guest. I felt like I was
going to puke.

Then something happened and I wasn't going on Letterman. They probably got a bigger name at the very last second. "But they're going to have you on
soon," Bobby said. "Maybe in a week or two." Just the thought of going on
drove me crazy. I continued to want to puke every time the subject came up.
Sure enough, a couple of weeks later, the call came and I was booked in ink. A
New York Times writer decided to follow me around that day. First I took another four-hour shower at the Flat Otel, trying to shake the urge to either throw
up or pass out. The *Times* guy picked me up in the limo at the hotel—I was extremely clean and shriveled up like a prune.

After arriving, I remember getting my makeup on and, from the makeup
chair, watching Letterman come out at the beginning of the show to do his
monologue. And at the end of the monologue, he said, "Tonight on the show
we've got so-and-so and we've got, from MTV, Tom Green. Tom Green." He was
subtly acknowledging my anonymity. It was hilarious. I mean, who the fuck
was I?

I was standing in the wings of the stage, and there was Biff Henderson, the
real Biff Henderson, doing the job of floor director or stage manager. Really
doing it. He had his headphones, he was talking to the booth, smiling at me,
and I'm standing there, starstruck by the stage manager. Again I felt like I was
going to puke. It's fucking Biff Henderson, you know? And I haven't even gone
on the show yet and I'm freaking out because there's Biff.

I'm standing there, looking at Letterman on stage. He looks over at me, or at least over in my direction, and I don't know how I mustered up the courage, but for some reason I just thought, I'm gonna do this. I stuck my hand in the air when he looked in my direction and I waved. He looked at me and waved back. I felt like that was it. I could have just gone home to Canada. I was done. I didn't have to go back to my own show. I had gotten to the Dave-Letterman-Waved plateau of life.

A couple of days before the show, I had gone down to South Street Seaport and bought a blue J. Crew sweater for forty-five dollars. It turned out to be a little small, but I didn't realize that until right before the show. I walked out on stage, sat down, and one of the first things I said was, "Wow, you know, I can't believe this, I even got a new sweater for the show." And Letterman said, "Yeah, what was that, like forty bucks at the Gap or something like that?" That got a big laugh, which was good. I had set him up for a laugh. I was scared shitless; he was laughing.

After that, the appearance went well. We showed the Slutmobile piece, and Dave leaned over to me while it played and said, "Are they really pissed? Are your parents really pissed?" It was an out-of-body experience. I didn't even feel like I was really there. I was just hallucinating the whole thing, like Rupert Pupkin from *King of Comedy* might have done. I just looked at him and said, "Yes, Mr. Letterman, they're really pissed." And he said, "Well, they look pissed." We came back off the clip and he asked, "Does anyone ever get mad when you do the pieces?" I told him about a piece we had just shot where a guy from Long Island chased me with a hammer. This reminded him of the time when he used to do street pieces, and there was an incident with a gun and a knife. He seemed to be enjoying himself. I couldn't believe it—I was fucking bonding with fucking David Letterman!

When my time was up, he said, as usual, "Thanks for coming on the show," and threw to commercial. I shook his hand and said, "Thank you, Mr. Letterman." I waved at the audience and Paul and everyone cheered, and this was really corny and lame, but I thought, Hey, I'm probably never going to be back here ever again. So I actually stopped, took a deep breath, looked up at the ceiling, and did a 360-degree turn with my arms out. I did a Mary Tyler Moore. (In case you don't watch *TV Land*, she was a big sitcom star in the seventies who started every show by doing a 360-degree turn in the street because she was so happy to be moving to Minneapolis.)

I watched the Letterman show in a bowling alley with the *New York Times* writer. After he left, I sat by myself in this empty room at the bowling alley for about a half hour. I couldn't believe what had just happened. I went home, went to bed, and didn't sleep all night. I remember thinking to myself, This is the most exciting moment in your entire life. And to this day, it's still close, right up there with the time I actually guest-hosted the Letterman show, not to mention the eight or nine times Jay Leno has asked me to come on *The Tonight Show.*

AFTER LETTERMAN, MY LIFE became kind of a blur. A good blur. The show continued to get good ratings on MTV—second only to *The Real World,* I think. They would run three old episodes in a row, then put on a new show, so if you were tuned in, you could get a constant dose of me. Besides shooting the studio show, we were doing a lot of field shooting and being pulled in a thousand different directions—interviews, promos, photo shoots for *Entertainment Weekly* and *Rolling Stone.* It was pretty insane.

Then one day I got a call from Pepsi; they wanted me to do this Pepsi One campaign. The idea was to do the kind of thing I was doing on my show, only with Pepsi One at the center of the antics. We'd been on the air for only a little while when this happened. In fact, if you weren't paying as close attention as I was—which 99.9 percent of the world wasn't, obviously—you might have thought I was the Pepsi guy who got a show on MTV. It happened that fast. Or you might have thought I was the guy on Letterman who then landed a Pepsi ad and then got his own MTV show.

I know a lot of people found out about me from those Pepsi commercials. It was a huge campaign that ran during March Madness and the NCAA Final Four college basketball tournament. Pepsi flew me to seven different cities to shoot a whole series of spots, again in a style I understood. I'd run around with a megaphone yelling and pouring Pepsi on people, 50 percent of whom were unsuspecting civilians and 50 percent sort of planted extras. I was blatantly against using actors on my own show, but this wasn't my show, this was a commercial—this was business. Plus, I was making more money than I had ever made in my life. And I was having a ball.

The director of those Pepsi commercials was a guy named Todd Phillips, and he was a cool guy. With Todd's encouragement, at least half of those spots were something I improvised on the shoot. We'd be in Cincinnati, for instance. And the setup would be that I walk into a library, talk to a cute girl, then pour Pepsi all over myself. I'd do that, then we'd break for lunch and I wouldn't stop. I'd jump on a snow-covered wall with a silly hat and start improvising a weird poem about Pepsi One. That turned into a spot called "Pepsi One Haiku with Tom Green," and it was probably one of the more obscure and confusing commercials ever made. It didn't have a lot to do with the taste of Pepsi One.

As I was starting to realize that all of this massive, instantaneous exposure wasn't normal, even for show business, so were the people at MTV. They perked up: Wait a minute. This guy hits the air and two weeks later Letterman has him on and Pepsi sticks him all over television. We just might have something here with this Tom Green.

I'm not sure they were thinking that, but I do know that making *The Tom Green Show* got a little easier at that point. There were still creative conflicts, but the atmosphere in which those conflicts were fought had changed. I don't think I quite understood at that point that I wasn't the only person who puts his livelihood on the line for this show. As scared as I was, and passionate and desperate and dreaming of making this thing a huge success, and afraid of it failing, so were all the MTV executives who had backed me. They were terrified of the show failing, too. They had just asked their boss for X millions of dollars to bring this goofball to MTV. Then they looked up, and not only was the show doing well in the ratings, Pepsi One was spending a lot of money airing spots on MTV featuring an MTV personality. This was good—this both doubled my exposure and fed their coffers. Everyone started to calm down a little and maybe even reconsider the content of the show. "You know, that cow-sucking thing? Well, jeez, if Letterman gets it and Pepsi One gets it, then it's probably what we should be doing. Tom, do more of that, will you, please?"

Virtually all creative control was taken away from us when we went to MTV. As they became more comfortable with the show, and the impact of the show, we began to slowly regain that control. And the more often something would happen—like a big magazine cover or feature piece, or a new ad campaign, or a movie role—the more control we got back. Soon it became the way

Me and Ray in Japan for the *Subway Monkey Hour* on MTV.

any good production should run—everyone working together for the good of the show and the mutual benefit of all.

The biggest problem at this point was simply the volume of material needed to fill a weekly show. It got very frantic; it was shoot, shoot, shoot, shoot. We had a big creative team trying to mass-produce this stuff, and it wasn't the kind of material you could just flip a switch and turn out like sausage. It's the kind of comedy that turns on spur-of-the-moment impulses, and accident, and the reactions of real people. You can't cast the old lady that I happen to fall on all bandaged up and swinging a crutch. She has to be there, in person, at the corner. On the old show we had the leisure of waiting for those situations to unfold naturally. On the MTV show, we didn't.

At the same time we were doing the show, I was also trying to adjust to a whole new life. I wasn't in my parents' basement anymore. I was now in a fully furnished apartment with a restaurant downstairs, a cross between a hotel and an apartment. It was the kind of place that divorced husbands moved into, though, at the time, I wasn't divorced yet. In fact, I had a nice girlfriend. I re-member waking up one morning and realizing, "Oh, I'm living in America now. I may be here for a long time. I have a girlfriend here. I have an apartment, a job, everything but a car and a dog. I'm *here*."

One day I was out and suddenly found myself in the middle of the St. Patrick's Day Parade, not realizing that it was such a big deal. Before I knew it, I was the focal point of an insane mob scene. It was the first time I'd ever experienced something like this. One kid saw me, shouted my name, then twenty kids appeared, then thirty, then a hundred. I realized the situation was quickly getting out of control. I started walking. Then it was three hundred kids, then a thousand. It got to the point where I had to run into a computer store, and the manager locked the door; there were a thousand kids banging on the window, trying to get in. It was a crazy moment—I was genuinely afraid.

Something outrageous was happening almost every day. Not two weeks after we were on the air, we got a call at the office from Puff Daddy. He liked the show and wanted me to drop by his studio for a quick tour. This type of "celebrity networking" was entirely new to me. Apparently "Puffy" just wanted to know that he knew me and vice versa.

Nothing much happened. I went to his studio with Bobby Maurer, the show producer, hung out with Puffy, and even talked about flying him up to Ottawa to wake up my parents. We never put that together, but the facts that (a) Puff Daddy was a nice guy and (b) he even considered coming on our show were more than I could handle at the time. It was all too weird.

Not as weird, though, as some of the pure media fabrications that began to pop up almost immediately. One urban myth about me grew to almost "Richard-Gere-gerbil-in-ass" proportions. One day a kid came up to me on the street and asked me if our show had been canceled. I said no. He said that he had heard that I had pulled a horrible stunt that got me arrested and subsequently booted off the air. The stunt was that I had dressed up as Hitler and walked into a Bar Mitzvah.

A few months later somebody else asked me about it. Then it began creeping up in conversation quite regularly. We would hear many different variations of the story. In one, I had dressed as Hitler and shot kids at a Bar Mitzvah with a paintball gun. In another, it was a water gun; another, a pellet gun, and so on.

Finally the story made the printed news. Some kids, I think in Boston, had been caught filming some stunt similar to the one described. When security guards asked them who they were, they gave my name. This lie made a small local paper and then, like all outrageous "celebrity" stories, spread like poison gas. People would ask me about it, I would deny it, and they wouldn't believe my denials. I started to get upset. It was not only a complete media invention, it was also a complete misreading of our comedy. I would never do a mean-spirited anti-Semitic joke like that—it's both abhorrent and not funny. The fact that people imagined I would do something so blatantly cruel and thoughtless was worrisome.

I ended up posting an elaborate letter on our Web site stating that this rumor was out of control and untrue. We even ended up discussing the rumor, and attempting to squash it, on *Entertainment Tonight*. It seemed to go away, but after I got cancer and I stopped doing the show, the story returned. To this day I still get asked about it, and it's annoying.

So again, for the record, it didn't happen. There is nobody on this planet that has ever seen this bit on tape because it does not exist. If it did exist, it would have certainly reared its ugly, hateful head on the Internet by now. But it won't, because it doesn't exist. I've never put on a Hitler costume. In fact, I've never even been to a Bar Mitzvah.

WHILE SHOOTING THE PEPSI commercials, Todd Phillips started telling me about this movie he was writing called *Road Trip*. He asked me if I might want to do something in it. I guess, like most people, he assumed that if I were doing a TV show, what I really wanted to do was movies. It's an easy assumption, since most TV performers dream of being in the movies. Then again, most TV performers don't consider it a day's work to be driving down the road, see a Mexican guy selling piggy banks, then all of a sudden be throwing piggy banks off the side of a hill and talking in a funny voice. This is not something that necessarily prepares you for a career in film.

A few months passed, and I got a call from Dreamworks; Ivan Reitman, the producer, wants you to do *Road Trip*, they announced. I read the script—the second movie script I'd ever read, after *Super Star*—and initially said, no, thank you. It was a scripted comedy and so anti-everything-that-I-had-ever-done at that point. But they kept calling and finally offered me the part of the narrator of the movie. This made some sense to me—I could shoot this part without interrupting the TV show, and as it turned out, it gave me some room to improvise.

I went down to Athens, Georgia, and shot all of my material in eight days. It was fun, it was quick, and the movie turned out great. It was a big change from yelling "You suck!" in *Super Star.* The marketing machine kicked in—the poster became me surrounded by the whole cast of the movie. They could use the TV show to market the movie, and MTV could use the movie to market the TV show. It was a marketing free-for-all.

Keep in mind, although I had been on a movie set before and of course had the TV show, this was all new. *Road Trip* was really the first time that I had ever had any lines in a movie. Todd Phillips was a young guy, about my age, and I felt comfortable because we had worked together before on the Pepsi commercials. But this had a script! I never had a script on my TV show. We improvised everything—I never had to memorize a thing. I was a little bit paranoid that I would have to memorize this entire script, not really realizing that on a movie you really only shoot about a page or two of script in a day. It was a slow process, and memorizing lines soon became a nonissue.

I was green. In part of the movie I played a tour guide. On the first day of shooting we were doing one of these scenes where I was talking to a group of people who were taking a tour of Ithaca College. The first time Todd yelled "Action," I instantly veered from the script and improvised a lot of crazy shit. I think it was okay with Todd, since we had largely improvised the Pepsi spots, but I'm not sure he wanted his movie to look like a Pepsi ad.

Eventually we found a place where I was able to work with the script and improvise around it. Even though I was petrified the entire time, because I really had no idea what I was doing, I was having fun. The one insane moment most people seem to remember is when I put the mouse in my mouth. Originally I was just supposed to be talking to the mouse as I held it by the tail in front of me. For some reason I got it in my head that I should swing it close to my mouth, and it eventually crawled right in. Everyone on the entire crew freaked. We had to do it about thirty more times from several different angles.

It turned out to be a really great scene, and I would do it again, even though that mouse did relieve itself in my mouth on a couple of occasions, and in more ways than one. I was suffering for my art, I guess. I think the mouse enjoyed it.

"MY BUM IS ON THE STAIRS, MY BUM IS ON THE STAIRS"

BACK TO TV: NOTHING BETTER ILLUSTRATES THE craziness of those early MTV days than the "Bum-Bum Song." The story goes like this: We went to Seattle on a field shoot. One of the bits planned was a four-mile swim across Lake Washington, the lake where Bill Gates lives. I was going to swim across that lake just to show Bill and everyone else that I was a hell of a swimmer. By this point, we were a well-honed production machine. We issued a press release to announce that we were going to hold a lakeside press conference. When I jumped in the lake, action-news "telecopters" followed my every stroke. It was intense.

Before the press conference and big swim, we thought it might be fun to record a song and film a music video, an homage to the Seattle grunge scene and bands like Nirvana, Soundgarden, and Pearl Jam. We booked the camera crew, planning to shoot the video on film, so it would look like the real thing. The machine went into full operational mode. It was on the production board: "Shoot a music video in Seattle, Music Capital of the World."

We got to Seattle only to realize we had one small problem—we didn't have a song. I hadn't written one and no one was going to write one for me. We were moving at a furious pace. I got up the day we were going to record the song in a studio, the day before we were then going to shoot the video on the streets of Seattle. I kept telling people, "Don't worry, I'll have a song, I'll have a song," which I didn't have. Then I thought of a song that I had improvised on a Spring Break boat trip in Cancún a few weeks before. This so-called song came out of a silly bit where I was going to wake up the captain of our cruise ship at four o'clock in the morning and offer him a fish sandwich. It was a gigantic hulk of raw red snapper between two pieces of bread. The captain was Russian. This was a high-risk ruse.

I never got to give the captain the fish, because a Mexican security guard interrupted the mission at the captain's door and began to haul my ass out of the bowels of the ship. There was, needless to say, a language problem as well as a behavioral one. As he was dragging me up the stairs, yelling, "You gotta get outta here, you gotta get outta here," I was doing everything I could to distract him. For some reason, with my bum pushed against the handrail of the stairs, I started singing this nonsense ditty, "Look, my bum is on the handrail, my bum is on the handrail." Then he dragged me a little farther, and there was a plant, so I sang, "My bum is on the plant, my bum is on the plant."

It was a catchy little tune. The security guard didn't care for it, but there was definitely a bum-bum buzz in the air. That Cancún special was our highest-rated show at the time, since it was Spring Break and a lot of people watch MTV at Spring Break. I'd walk down the street in New York and people would yell out of their cars, "My bum is on the plant!" It was an easy line to remember.

Pressed for a song for this Seattle recording/video shoot, I wrote "The Bum-Bum Song." Derek drove around Seattle, took Polaroids of anything mildly interesting or strange, threw them on my breakfast table, and I wrote the song on a napkin. I'd see a Polaroid of a weird medical supply store with a big sign reading "SWEDISH" and would write, "My bum is on the Swedish, my bum is on the Swedish." There's even a line in there that reads "My bum is on the cheese, my bum is on the cheese, if I get lucky, I'll get a disease." It was kind of prophetic in a very disturbing way.

We went into the studio and recorded the song. We then headed for a radio station to promote the Lake Washington swim-a-thon that was going to take place the next day. I just happened to have the "Bum-Bum" CD with me, so I said to the jock, facetiously, "Hey, I just recorded a great song right here in Seattle and it's going to be a big hit. Want to hear it?"

We played the song as a joke, and the phones started to light up. The station had a top-ten request show every day, and by that evening "The Bum-Bum Song" was number eight. We hadn't even shot the video yet. As we were shooting it the next day, the song made it to number two. I ran around town in a super-hero costume and stuck my bum on all sorts of things. By the time we left Seattle it had made it to number one on that station. I also made it across Lake Washington, something I still consider a personal triumph.

We got back to New York and everyone at MTV was talking up the song. Then we thought, Hey, let's try to make this joke song the number one song in America. Legitimately. We played the edited video on our show, after which I said that my dream was to have a number one song, and although you can't buy this record and I'm not going to make any money on it, this is my shot at music immortality. I encouraged all watchers to call the MTV show *Total Request Live*, request "The Bum-Bum Song," and make my dream come true.

After it hit number eight on *TRL*, I went on the show and said, "Hey, let's get this to number one! I have a lot of respect for 98 Degrees and Britney Spears, but now it's time for my shot." The youth of America responded with gusto. The song took off like a frigging rocket ship. On Thursday night of that week, we got a call from MTV: by the next day the song was going to hit number one on *TRL*. It was taking the country by storm, one bum at a time.

Then the MTV people announced calmly, "We want you to come on the show tomorrow and retire the song." They do this when a song stays on top for too long, like five or six weeks in a row, and keeps other songs from getting heard. But we were only on top for one day—why retire what America was crying for? The reason was simple—Carson Daly was going out of town for a week, and they had already pretaped the whole week's shows. If "The Bum-Bum Song" wasn't on those shows, the audience would know the shows were not live. I said to myself, Wait a minute. That kind of negates the idea of both "live" and "request." Why don't they just call the show *Total*?

But I got the point, and being a team player, I went on that Friday and made a big song-retirement speech. I said I felt bad for real performers like Britney and N'Sync who were getting pushed aside because of my song and it was time to "give back" to the artists who brighten our lives with song. It actually was a good way to bow out. We shelved the song before the audience became totally bored with hearing it.

There's one more level of ridiculousness to the Bum-Bum phenomenon, one more crazy twist in a completely crazy year. A good while after the song first appeared, Eminem's second big song came out, and I became the subject of part of his rap. He said, in part, that it wasn't okay for him to let loose on TV, but it's okay for Tom Green to hump a dead moose. Then he went on, "My bum is on your lips, my bum is on your lips. And if I'm lucky, you might just give it a little kiss." There it was—the world's most famous rapper mocking, or perhaps paying homage to, "The Bum-Bum Song." During the video he even wore the same superhero outfit I wore in the Bum video. So, again, the evolution—from a stupid impromptu bit on a Russian cruise ship, to something jotted on a napkin in Seattle, to *Total Request Live*, to Eminem's Grammy Award–winning CD. He was no doubt dissing me, but so what? I was happy to make his diss list, as any red-blooded rap lover at the time would have been.

After the Bum-Bum song, record companies started calling. I remember meeting with David Wolter and Keith Wood, two high-level A&R guys from Virgin Records, at a restaurant on Broadway. This was kind of a sly move. I was by this point unable to go out in New York without getting mobbed by MTV-watching tourists. Throughout our lunch meeting, fans kept swarming the table for an autograph. After lunch they shouted from their cars as we walked down the sidewalk. It worked! I got a big record deal with a big international record company! Virgin signed me the next day. Everything seemed to be happening at once. They paid me a whole bunch of money, and when I moved to Los Angeles, they built me the dream home-studio I had always wanted. Now all I had to do was write some songs. Unfortunately (and I apologize to Dave, who is still my friend), I still haven't completed the album. Something bigger and more life-changing got in the way. But I'm getting ahead of myself here.

"YOU KNOW, YOUR LIFE'S GOING TO CHANGE"

BEFORE "THE BUM-BUM SONG," RIGHT AFTER THE TRIP to Cancún, I was walking the four blocks from my apartment to the production office one day when a big black suburban pulled over, the tinted window rolled down, and Kevin Spacey yelled, "Tom! Come here!" I looked at him and I said—I remember how weird it was—I said, "Hey, Kevin!" I walked up and shook his hand, and he said, "I just wanted to say I love your show and I love that Spring Break thing on the boat, that was hilarious. And I just wanted to say hi." And I said, "Cool, well, thanks, man." He drove off, and I went back to the office and told everybody and they all freaked out. It was a shock to all of us that someone like Kevin Spacey even watched the show, let alone liked it.

Then a couple of weeks later Kevin Spacey's assistant came by the office. He was putting together a happy birthday video for Kevin and he wanted me in the video. He showed me some of these people he'd shot—Bono, Bill Clinton, etc.—saying, "Happy Birthday, Kevin." What was I doing on this tape? Nevertheless, I played a little song on guitar and spilled a bunch of milk all over myself, and they put it in his happy birthday video.

Around the same time, I was doing an interview with *TV Guide* and the reporter told me that Drew Barrymore was a really big fan of the show. "I've just done an interview with her," he said, "and she loves the show. She couldn't stop talking about how great it was blah, blah, blah. . . ." I was completely amazed in the same way that I was about Kevin Spacey. I went back to the office and told everybody, "Oh, my God, you won't believe what I just heard. *TV Guide* just told me that Drew Barrymore loves the show." Same reaction. No one could quite believe it. Then someone said she had actually called to talk about doing something on the show. I didn't believe it for a second. She was from L.A., after all—a completely different world.

Six months later—I'm skipping ahead here—I took a trip to L.A. It was becoming increasingly impossible for us to shoot on the streets of New York. We'd have to pile in a car and fight traffic all the way out to Long Island or somewhere to shoot a simple bit. Manhattan was too crowded and too media-crazed. Every time we went out to 59th Street or the like, it was St. Paddy's Day all over again. I mean, who wants to drive four hours to barge into a convenience store and suck milk out of a cow's udder? So, at my manager Howard Lapides's urging, I decided to check out L.A. First of all, I needed a show-biz agent, and that's where they all lived.

I flew out on a Friday and over the course of a weekend, I met some prominent agents and heard their pitches about how they were going to make me rich and famous. I had the TV show and had already shot *Road Trip*, so in their minds there was nothing I couldn't do. I ended up signing with the then-head of the William Morris Agency, Arnold Rifkin. In Hollywood circles, he is a powerful guy. I remember walking into his office, and he stood to meet me in probably the best suit ever made. He had on an exotic watch, and he was tan, gracious, and more self-assured than any person I'd ever met. This was Hollywood, I told myself. I had never been in that kind of world. Arnold Rifkin seemed to embody the whole idea of American entertainment. He looked like Frank Sinatra. I felt like I was meeting Frank Sinatra.

He took Howard and me over to the Beverly Wilshire Hotel for a drink, and when we arrived, they made me put on a complimentary jacket that they provided for slobs like me. It was a house rule—no jacket, no serve. As we sat there, Mr. Rifkin gave me a speech that struck me as insane at the time.

He said, "You know, your life's going to change. Everything that you consider to be normal now is not going to be normal in a few years. Anybody you consider to be a close friend now may not be your close friend in a few years. And that's what this business does, and you're about to wade into the deep end of it." In other words, I was getting on a rocket ship. At this point, of course, there was no sign of the rocket ship turning into the Space Shuttle *Columbia*, you know what I mean?

Everyone I met in Hollywood on this trip was saying ridiculous things that I didn't believe and wanted to believe at the same time. Someone had the gall to say, "Hey, you know they're kind of angling you towards becoming the next Tom Hanks." Excuse me? "You know, *you* started out on TV and in funny comedies like *Road Trip* and *he* started out on TV and in funny comedies like *Bachelor Party*, and that's going to be the arc of your career, just like his." They babbled on, and I was in a daze. "I'm going to be Tom Hanks? Wow! *Philadelphia?* Academy Award? Holy Shit! I'd better go buy a new suit so when I meet my agent I don't have to wear the house knockoff jacket." Everything was happening at once—meeting Frank Sinatra, getting movie offers, being compared to Forrest Gump—it was crazy.

This was the first time, mind you, that I'd been back to Hollywood since the four-hour shower at the Mondrian and the show pitch I gave at the House of Blues. I'd been in town for maybe an hour when Howard's phone rang, and it was Drew Barrymore's office calling. Drew wanted to meet me. She wanted to talk to me about a part in this new movie she was doing, *Charlie's Angels*. I ended up not meeting her on that trip because both of our schedules were screwed, but it wasn't too long after that that we finally connected. I went back to New York to resume doing the TV show, but the seed had been planted. I was going to move to L.A. We were going to move the whole show to L.A.

"WELL, WHAT IS IT, IS IT THE CHAD?"

THREE MONTHS LATER, WE PACKED UP AND MOVED west. My New York girlfriend and I decided to break up. She didn't want to leave New York and move to L.A., and I wasn't sure I was ready for the kind of serious relationship that can be sustained over three thousand miles. I was completely overwhelmed by everything going on with my so-called career, and I thought a serious relationship was more than I could handle under the circumstances. Of course I then went to L.A. and got married, but I'm getting ahead of myself again.

I was still on airport property when Drew's office called again. She wanted to meet me for a drink at the Le Colonial Restaurant, and she wanted to bring along the director of *Charlie's Angels,* McG. So Howard and I went over there to meet them. McG was very nice, and Drew couldn't stop talking about my TV show. I felt I was being seriously schmoozed. I liked it.

She then asked me to be in her movie. There were three boyfriend roles in the film, and I could pick one to play. They gave me the script and asked me to read it and make a choice. When the meeting was adjourned, Drew gave me a hug and a kiss on the cheek that I thought was a bit longer than I would have expected from Drew Barrymore. I left completely starstruck. "What the fuck, you know, like Drew Barrymore just kissed me on the cheek, that's pretty cool!"

I read the script, and my honest reaction was, This is the biggest piece of shit I've ever read in my life. I thought *Road Trip* didn't make any sense—this thing sucks! I was not good at giving scripts a fair shake. The next day Drew herself called me on my cell phone to tell me how much she enjoyed our meeting and how she hoped I'd like the script. I said nothing about the script. We ended up talking for half an hour on the phone. This was business-cum-flirtation or something.

A couple of days later she called again and kept up the pressure. She again said she wanted me in the movie, but, unfortunately, they couldn't pay me like I was paid for *Road Trip.* It was only a cameo and a one-day shoot, and even though the movie had a $120 million budget, there was no money there for my role.

I honestly couldn't tell what was going on. This was Drew being a producer and a smart one. Maybe she was flirting with me to get me in her movie for free, or maybe she actually liked me. I knew she liked the show, even before the movie came up. And she was very nice. And, hell, I was interested. Okay, I was really interested.

What's funny about all of this is when that movie came out a year and a half later, the media spin was that I was a jerk who had seduced America's Sweetheart so I could get a role in her movie. I distinctly remember some bitchy, bottom-feeding reporter saying at the premiere, "Oh, you knew who to sleep with to get this movie, right, Tom?" (nudge, nudge, wink, wink). And I felt like saying (but of course didn't), "You know what, man? She practically had to sleep with *me* to get *me* to be in this thing."

Anyway, I signed on for my one-day cameo. I played this tugboat captain, "The Chad," who Drew wakes up next to one morning. She looks over and I'm making eggs and it's The Chad. Before we did the scene, I had an idea. I went up to McG and said, "When I'm standing on the front of the tugboat and she walks up and I'm saying, 'It's the Chad,' what if I just fall off the boat into the water?" McG said no way. "Man, you can't just do that. These people will freak. You need to have a stunt coordinator and insurance and three changes of wardrobe and shit." I wanted to do it, was willing to do it, but given the extreme tight system in which big-budget movies are made, it seemed stupid and dangerous to McG. It probably was stupid and dangerous, but I still wanted to do it—I wanted to fall into the water with my spatula and my pan of fried eggs.

We were about to do the last take of this scene where I stood on the bow of the boat, a good twelve to fifteen feet from the water. It wasn't a little fall, but it's the kind of thing I would have done on the TV show without thinking twice. At that point, I had never met a stunt coordinator and didn't need one. McG came up to me right before the take and said, "Give me your mike. We don't want to fuck up your mike." I was going to do it. We took my mike off secretly, told no one what was about to occur, and began to shoot the bit. Drew walked by, and I said, "Well, what is it, is it the Chad?" I'm doing a scene with somebody who's been acting since she was four years old. I didn't know what I was doing, but I knew how to fall into the water. So I did, eggs, spatula, and all.

I got out, and all hell broke loose. The first assistant director was screaming, "What the fuck is going on? You fucking can't do that, you idiot!" And everybody on the set was freaking out. I'm sure people were calling the studio and checking the pollution levels of the water and were ready to kick me out of show business. McG, on the other hand, was elated. And when I looked for Drew's reaction, she was laughing her ass off. I think she thought it was the coolest thing in the world. I know I did. And, of course, that's the take they used in the movie.

Afterward, Drew asked me to join her and a couple of her friends/assistants for a drink. "Sure, yeah, okay." She wrote down her name and cell phone number with a little heart on a scrap of paper. We were traveling in two cars, and she wanted me to have the number in case we got separated. Later, while we were driving to the bar, she jumped out of her car in traffic and jumped into mine. I guess she really didn't want us to get separated.

We went to a gay bar with her two assistants and had a drink. I of course had no idea why we were in a gay bar, but just figured that was the hip thing to do. It didn't take me long to realize that Drew wasn't just being nice so that I would be in her movie. I'd already been in her movie, and she was still being nice. Nonetheless, the situation didn't make a whole lot of sense to me. I did the math, and it didn't really compute. I wasn't complaining, just confused.

I drove her home to the Chateau Marmont in West Hollywood, where she was staying at the time. She didn't feel comfortable being alone in her own house in Coldwater Canyon then, so she drove down the hill and moved into this hotel. As I was saying good-bye, she leaned over to kiss me, and my instinct was to turn away. As I said, I was confused. I was still in my professional-actor working mode. This woman about to kiss me was not only my professional actor co-worker; she was my boss! I felt like if I returned her kiss, I would be doing something inappropriate and unprofessional. I mean, you get invited to be The Chad for one day in a big Hollywood movie, and all of a sudden you're hitting on the star of the movie, who is in fact a major movie star since the age of six and a household name in Kansas? It just struck me as weird.

I tried, awkwardly, to give off the aura that I wasn't interested in pursuing this unprofessional, inappropriate little tête-à-tête when of course I was. She leaned over to kiss me, I kind of turned my head, and she ended up kissing my cheek, sweetly. Then we both recovered and shared a quick little peck on the lips.

Ottawa Stallion that I was, I said, "Boy, that was fun tonight, you should, you know, give me a call sometime, you know, give me a call on my cell phone. You already have that number." She looked at me like, You prick, I'm not good enough for your *home* number? Of course I later found out that I had just committed a felony-level faux pas in the handbook of modern courtship. You don't give a girl your *cell* phone number. How stupid can you be? To offer up your cell phone number is tantamount to saying, "I don't really like you that much, so I'm not about to give you my *real* phone number. Catch me on the cell. Maybe I'll pick it up."

I fumbled around and quickly gave her my home number, but I still felt foolish. She now looked up and said, "Well, you want my number or anything like that?" And all of a sudden, when she said that, it struck me pretty hard: Oh, wait a minute, this is, I think, this could be . . . we're really flirting here, we're making contact here, we're exchanging sincere good-night pecks and passing out *home* phone numbers!

I guess I could have come to this realization during any of the three or four hours we had just spent together, but I hadn't—maybe my brain was affected by the fall into the ocean. So I just said, "Hey, give me a call. Or maybe I'll call you." Actually I didn't know what I was saying. I was a little dizzy.

My bum is on the cheese,
my bum is on the cheese.
If I get lucky,
I'll get a disease.

9.

CANCER!

—

"It was like a storm, like a tornado, and he realized the storm was coming, so go chase the tornado and get it on tape, you know? Because it's probably going to kill me anyway and I can't really leave the area. I might as well turn the camera on so that someone can watch that footage later."

—Phil Giroux

I LEFT THE VERY NEXT MORNING FOR A PRODUCTION trip to Northern California. The pace of the show was still frantic. We had to generate more material faster than we ever imagined. I wondered out loud to the guys about whether or not I should call Drew, or whether or not they thought she would call me. They chastised me mercilessly about the whole cell phone number fiasco. "She's not going to call you on your cell," Derek would say. "It can be uncomfortable calling someone's cell phone at first because you never know whether you are interrupting them. You don't know their schedule...." Jeff the producer would chime in, "For all she knows, you could be in a meeting, or just busy, or even in bed with some other chick." This non-stop Seinfeldian banter went on all day. I was annoying everybody in sight with constant questions on my high-profile courting dilemma.

I don't think we came to any intelligent conclusions, but I knew one thing. I couldn't get her off my mind.

Feeling like a complete idiot, I waited about three days before I called her. We were shooting every day and she was shooting a movie and I didn't know quite what to say. I got her answering machine and left the following message: "Oh, I'm here in the Sequoia National Forest . . . Sequoias! Sequoias! Sequo-oias!" I just repeated the word nine times and said something like, "had a good time, give me a call." And this was the beginning of the next two years where I was completely overwhelmed by Drew Barrymore. I was in the throes of the greatest infatuation of my life.

I waited anxiously for a return call, and a couple of hours later it came. I

The baby segment for MTV, shot in Sequoia National Park.

went back to my hotel room and we talked for six or seven hours. It was ridiculous. We were like eighth-graders experiencing our first crush. If we both didn't have work to do, we probably would have talked all night.

On the same trip, at exactly the same time, something else was happening. My right testicle was beginning to hurt badly. This had been going on for a few days. I can't remember exactly when I first noticed a problem, but I remember the feeling. At first it wasn't a lump, it was a dull pain, a dull pain that never seemed to go away. I kept poking around down there, all the time telling myself that nothing seriously was wrong. When in doubt, practice denial.

Soon I could tell that my right testicle was larger and harder than my left one. I kept this information to myself. After a lifelong habit of taking showers, I began to take long, warm baths. I think I actually believed that the warm water would melt or dissolve whatever disease had entered my body. I remember that every night I would go to bed and pray that the swelling would magically disappear by morning. I was afraid. I knew something was terribly wrong.

I wanted to get back to L.A. for two reasons: to see Drew and to see a doctor. I set up our first real date and my first trip to the doctor's office at the same time. The doctor didn't say right off that it was cancer. In fact, I don't think the word "cancer" was mentioned during that first visit. The initial diagnosis was infected epididymitis, an inflammation of the long, tightly coiled tube behind each testicle (epididymis) that carries sperm from the testicle to the spermatic duct. This sounded serious but not life threatening. He put me on antibiotics and sent me on my way. It took three weeks before the diagnosis was changed to testicular cancer.

Feeling a little better, I went on the date with Drew. I showed up in my date mode, not work mode, wearing a leather jacket and drenched in cologne. We went to a restaurant near the ocean, and since I'd never seen the ocean in Los Angeles, we decided to go down to the beach. We took our shoes off, walked in the sand, and climbed atop some rocks. Then we kissed. It was one of those perfect first dates. It was as far away from the one I had with the Ottawa stripper as you could possibly get.

Meanwhile, of course, I had cancer. It was as if somebody were looking down and saying, "You know, falling in love is falling in love, but we want this book to have a good story arc to it, so we're going to throw in some totally negative shit, okay?"

I was suddenly taking the Drew affair very seriously. On that first date, she told me a silly story about going to Hawaii and regretting not buying a shirt at the airport that she really liked. So, the next day, I called the Honolulu airport, described the shirt to concession people there, and they FedExed it to me. On our second date she opened it and loved it. I figured, hey, this is a big movie star, it probably takes more than a movie and popcorn to keep her interested. I wasn't going to run out of ideas.

When we were at the restaurant that night, Drew saw some lobsters in a tank and announced that she would love to free lobsters trapped like that. The next day I picked her up and said, "Hey, let's go free some lobsters today." We drove up the Pacific Coast Highway, found a fish store, and loaded up on lobsters and crabs. We drove out to the beach to free these shellfish. We both loved taking pictures, so we brought along a retro Pentax K1000 student camera, and while I released the freedom-loving creatures back into the sea, Drew took pictures and then we reversed roles.

For our next date, I had the pictures framed into a kind of visual story. I also included a plaque on the frame: "PETC," or "People for the Ethical Treatment of Crustaceans." It was one thing after another. It seemed like every date we had, I planned some ridiculous sideshow. It was a creative exercise every bit as important to me as inventing pieces for our show.

Sometimes my little gifts were a way out of trouble. Soon after we started going out, Drew asked me if I was interested in a little marijuana. This is common enough among people my age, and people living in L.A., but I'm not a regular consumer of drugs. In fact, if I had been with anyone else in the world, I would have said no, but, hey, I was in Hollywood now. I had smoked pot once in my life, when I was twenty-three or so, and did not enjoy it. All I'd ever known about drugs was fear—i.e., "This is your brains on drugs."—so, on that first occasion, I went from laughing at my hand for twenty minutes to thinking I was about to die and curling up in a fetal position under the bed.

With Drew my reaction was equally unsettling, especially to her. Immediately my brain was flooded with the insanity of the situation: I'm in Hollywood, sitting here with Drew Barrymore, I probably have cancer or something equally frightening, and I'm stoned! I explained to Drew that I was a novice at altered states of consciousness. I then started talking to a cup of water for forty-five minutes, after which I began to think that my head was no longer on my shoulders—it had been mysteriously lobbed off and replaced by the head of an Irish setter. Marijuana makes some people paranoid. It made me *insanely* paranoid. I thought that the squirrels in the trees were out to get me.

When all of this became apparent after I came down, I was very embarrassed. Drew was nice about it, but I'm sure she thought I was both a danger to myself and to her.

The next day I was even more freaked. I liked this girl so much and certainly didn't want to leave her with the impression that I was a drooling idiot. I decided to turn the whole thing on its head and make an oil painting of my crazy hallucinations. The fact that I had never done an oil painting in my entire life didn't deter me. I bought the paints, the canvas, and the hardener and flipped into a Van Gogh state of obsession. I whipped up this primitive, naïve masterpiece of a guy standing under a tree with an Irish setter as a head and a tree full of squirrels staring him down. I then got it framed in a gaudy, gold-flecked, over-the-top, faux-Louvre frame and gave it to her on Valentine's Day. She cried. I felt great.

Meanwhile, the swelling in my testicle had not gone down. The doctor had said it would take about two weeks. Two weeks later I was back in his office with the same painful problem. He said, "Let's switch to another antibiotic." I of course thought that must be the whole problem, the wrong damn antibiotic. What else was I supposed to think?

As if things weren't weird enough, I then took off to Ottawa to pay a surprise visit to my parents on the arm of Monica Lewinsky. Here's how this happened. A few months before, the night I was getting on a plane to Athens, Georgia, to film my part in *Road Trip,* I got an urgent call from Tony Hawk. As I mentioned before, Tony was first one of my teenage idols, then a guest on the show, and now a friend. He was calling from a party in L.A. to tell me that he had just met Monica Lewinsky—the then-planetarily-famous Monica Lewinsky—and that I should come over right now to interview her and maybe get her to be on my show.

I couldn't cancel the flight, so Glenn and one of our field producers, Jeff Boggs, went to the party to woo Ms. Lewinsky. Jeff ended up going on a couple of dates with Monica and, during that time, introduced her to Derek's wife, Tammy. Tammy and Monica became friends and, through this web of connections, Monica agreed to come to Ottawa with me as part of the show.

It turned out that Monica's brother was a big fan of the show, and I'm sure that helped convince her to do something. My thought was, rather than just shoot a small bit with her, why not get on a plane, fly up to Ottawa, and meet the folks. It soon became more elaborate than that—in fact, it morphed into a one-hour special—but that was the original impulse.

Given Monica Lewinsky's incredible media saturation at the time, we decided to fool with the insatiable media machine that stalked her every move. The plan: we would arrive in Ottawa, surprise my parents, then go to the local community cable station, the very station where I got my start, and announce that, the following day, we were going to make a very important announcement. We knew by the time we got ready to make the second "major" announcement, the worldwide pack of Monica leeches would be hanging on our every word. "Are they getting married?" "Is Monica going to write a tell-all book?" "Are they going to pull some embarrassing prank on the president of the United States?"

We flew into Ottawa and went straight to my parents' house. Unfortunately, the shock effect of barging into their bedroom had worn off by then. Though they had absolutely no idea that we were coming, my dad woke up and instantly quipped, "Oh, Monica, hi. How are you?" After a thousand such intrusions, not to mention their own stardom on *Oprah*, etc., my parents had become extremely media savvy. They knew that Derek's wife, Tammy, was a friend of Monica's and quickly put two and two together, even at four in the morning in their pajamas.

The next morning we did the preannouncement at Rogers 22: "The announcement that we want to make is that tomorrow, on the roof of the Little Beaver (pun intended) Restaurant in Ottawa, we are going to make a very important announcement." Of course the instant rumor was that we were going to announce our engagement. We went to lunch with my parents at the Château Laurier, the fanciest place in downtown Ottawa, and suddenly twenty-five cameras greeted our arrival. Remember, we're in Ottawa, Canada—where did these paparazzi come from? But we knew this would happen and were ready for it.

I put my loving arm around Monica and my hands in front of the cameras as we hustled into the restaurant. "Stop filming us!" I shouted. "Stop filming us on this special day! You animals! You media, you're all animals!"

By the next morning every radio station in Ottawa, and probably Canada, was announcing the Little Beaver event. The restaurant was, in fact, a trailer. We got on top of it and faced a sea of cameras, microwave antennas, and satellite transmission trucks. It was worse than O.J. Derek and I looked at each other in absolute amazement. We had successfully talked Monica Lewinsky into giving a press conference on a building with the word "beaver" in the title.

Then came the announcement: We were there to announce Monica's new line of handbags. As the world soon learned, Monica was going into the handbag business, and to illustrate this important breaking news item, we even fashioned a Monica-designed handbag out of some of my parents' sheets.

**In this picture Monica and I are being swarmed
by the vicious Ottawa paparazzi!**

You could see the collective face of the world media drop when I said "handbags" instead of "engagement." They had to run the story. Anything with Monica was defined as news, even a stupid media stunt made at their expense on the top of a portable restaurant in Ottawa, Canada. All of a sudden, in the Monica media circus, *they* were the trained animals.

I rushed back to L.A., edited the Monica special, and got it on the air. Unfortunately, sometimes cable channels aren't equipped to deal with a TV event like this. Barbara Walters herself couldn't get Monica to do an interview at the time, but we had an entire hour with her making fun of the very media that had pilloried her for months. For whatever reason, the show didn't get much promotion. When Barbara Walters did finally land Monica, it was on the side of every bus in America. Our little Monica moment aired without much fanfare.

Holding a press conference on the roof of the Little Beaver Restaurant with Monica Lewinsky.

**A newspaper cameraman took this picture of my parents,
Monica, and me in Ottawa.**

Meanwhile, I was checking in regularly with the doctor. Everyone I worked
with could see that I was becoming increasingly edgy. I told them I had a stomachache. A really bothersome, chronic stomachache.

There was too much going on at once. I was, through it all, madly in love.
Drew would call and leave long messages on my phone daily. She'd say very
airy, Drew-like things like, "Whenever I think about you it's like a thousand
butterflies floating through the fields." How would you like to hear that on
your answering machine? Swollen gonad aside, I was feeling that the whole
world was a thousand fucking butterflies floating around my head.

When the Monica special aired, MTV threw a party at a nightclub in Hollywood where everyone watched the show on a big screen. It was the first public event at which Drew and I appeared together as a couple. For some
reason—probably because of the reams of fake media speculation—Drew got
it in her head that I was also seeing Monica Lewinsky at the same time. It took
me years to convince her that that was ridiculous.

Hollywood premieres, a beautiful girlfriend, fame, success . . . and cancer.
After the second antibiotic failed to have any effect on my diseased right testi-

cle, my urologist announced that we were going in for an ultrasound test, "just to see if this is cancer." He actually said the word. I thought I was going to choke on my tongue. It turns out that testicular cancer is not something seen as a matter of course by most doctors, so it is not the first thing that pops into their minds when they see a scrotum infection. There are maybe four thousand cases a year diagnosed in the United States. By comparison, there are more than sixty thousand new cases of breast cancer reported yearly. Testicular cancer, as cancers go, is rare.

By this point my testicle was swollen, hard to the touch, and increasingly painful. It grew to the size and shape of a golf ball. Before the word "cancer" was seriously mentioned, my greatest concern was that this growth in my pants didn't appear freakish, with or without my clothes on. After the ultrasound, appearance was no longer a big concern.

"You have cancer," the doctor calmly announced, "You have testicular cancer."

When this message was delivered, the first thing that went through my mind wasn't, Am I going to die? That was actually the third thing. The first was, Am I going to lose my testicle? Facing the world with one testicle is a very big deal before it happens. It is in fact a shocking possibility to a twenty-eight-year-old, red-blooded, sexually crazed, and occasionally sexually active male, males being the only people, of course, who can get *testicular* cancer and thus face the possibility of losing a testicle. At the time, you have no idea what losing a testicle means, but there's not a chance in hell of it being a positive development in your life.

The second thought was obvious: Am I going to be able to have children? Am I going to be able to have *sex?* The answer to these questions, fortunately, was yes. Throughout the whole ordeal, my sexual performance was never really affected. Apart from about three or four weeks after my lymph nodes were removed, I was always pretty mobile. My sex, and romantic, life survived intact. I am functioning to this day as well as, if not better than, ever, thank you very much.

Once you get these concerns out of the way, it then hits you hard. This is cancer. People die from cancer. All the time. Am I going to die? The mortality question came last, but it was a damn big one.

As someone who had rarely contemplated his own death, and certainly not death from cancer, I had to educate myself quickly. As I soon learned, testicular cancer, as I mentioned, is considered rare, and the number of deaths from this form of cancer has decreased considerably over the last thirty years because of better detection and treatment.

Who stands a chance of getting it? Males, obviously, and most commonly, males between the ages of fifteen and thirty-four. It is, in fact, the most prevalent form of cancer for males in this age group. Men with a family history of the disease are at higher risk, as are men with an undescended testicle, i.e., a testicle that hasn't naturally descended into the scrotum. It's more common among white males than other racial groups. And if you've had one ball removed, like I did, the cancer can possibly come back in the other one, though it is extremely rare.

As with many cancers, early detection is the key, and most of the time this means *self*-detection. Sure, a doctor might spot a testicular abnormality during a routine physical exam, but how many sixteen-year-old kids, or twenty-eight-year-old men for that matter, get routine physical exams where their balls are a subject of conversation? The best thing to do is just check yourself—squeeze, pinch, poke, make a day out of it—and if your testicle feels hard or swollen or hurts like hell, see a doctor.

The fact is, testicular cancer, especially if caught early, is one of the most highly curable forms of cancer. Specialists know exactly how it spreads—it spreads in a very predictable fashion—and they can both trace its progress very systematically and cut it off at the pass, so to speak, before it spreads further. For one thing, it rarely spreads directly from one infected testicle to another uninfected one. A man's testicles are in two completely different chambers and essentially protected from each other. This was a piece of very good news when I first heard it. My left ball was safe and secure.

Testicular cancer spreads from the infected testicle to lymph nodes in your stomach and if not caught before that, on to the lungs and finally to the brain. It spreads upward. Cancer, you quickly learn, is a "game" of percentages. The more the cancer spreads, the lower the percentage that you will be cured. If they catch it in the testicle before it has moved into the lymph system, then the cure rate is 98 percent. If it hits the lymph nodes, the rate drops to around 75 percent. Though this form of cancer is also very responsive to chemotherapy, if it reaches the brain before detected, you're in serious trouble. I don't think I ever asked about those percentages.

I had immediate, next-day surgery to remove my infected testicle. After that relatively uncomplicated procedure, my doctors, led by the incredibly competent and knowledgeable Drs. Donald Skinner and Matthew Dunn, offered me two options. An MRI test didn't show any cancer in my lymph nodes, but there was still a 10 percent chance that the cancer was there. The two options were to undergo surgery to remove that 10 percent doubt or to continue with frequent checkups and MRIs until they could be certain it had not grown to a detectable size.

It was like Monty Hall in a white lab coat, except it wasn't a new Volvo behind Door #2—it was my life. I opted for the lymph surgery even though I knew I would be bedridden and in pain for several months after being cut open. I had to know for sure. Even a 10 percent possibility that a cancer was growing inside of me would have driven me up the wall.

There was one more percentage to throw into the mix. With the lymph surgery, there was a 5 percent chance that I would never be able to ejaculate again. So I mathematically weighed all these factors like some kind of rocket scientist that I'm not and decided to go with the surgery anyway. Of course I had no idea what I was getting into. The biggest medical procedure I had ever gone through before this was a hernia operation after flipping a desk over on the Community 22 show.

There was a twenty-four-year-old kid with testicular cancer in the hospital room next to mine while I had the second, larger surgery. He was a big fan of the show, so when I was recovering from my operation, I hobbled over to his room with my IV hanging out of my arm and chatted with him and his girlfriend. Like me, he was a skateboarder, and it was easy to talk to him. I wasn't some "celebrity" dropping by the cancer ward. We were just two unlucky guys with testicular cancer.

Six months later, when I was back at the hospital for one of my periodic checkups, I asked about my friend. "Oh," someone said, "he died a few weeks ago." I was pretty much out of the woods by then, but the shock was still very real. You can indeed die from testicular cancer. This twenty-four-year-old kid died from testicular cancer. And I was one room away and maybe two or three weeks earlier in detecting my cancer and dealing with it.

I think I understood all of the medical information I was being given, but I didn't really understand the impact that having cancer would have on my emotional life. I figured, at least in my most clear-headed moments, that I would either die or I wouldn't die. I assumed that if I continued to live, I would just pick up where I left off and continue on. That didn't happen.

Getting cancer, I came to discover, wasn't just a matter of being confined to a bed for a few months. Getting cancer was a very scary proposition. And that fear changed my path. It muddied my vision and skewed my focus. It didn't just rearrange my body. It rearranged my life.

"I DON'T BELIEVE YOU"

THE FIRST PERSON I TOLD ABOUT THE DIAGNOSIS was my manager and friend, Howard. He understood that this was a real predicament that I couldn't talk my way out of, unlike the dozens of self-made predicaments I had done for laughs. Then I started down the list, one good friend at a time. This may sound strange—or demented—but it got to the point where I actually enjoyed telling people that I had cancer. I can't explain it, but other people with life-threatening diseases have told me the same thing. It may have something to do with the relief that comes with unloading the information and being reassured that others will help you through your ordeal. Or maybe it's something more selfish, i.e., "You've *got* to take me seriously now. I've got *cancer*, for chrissakes!"

As I replay it in my head, I can remember exactly how I told my closest friends and family and how they reacted. When I told Drew, I first asked her to come over to my house. I remember lighting a cigarette—I wasn't a smoker—and even noting to myself the absurd irony of smoking a cigarette while telling someone you had cancer. It's like having a drink while announcing you have cirrhosis of the liver. The real reason for the cigarette was that I was freaking out. I was afraid of losing her. I was afraid she would have a tough time dealing with the fact that I had to have one testicle removed. Especially since this would undoubtedly become grist for the tragedy-loving, exposé-hungry media hounds sooner or later. I sat on the couch and told her the whole story, afraid about everything, including my life. As I said, it's as if all of this happened a minute ago.

Drew handled it well. She was instantly supportive. I was so relieved that she didn't say, "Testicular cancer? I'm out of here. I need a boyfriend with *two* testicles!"

Derek came over to my rent-a-house the next day and sat on the kitchen table as he heard the news. I tried to play with him a little. The movie about Andy Kaufman, *Man on the Moon*, had just come out. As you may recall, Andy Kaufman died of cancer, but not before it was widely believed that he was faking the whole thing. I'm sure there are people out there who still think he was playing a huge joke on the world and is living happily in the Philippines or something, laughing his ass off.

With *Man on the Moon* on my mind, I said to Derek, "Hey, you know how everyone says we're doing Andy Kaufman–type of stunts, like driving people home after a show or faking being sick or injured? Well, I got another good one for you." Derek thought this was pretty funny until I began to break down. In fact, every time I initially told somebody, without fail, I'd get choked up and start to cry. This wasn't "Hey, I got bronchitis" or "Hey, I got the clap." It wasn't even, "Hey, I got cancer, but we're going to make a joke out of it." It was, "Hey, I got cancer and I may die." The fact that Andy Kaufman and I both contracted cancer seemed ironic in a perverse way. Or maybe it was just perverse. It took Derek a few minutes to take it all in.

Glenn just flat-ass didn't believe me. He was in Canada at the time and couldn't see the expression on my face. He said, "That's right, I don't believe you. And I'm not going to believe you until I come down there and see you in the hospital, and even then, I won't believe you." Then I started crying on the phone, and Glenn could hear the crack in my voice. His response was classic. He said, "Holy shit, you're serious. I know you're not a good enough actor to pull off crying like that." He was exactly right. I couldn't fake cancer.

Of course my parents were the first call to Canada. My mother believed me instantly, as she always does, which has always made her such a good foil for the pranks we do. Both of my parents always buy into the goofy setups because, basically, they think that I would never lie to them. Which I wouldn't. Except to set up one of dozens of practical, parent-bashing jokes.

I am constantly amazed at my mother's credulity. I could call her up right now and tell her that I was in the L.A. County Men's Jail and had only one call, and she'd believe me. "Mom, I got drunk with Glenn last night and I threw a trash can through a store window and now I'm in jail facing felony assault charges." She would buy it without question. She thinks my life down here is so crazy that anything could happen. To her, Hollywood *is* Babylon, and of course she's about half right.

But she also knows that there are certain things about which I would never have the impulse to lie. Getting cancer is certainly one of those things.

My parents immediately flew down from Canada and moved into the guest room in the house I was renting from, of all people, William Shatner. They were there to help, of course, but their presence only added to the fear I was feeling. I remember lying in bed later at night, curled up, with all the lights on. I was sure I was going to die. I had listened to the doctors, I understood my odds, but none of that really mattered. I was sure I was going to die. I am by nature a pessimist, and when a pessimist gets cancer, look out. I mean, what are the friggin' odds that I would get testicular cancer in the first place? Ridiculously low. If I had already lost at that game, then in the big picture, the odds were that I was fucking dead.

From that fetal position, it all kind of made sense. I was riding the wave of the biggest success of my life. *Entertainment Weekly* had me on its "It" list of the 100 Most Creative People in Entertainment. The TV show was a hit. *Road Trip* had a big buzz. I had just been smitten by this beautiful, vivacious woman.

Everything was perfect. So, of course, something had to go terribly wrong. It was a joke that I hadn't thought of.

Sitting there, numb from the ridiculousness of my circumstances, I didn't know whether to laugh or cry. I remember thinking that if the cancer had struck only a year earlier, my life would have been completely different. The TV show would have never been picked up by MTV and taken off. I would have stayed in Canada and recovered from cancer, or not. My fifteen-odd years of struggling to make it would have been in vain. The cancer would have completely blown my shot.

So, I thought, Hey, God does have a sense of irony after all. He didn't want me to fail from the start. He wanted me to have a taste. And, thankfully,

I did. But now I was scared and pissed off. It was like I had run the entire marathon and was a hundred feet from the finish line when someone stuck their foot out and tripped me. I was sprawled all over the pavement going, "Hey, what the fuck?"

"CANCER SIDELINES ZANY COMEDIAN"

AFTER THE INFECTED TESTICLE WAS GONE, I DIDN'T feel that different. I was happy that they didn't cut open my scrotum to remove the testicle. An intact "normal" scrotum was important to me. To anyone who cared to know, I explained that they entered the scrotum from the top down with a small incision in my lower abdomen and shucked the infected testicle out like an oyster. For reasons I can't explain, I didn't want people thinking I'm walking around with a scarred scrotum. There is no scar on my scrotum. If you remember anything from this book, remember that, please—my scrotum was never touched.

Needless to say, this was very traumatic, even though the surgery itself was neither complicated nor life threatening. At the same time I decided to stop production on *The Tom Green Show*. It just seemed like the right thing to do at the time. No one knew what the outcome of my illness would be, but it no doubt would involve a long recovery period. On top of that, my doctors didn't want me involved in any unrehearsed physical activity like flailing around on a street corner. My fallback at the time, assuming the cancer became a nonissue, was movies. Movies, for one, were staged. All movement could be planned beforehand. *Road Trip* was about to come out and there were other movie offers on the horizon.

Of course, I still had my life to think about. After the cancer had been diagnosed and I had had my first operation, the doctors suggested that I go to a cryogenics clinic and donate some sperm to be frozen. It was just as a precaution. Although my left testicle would not be touched by any surgery, it was still suggested that I freeze some sperm for future use. There was now a second, lymph node procedure in the offing, and there was this remote possibility that I could be rendered impotent. Why take a chance? It's always good to have some savings in the bank.

Planning this precaution, I was, for the first time, forced to confront my desire to have children. I had always thought of the idea of getting a girlfriend pregnant by mistake was the worst possibility I could face. But when the prospect of never being able to procreate came up, I was suddenly very afraid. I knew at that moment that I desperately wanted to have children someday.

I went to the sperm bank, and my new girlfriend came with me. It was something of a watershed event in our relationship. A nurse asked me to fill out some forms, and one of the questions was, "Who would be receiving your seed, should you die?" I had been going out with Drew for a couple of months and all of a sudden I was being asked to deed her, or someone, my sperm. We giggled and looked at each other, but we both knew it was too early to make that kind of commitment. I wrote down, "Nobody."

In case you ever visit a sperm bank, the basic idea is that you go into a room with a little plastic bottle, and you come out with your deposit. It's just like you see in the movies—they have a little TV playing porno movies and, for you readers, a stack of dirty magazines. It was strange and fun, especially with my girlfriend there. Although this was a scary time, and there were a lot of scary conversations of mortality being bantered around, this particular occasion was kind of a respite. It was, in fact, intensely romantic for a relationship so young. Without sounding hokey, when we left that cryogenics facility, having just placed my sperm in a permanent state of hibernation, we felt almost like we had procreated. The seed was there—if it was ever needed, it would be used for having a baby together. We went out for lunch and then drove home, very much in love.

"FEEL YOUR BALLS, . . . SQUEEZE YOUR BALLS"

I DID DECIDE TO DO ONE MORE SHOW FOR MTV—THE cancer special. The focus of that show was the second surgery we decided I needed to remove all doubts about the extent and spread of the cancer that had begun in my testicle. This was a much more complicated, and bloodier, procedure. There was no public announcement about the initial surgery, but there was no hiding this one. The media rumor mill was already in motion.

There were at least two good reasons for documenting this second surgery. One, it would help me deal with it by doing what I had been doing for years—

exposing my life on tape and making jokes about it. The second reason is that testicular cancer, as I said, is a disease of young men. This group is a big chunk of my MTV audience. It might be the only way some of them at risk would ever find out about this horrible disease. I'm not much of a crusader, but, hey, I had this cancer, and it was the least I could do to tell people about it. Especially some fifteen-year-old kid out there who thinks his left ball is red and swollen because he masturbates too much.

The cancer special began with a frank admission of the situation. "And I had my right testicle removed. And it was pretty embarrassing, because now all of a sudden I got one ball." Glenn: "Yeah, but it works." Tom: "All of a sudden I'm the guy on MTV with one ball, one nut." Glenn: "It's a pretty delicate thing to talk about." (LONG PAUSE) Tom: "Ah, yeah."

We then showed an *Entertainment Tonight* story on "Tom's battle with cancer," for which, they said, I should be prepared to fight because, in their words, "laughter is the best medicine." As the cancer special continued, I got fitted for my burial suit, joked about dying with my parents, and invited my urologist on stage to demonstrate on Phil Giroux exactly how to diagnose your-self for danger signals. Phil was cajoled into dropping his pants and exposing his gonads as Dr. Dunn showed him how to check for lumps. Phil, we were happy to report, had healthy balls.

We documented every minute of the surgery, beginning with the pre-op nervousness and then going to a "Last Supper" at a nice Italian restaurant with my friends and family. When I announced to the waitress that I had cancer and "hopefully I'm not going to die," her stunned response was, "You want to see the wine list?" I showed some fans who dropped by the table my abdominal scar from the testicle removal. I think I was the only person in the group who thought any of this was funny. Glenn and Phil almost hid their faces in shame or sadness or both. I kept laughing way too hard. What else was I to do?

The surgery was both frightening and gruesome. "This is going to fucking suck," I told Glenn, and I was right. Right before I went under and they sliced me up, I said something stupid like, "Can we get some firefighters to run by the bed as soon as I wake up?" Accompanied by the theme song from *St. Elmo's Fire*, they pulled out my internal organs on tape as Phil and Glenn watched in horror on a monitor. My own later comment was, "Gosh, I was hoping it would have been funnier in there." The doctors didn't mind that my lymph nodes weren't funny—they were, it turned out, cancer-fucking-free.

Unfortunately, I wasn't pain-fucking-free. In fact, for the first two days after the operation, I was in the worst pain of my life, curled up on my side, screaming in agony. The documentary crew took one look at me and said, "This might not be that humorous." By the third day, the morphine had kicked in, and when Glenn greeted me in a firefighter's outfit, I loved the joke.

I wrote a feel-good cancer song for the special that I'm sure many of you hum on a daily basis. It's called "The Cancer Song" and goes like this:

**Hey, kids, feel your balls,
So you don't get cancer,
FEEL your balls, SQUEEZE your balls,
TEASE your balls, PLEASE your balls.**

"Rub your balls," I exhort, "while masturbating or while not masturbating." This was the best advice I could give to the male youth of North America. In fact this was the only advice I had ever given publicly on any subject. I felt like Dr. Phil.

After some other silliness like Glenn inspecting my diseased right testicle in the lab and getting kicked out of my post-op room in his fireman's outfit, the cancer special ended with a public appearance in front of eighteen thousand screaming college kids at a sports facility at the University of Florida in Gainesville. I just stood on stage and told my cancer story. While I talked, kids held up signs like "I SUPPORT TOM GREEN'S NUTS" with the s crossed out and asked questions like "Can Glenn help me see if I have cancer in my testicles?" I told them I wanted to use my amputated ball as a mike cover for man-on-the-street interviews, but the hospital said no. It was a disgusting image the whole crowd appreciated.

The irony was, it was easier, and more fun, to talk about this embarrassing ordeal in front of eighteen thousand people than to talk about it with my girlfriend. Making it into a public spectacle, however much it helped me distance myself from the reality of getting cancer at twenty-eight, only added to her own distress and confusion.

In the face of this prolonged trauma, she seemed to move away from me. Our relationship, after all, was a few months old. What was light and fun and frivolous—a budding romance—all of sudden became dark and serious, a budding romance with someone with *cancer*. It is not at all unusual, I've been told, for couples to have a tough time when one partner becomes seriously ill. We were barely a couple. I was madly in love with her, but our couplehood had not even been tested by a good argument, let alone a life-threatening disease. Plus she was in the middle of a very big movie, *Charlie's Angels*.

The cancer media train, at this point, was unfortunately unstoppable. Special or no special, there was no way *not* to talk about it. I just had to handle it the way I handled anything. I was popping jokes, trying to smother the awkwardness and embarrassment in black humor, but I was also in a lot of postsurgical pain. I was putting a good face on it, including appearing on the cover of *Rolling Stone* and telling them the whole story, and Drew was putting a good face on it, politely answering the millions of questions about it that were constantly thrust at her. The truth was, we didn't become like some TV-movie couple who overcame a horrible adversity and were bound together by it—we grew distant.

One of the exciting aspects of being with Drew was that she had her own rich, crazy, fascinating life. With no offense to other mates, before or after, this was the first time I'd ever been with someone whose work genuinely interested me. In most cases, I have gone out with women who had day jobs that didn't intrigue me in the least. I didn't want to sit around dinner and hear how it went down at the insurance office that day. Remember, I suffer from what most performers suffer from—an inflated sense of themselves and an obsession with their work. Which makes me, like most performers, a selfish bastard.

When Drew talked, I listened. First of all, she was charming, and second, she had been working in Hollywood since the age of four. She had led a textured life. She was the first person I ever dated where I was actually as interested in what she did all day as I was with what I did all day. We had no trouble finding common conversational ground. We lived and breathed common conversational ground.

The subject of cancer, difficult to talk about even in the abstract, was something we didn't have in common and couldn't talk about in a free and easy fashion. It had emotional repercussions neither of us had ever dealt with before. I felt I was walking on eggshells every time the subject came up. I was as confused as she was. This cancer shit had taken over my life.

The parts left out of the cancer special were the most painful—the epidural

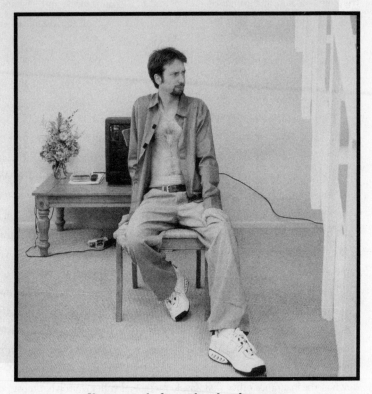

**About a month after my lymph node surgery,
in my sparsely decorated rental house in L.A.**

in my back, the morphine and other painkillers flooding my body, and still the intense pain. Post-op, my body felt like it was on fire, and all the discomfort and body dysfunctions went on for months after that. Upon returning home, and with the requisite medication to keep me going, I tried to resume a normal life, keeping in mind I'd been living in L.A. for only a couple of months. It's overwhelming enough to move to L.A. and rent William Shatner's house without the cancer. Everything seemed a blur, but I had to keep moving. The lengthy recovery coincided with some important decisions I needed to make. "Cancer" sat at the table for every one of those decisions.

This disease is no longer something I think about every five minutes, but in retrospect, I think it had a profound impact on the events of my life that followed. As I said, getting cancer is a scary proposition, and the fear, doubt, guilt, and anger that it engenders enter every decision you make. For instance, if I hadn't gotten cancer, would I have ever married Drew? After I was diagnosed, I became very needy. Not only was I needy because I was sick, stuck in bed, and lonely. I was also heavily medicated on morphine, Vicodin, Percoset, and a whole host of other meds. This stuff makes you crazy, and in my case, crazy with need. When Drew seemed to move away in the face of this awful illness, I freaked. I needed her, badly, and I worked like hell to get her back. But what if I hadn't been in that cancer state? I wouldn't have been that needy soul and there wouldn't have been that live-or-die desperation hanging over everything. We might have gone out for a few months and then drifted apart. Or just eased into a longer relationship without the spectrum of disease and death hanging over our heads.

Also, what about my TV show? If I hadn't gotten sick, I would have certainly continued doing it, on MTV and perhaps, in time, on even a larger stage. The team was in place, the machine was working. Of course the cancer shut us down, the long recovery delayed things further, and I stopped the show. Soon after I got sick and we stopped production, the entire crew left for other work. Half of them started work on this new show called *Jackass*. By the time I was cured of my disease, they were all gone.

I remember the first time I saw *Jackass*. I was, to put it mildly, surprised. We weren't doing the show anymore, I was in the middle of shooting *Freddy Got Fingered* (we'll get to that later), and I started hearing about it. I immediately noticed what I thought was the blatant borrowing of many of our ideas. Waking up parents, putting animals in parents' houses, falling down on crutches, swimming with sharks, and crashing into stuff in an electric wheelchair while dressed as an old man—the list went on and on.

Initially I was a little bit upset, but then I got used to it. The thing that really stung was the fact that the show was actually produced by many of our show's staff. When I had gotten sick with cancer, these people needed somewhere to go. They took along with them our ideas and the shooting method that we had created. What we had taken years to come up with in Canada was basically lifted and re-created in a moment. In the end, though, most people seemed to notice the similarities, and I now take it as a compliment.

I've become a huge fan of *Jackass*. I loved the movie and the show. It's fun seeing them take the stunt side of things to such an insane extreme. I actually worry about Steve-o and Pontius and Bam. We always said on our show, it's all fun and games till somebody loses an eye, so, please, be careful. I've also come to realize that what we did may have been more performance driven and their show far more stunt oriented. Like myself, some of those guys skate, and it seems to be a show that derived from the skateboarding subculture of *Big Brother* skateboard magazine, so there is really no way I couldn't love it.

In any case, we were back to square one, just Glenn, Derek, and me. So I decided to try something different. I decided to make a movie. And if I want to be honest with myself, I soon got sucked into that world. Cancer forced a turning point. TV was out of the question for the moment, and making movies was the next logical step.

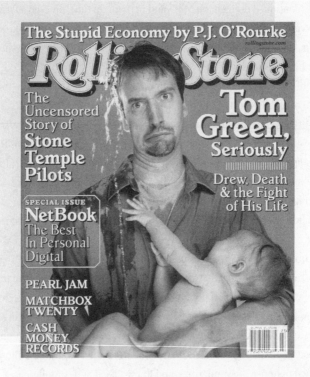

10.

STRAWBERRY FIELDS FOREVER

—

"**H**e got sucked into her world and all of a sudden he's meeting big Hollywood movers and shakers. Now there are people who he doesn't want to make fun of himself in front of. I mean, when he went in to pitch the show to MTV, he covered himself in milk and splashed around and made a fool of himself. With her taking him to this ridiculous level instantly, yeah, it had an effect on him, for sure."

—Derek Harvie

THE YEAR THAT FOLLOWED THE CANCER WAS ONE OF the best of my life. First of all, you can't help feeling good after you "beat" cancer. I love the phrase "beat cancer." It sounds like a WWE Death Match where you and some gorilla are chained together in a steel cage and only one of you will come out alive. I survived cancer, for sure, but I didn't beat it. It got cut out of me, thank goodness, and I survived.

The recovery, as I said, took a while. After I got out of bed, I still wasn't all that mobile for about five or six weeks. I hobbled around my rented house, wincing with the pain in my abdomen, and I tired easily. I was in a Vicodin-induced fog. Vicodin is a combination of the drugs acetaminophen (Tylenol) and hydrocodone, known in the trade as a "narcotic analgesic." A popular painkiller, it can become addictive if taken regularly and in excess over a long period of time. In some Hollywood circles, it's considered a chic drug, since it makes you feel good and you can still function. It made me feel goofy, and I could barely function.

Soon into my recovery I started getting calls for work. I was still in bed, in pain, and on Vicodin, when I got a call about a Right Guard commercial. "Hey, I'm sick," I shouted into the phone. "Hey," they shouted back, "they want you to go down to Zuma Beach for one day, and they plan to pay you more money than you've ever seen." I figured, hell, I can get out of bed for that. I'm no malingerer. I'm not going to let a little thing like two major surgeries from testicular cancer keep me from earning a living pitching deodorant.

So I spent a day or two on the sand applying roll-on deodorant to the foreheads of Venice Beach–type bodybuilders. If I hadn't been sick, I might have passed on the assignment. Sometimes, making commercials feels like selling out, because it *is* selling out. But it beats lying in bed and feeling sorry for yourself.

With some of that funny money, I went and bought a brand-new Porsche. I was already driving a brand-new Range Rover, but for some reason, I thought I needed to treat myself after being so sick and so scared. Plus, the windfall from the commercial made spending that kind of money seem perfectly reasonable. Money, cancer, Vicodin—they all distort your view of things.

I felt a huge amount of pride when I bought that car. It was ridiculous—why the hell did I ever think I needed two cars, let alone an over-the-top European SUV and a Porsche? The reason, I told myself, was that I had just gotten cancer and I was pissed off. I had been robbed of my health, and in my twisted logic, I was going to get revenge by indulging my automotive fantasies. I had the money, and I wasn't going to die without buying my first sports car.

I drove it over to Derek's house and I parked it on the street, a few doors down from the place Derek and his wife were renting at the time. I popped in, as I often did, and just sat in his kitchen shooting the shit and drinking a beer. I was bursting at the seams to show him the car.

Finally I dragged him outside and we walked down the street *past* the Porsche. We kept walking until Derek asked me where the hell we were going. "Oh," I said, as we circled back, "want to take a ride in my new Porsche?" He didn't believe me until I hit the key remote and the lights flipped on. We put the top down and took off down Mulholland Drive, fast. It helped me think about something other than my illness, and even though I was driving like a maniac, for a minute it was hard to be scared.

I now had a little money, but money, it turns out, is a far more complicated thing than I had ever imagined. When I was broke, I used to think how amazingly simple everything would become if I had money. And of course having money is great, it affords such wonderful things in life. But I have to admit I had never even considered the possible evils.

It's not like I have made insane J.Lo money or anything like that. But I certainly made a lot more money in a short period of time than I or anyone around me expected. It is a very confusing wrench that gets thrown into one's life, getting fast money. I guess what happened to me was somewhat equivalent to winning the lottery, without the absolute luck. On the good side of things, I could now afford luxuries I would have never considered. I soon owned two homes. I owned some expensive cars. I was able to give my parents nice things. I built a professional recording studio in my guesthouse and have picked up a bunch of cameras that I always wanted.

But the biggest difference about having money isn't really the access to material things. It shifts your point of view. You feel guilty. You're suddenly in a different financial league than your best friends. There is a definite bond that gets created between people when everybody is broke. My friends and I would all laugh about how we lived in our parents' basements, how we were "losers." Suddenly that whole self-deprecating stance just didn't work anymore. You can't really call yourself a loser when you're sitting in front of a ten-thousand-dollar TV in your fancy bachelor condo.

There is a saying that my manager Howard is fond of repeating: "Money fucks the brain." Not only can it fuck your own brain, but it can fuck everyone's around you. It eventually goes to the extreme where you start to notice certain "friends" who revel in your failures. There are some people from whom you hear only after a movie bombs or a show goes off the air. They are calling with condolences, although you can hear in their voices a distinctive "Ha ha sucker! You may have a nicer television set than me, but that movie sucked!"

Money fucks the brain. Cancer fucks the brain. Love fucks the brain. My brain was getting screwed right and left.

MEANWHILE, DREW AND I were still distant, which was driving me crazy, probably crazier in my drug-clouded brain. She was under an enormous amount of pressure, both producing and starring in *Charlie's Angels*. We'd talk on the phone, but I didn't feel that she cared enough about my plight. She probably thought I was being excessively needy, which I was. It was weird.

About this time, *Road Trip* finally came out in theaters. This modest little college comedy made $15.5 million the first weekend and went on to make over $120 million in worldwide theatrical release. It was a huge hit. Jeffery Katzenberg, one of the three partners of Dreamworks and one of the most successful movie producers of the modern era, called me at home to congratulate me. I don't think anyone expected this, least of all me. It's just one of those amazing things that happens sometimes in Hollywood. Something actually works.

Road Trip was a blessing in more ways that one. It was something that Drew and I could talk about and feel good about, something much more exciting and full of possibilities than the progress of my cancer. As things often work in the movie business, all of a sudden the studio making *Charlie's Angels* wanted me to shoot more scenes. They wanted me to expand the role of The Chad. Drew called to urge me to shoot another day. Maybe it was the Vicodin, but all of this made me feel a little paranoid. The way I saw it at the time, I was kind of cancer-victim-non-grata until I had a hit movie, and then all of a sudden I'm the flavor of the week. I was slightly confused.

So I did the second day on *Charlie's Angels*, knowing that it couldn't possibly hurt my relationship with Drew and would probably help it. If you watch the movie closely—assuming you have the free time to dissect a movie as carefully as one of its actors watching *himself*—you'll see that I'm about thirty pounds lighter in the second scene I'm in than I am in the original, falling-off-the-boat scene. And I wasn't that fat to begin with. I went from geeky-thin to cancer-victim-thin.

My recovery, the success of *Road Trip*, doing more work on *Charlie's Angels*—it all helped reduce the stress and intensity of what both Drew and I had been going through. In fact, that *Charlie's Angels*/cancer period may have been the most intense time in both of our lives. It certainly was in my case.

AND ON TOP OF all of this, we had sold a script that Derek and I wrote on our own—*Freddy Got Fingered*. Long before I had met Drew or moved to Los Angeles, Derek and I had had the idea for *Freddy Got Fingered*. While doing the MTV show in New York, I was getting movie scripts sent to me all the time, and most of them I hated. They were pat, predictable, "zany" youth comedies that I rarely found funny. They were mostly movies patterned after, or copied from, other successful movies and had nothing in common with what we were doing on TV.

Reading these scripts, we got the idea of writing our own comedy that would be a mockery of conventional comedies. I had seen a video biography of Jim Carrey where he talked about doing *In Living Color* during the day and staying up all night working on *Ace Ventura—Pet Detective*. We adopted the same routine. We'd work on the TV show until everyone else left at around eight or nine and then switch to the movie script. We had no family or friends in New York other than the people we worked with, so we used the isolation to get something done.

We mapped out the whole story from beginning to end. It was vaguely autobiographical and vaguely nonsensical at the same time. The main character is a small-town boy from Oregon, not Canada, who tries to prove himself to his dad by coming to L.A. to make it as an animator, not a comedian. But that was only half of it. We spent just as much time coming up with insane scenes that would never appear in a hometown-idiot-boy-makes-good story. Most of our creative energy, in fact, went into scenes that had only a tangential relationship to the main story—cow-udder-sucking scenes, horse-masturbating scenes, delivering-a-baby-and-slinging-it-around-my-head scenes. That's what people would be walking out of the theater talking about, or perhaps cursing about.

The script was first bought by the Disney/Touchstone studio—specifically, Joe Roth and Todd Garner, who left shortly thereafter to start Revolution Studios. After a few "what are we doing here" meetings with their successors, we realized that we were never thinking about the same movie. The script went into what is known as turnaround, which means the studio offers it up to other studios to pick up, pay for, and produce. Only one day after it was offered up, the script sold to New Regency Studios, run by a legendary Hollywood figure named Arnon Milchan. Something of a mystery figure, reputed to have been, at one time, an international arms dealer, Mr. Milchan was also a very successful and highly respected movie producer, having produced such noted films as Scorsese's *The King of Comedy,* Terry Gilliam's *Brazil,* and Garry Marshall's *Pretty Woman.* I wanted to add *Freddy Got Fingered* to that distinguished list.

We quickly realized that the New Regency people wanted to make the same movie we did and were ready to move. About the time we got the script into a polished state was when I got cancer. I was of course both deflated by the cancer and by the prospect that the movie would get put in a drawer and never brought out again. Then, after I had survived the two surgeries, I got a call one day on my cell as I was driving down Sunset. It was Arnon Milchan and another executive, David Matalon. They were calling to say, "We're behind you all the way. Just get better. We still want to make this movie." So I went through the recovery process knowing that I had something to do when I got well. That was an enormous boost to my spirits.

The second I felt good enough to sit up straight in bed, I started meeting people about the movie. Originally the idea was that I would star and someone else would direct. So I sat there in my bedroom with an IV stuck in my arm and interviewed potential directors. Candidates would come over to my house and listen to my slurry, drug-addled explanation of this clearly outrageous movie in the making.

The point that I tried to stress in every one of these chats was that I didn't want to make a mainstream Hollywood comedy. I didn't want to make the style of watered-down feel-good farce where a few good jokes, if that, are overshadowed and diluted by a patently bogus love story and a pat ending where the crazy guy in the middle both gets the girl and kicks the winning touchdown and you can see it coming in big cookie-cutter steps sometime around the opening credits. I didn't want to do that. I wanted to make something where people walked out of the theatre saying, "What the fuck was that?"

My reference point was not a Hollywood youth comedy—it was something like Monty Python's *The Meaning of Life*. When the fat guy in that movie vomits, there is a lot of vomit coming at you. When he blows up, there is a beating heart in his chest with his rib cage showing, and when they take out his liver, the guts they extract look as real as my own guts in the MTV Cancer Special. *Freddy* was replete with images of bloody bones being licked and babies being swung around by their umbilical cords that I didn't want to be either omitted or reduced to the level of a family-friendly sitcom joke. Remember in the Python movie *The Holy Grail*, where a character gets both arms and both legs sliced off with a sword? That's the kind of bloody comic reality I was going for.

I met a lot of first-time feature-film directors, directors just coming off of a hot commercial campaign, music video, or TV show. They all seemed to come from the same place. They wanted to make a typical *SNL* teen movie. They saw me as the next box office star of that ilk. They all were older, midthirties versus twenty-eight, and they had a more "mature" mindset. I wanted to make sure that they were the type of people who would protect all the craziness of the script, and in every case, I felt like they weren't. They were all saying, in so many words, Hey, this is my big chance. I've waited years for this. This is my first job as a big director, my first feature, and I'm going to have to play ball with the studio.

I could see their point. You don't survive long in Hollywood if you get the reputation as a troublemaker on your very first feature film. Even if you're good, studio execs don't want the grief. If you're just okay, you better have a can-do, get-along temperament if you want to be asked to direct a second feature. This was a very adult, healthy attitude—it just didn't have anything to do with this movie. This movie was made to be rude. It wasn't can-do, get-along material.

With the bravado of someone who, despite the trauma of the last few months, had always taken ridiculous risks, I decided to pitch myself as the director. I had been "directing" my own comedy bits on TV for years—conceiving them, story-boarding them, at least in my head, and editing them one cut at a time. I saw *Freddy* as a direct extension of that self-crafted humor. And I was a lot more passionate about the material than anyone wandering in from the outside. And, hell, I had just beaten cancer—I could do damn near anything!

The producer of the movie, Larry Brezner, said there was no way that the studio would let me direct my first starring vehicle. But I walked in and mounted my best pitch since the MTV pitch at the House of Blues. The studio executives in charge, Sanford Panitch and Peter Kramer, thought about it and said, "Yeah, sure, you can direct the movie." It was great. It was cool. No one could believe it. I couldn't believe it.

The next step was a one-on-one meeting with Arnon Milchan to confirm the arrangement. On one side was this billionaire, former-international-man-of-mystery producer and on the other side was this Canadian kid known for humping a dead moose. I was completely intimidated. I talked about the swinging-baby bit. He talked about hanging out with Canadian Prime Minister Pierre Trudeau. I talked about disemboweling a deer. He talked about the evolution of Picasso's work. He then said go and make my movie, and I was ecstatic.

MEANWHILE, AFTER THE TRAUMA and confusion of the cancer started to subside, I was slowly getting back with Drew. I wanted to make it work—I wanted both her affection and her respect—and I thought the fortuitous chance to direct a movie would help my cause. I was impressed, and I hoped she'd be, too. It was a whole world I was trying to plant my flag in—the movie world. It's like joining the country club in your hometown. With certain exceptions, TV was the local health club; film was the exclusive, by-invitation-only eating club. And I got sucked in. Talk show be damned, I wanted to be part of that group where it's all about movies, all anyone talks about is movies, and the only thing that counts is movies.

Part of the appeal of movies is financial. If you can build a movie career, you can make two movies a year and spend the rest of your time playing with your dogs. At this point, I didn't have a TV show to go back to, but even if I did, it would be a lot more work for a lot less pay. I really wasn't looking at movies versus TV at this point. I was looking at movies versus nothing. It wasn't a matter of whether or not it was a good creative fit. It was a matter, as are many things in Hollywood, of making some dough and having some postcancer stability in my life.

As Drew and I got back together, our bond felt stronger than ever before, and we both entered a kind of stable, predictable period in our lives and careers. She was through with *Charlie's Angels* and beginning to prepare for her next movie, *Riding in Cars with Boys*. I was almost through with my recovery period and in preproduction on *Freddy Got Fingered*. It was a good six months before the movie would start shooting, six months filled with production meetings, casting sessions, picking out props and costumes, i.e., all the stuff that goes into a movie. It's an enormous amount of work, but it's work that begins at nine and ends at six. It's like an office job.

The movie was budgeted in the range of $15 million. We basically had all the money we needed to make the movie. By Hollywood standards, it was low budget. By *The Tom Green Show* on MTV standards, it was pure luxury. And we put it on the screen. We built huge outdoor scenes. We mounted a house on a pole on the back of an 18-wheeler. We dropped boats from helicopters into wood chippers. The scale of things was both exciting and frightening to me. It's not like I had dreamed of making a film on this scale since I was a little kid, but when it was offered up, I threw myself into it with abandon.

I'd get up every morning, drive down to our production office in Santa Monica, and put in a full day dealing with all those preproduction details. At the same time Drew was prepping as an actress for her movie. Our lives were in sync. At almost the exact same time that I was going to go to Vancouver to shoot my movie, she was moving to New York for six or seven months to do hers. We were both busy but neither under the horrendous stress of actual production. We'd go away every weekend on little trips up the Pacific Coast Highway or the like. We compared cameras and snapped pictures. If it sounds like normal behavior, that's because it was. It was probably the first time in my adult life where I felt normal with someone. It may have been, as I look back, the happiest six months of my life.

This was also a time when the press still treated me as the new wonderboy of outrageous comedy, and they tended to think that this new Hollywood sighting of American's princess with the zany MTV clown was charming. Later, the story became "Beauty and the Beast" or "Hollywood Royalty and the Bottom-Feeder." For now, it was something new to fill up TV time, a new celebrity coupling, crazy, clean-cut kids having the kind of fun all of us *Access Hollywood* watchers yearn for.

Naturally, you don't want something like that to end. I kept saying to myself, and to her, "Hey, this could be a great life." As the end of that period came and we were both about to go our separate ways—Vancouver and New York, respectively—I began to fear that the whole thing might dissolve in the months we would be apart. I had found something and didn't want to lose it. That's when I decided I was going to ask her to marry me. I thought that if I did it before we both went away, at least she would know that I was willing to make that kind of commitment, a commitment for life.

Drew had to go to Utah for a few days to film a bizarre photo shoot for a magazine. It was a promotion for *Charlie's Angels*, a movie that wasn't coming out for a year. The idea was the three angels roughed it in the desert for three days, eating plants and drinking cactus water, I guess, and a photographer would get it all on film. Welcome to Hollywood.

While they were gone I went with Derek down to Rodeo Drive to buy an engagement ring. I wrote the biggest single check of my life for a big diamond ring. I put it in my pocket and left the jewelry store. Then I realized I was walking around with a fortune in my pocket. I was afraid I would lose it and ruin everything. I planned to spend the rest of my life with this person, and I didn't want to blow it over losing the ring on the way home.

It all made perfect sense. We'd been together for almost a year—longer than my parents were together before they got married thirty-two-plus years ago—and we were just getting engaged. In fact, my dad told me at one point while we were dating, "You know, you better ask this girl to marry you—she's not going to wait around forever." Like she was on pins and needles or something.

Anyway, we had talked about it a little. We took a trip to Bora-Bora where I brought up the subject, casually, only to discover that she had been married before. I probably knew that but had blocked it out. She'd been married for nineteen days to someone she met when she was twenty. It was obviously a mistake. So I thought, Oh, well, error in judgment. I'm sure that wouldn't happen again. Not with me. Our marriage lasted a lot longer than nineteen days—

it went all of five months. We beat the record by almost four and a half months. I can't help but feel good about that.

Given that Drew had thought that her first marriage was perhaps the biggest mistake of her life, I knew she wouldn't be in the mood to rush into another one. And neither was I. If we got engaged, we both knew, at least intuitively, that the engagement would last a year or more. We weren't going to drink too much wine, go crazy, and drive up to Vegas for a wild weekend and issue a Monday-morning wedding announcement to family, friends, and *USA Today*. In retrospect, after the marriage and divorce, it made good tabloid copy to say, "Oh, look, they got married, then, boom, they got divorced. Boy, these people are so irresponsible." It wasn't like that. The marriage didn't work, but it wasn't because we rushed into it like two sixteen-year-old kids from Kansas. We were together almost two years before we actually married.

The proposal was, however, time-bound, so I didn't have much of an opportunity to plan something clever or elaborate. I was leaving in a week. I wanted to get this thing resolved. Plus, I was afraid of losing the friggin' ring. I wanted to shift the onus of responsibility.

We ended up driving up the coast and taking a walk on the beach, which, of course, sounds like something out of a bad romance novel. I'd had my share of intense moments of late—going on *Letterman,* cancer, lymph surgery, etc.—but this was, in its own way, the most intense of all. I never had even thought about getting married before, let alone actually going through with it. It felt like a slow-motion dream. I actually got down on one knee, slowly pulled the ribbon off the box, opened it up, picked up this ridiculous rock, and held it up like a jewelry salesman. It was a powerful moment. It took her a couple of seconds to say yes. It felt a hell of a lot longer. She was at a loss for words. She didn't know it was coming. Of course she did note that I had been acting particularly weird for the last twenty-four hours, but she didn't know why. Now she knew.

SO, HAPPILY ENGAGED, I took off for Vancouver to direct my first movie for the next three months. I spent one last weekend with Drew in New York before going to Canada and we tried to get together every chance we could after that. And when she wasn't around, I was thinking about her. I was making a movie, a crazed, obsessive task under any circumstances, but I was probably spending as much time planning my next love letter or trip to New York. This may explain why the movie got a record five Raspberry Awards. I had my head in two places at once.

The first time I had to say, "Okay, action," I was thoroughly intimidated. I had thrown myself into something that was both foreign and large. There were all these stone-cold movie pros on the set and I didn't know many of the mechanics of movie making, but people were really supportive of what I was doing. I think everyone who'd read the script knew that this was going to be different and insane. I felt like I had the good faith of the crew. I didn't get the sense that the key grip or the best boy was watching me stumble around and rolling his eyes after every amateurish misstep. This wasn't just another first-

Getting ready to shoot the skateboard sequence for *Freddy Got Fingered*.

time effort. Scenes were much bloodier and more ridiculous than the standard comedies these people were used to turning out. I think the mood on the set was that this thing was going to be huge. Or maybe that was just my mood.

The daily routine went something like this. There would, for instance, be a scene where I slit open a deer and the guts would come pouring out. The prop people would show me the guts they had picked out for the gag. To my eye, they looked like plastic, too-perfect, Hollywood-style guts. I'd say, "No, no, I want real guts. Can't you go down to a butcher shop and bring back a trunk full of bloody leftover intestines?" They'd look at me like I was slightly insane but went after the guts.

We had already built this fake deer with a compressed air device to push the guts out. The real guts, of course, made the whole bit work. Blood was everywhere, and I used the occasion to improvise a few moves where I covered myself in cow intestines. All in a day's work—taking an intestine bath, whacking off a virile stallion. The movie bombed, but we had a great time making it. Maybe we should have simply done *The Making of "Freddy Got Fingered"* and released that version.

Bonding with the elephant right before the "money shot" on the set of *Freddy Got Fingered*.

As much as I liked the work, every time I yelled "Cut" on the set, I would go back to my trailer and check my cell phone to see if she had called. Every day I would get home from work and write her a three-page letter full of gushy thoughts and mail it. If I had three days off, I'd rather fly to New York than get some rest. Or if she had a free weekend, she'd fly to the set. One occasion sticks out. I'd just finished shooting a scene with a Bell 101 Huey helicopter when she arrived in Vancouver. It was all very cool—it was my set, my movie, and my fiancée had just pulled into town. So I said, "Hey, let's go for spin in the Huey." We flew above Vancouver, over the famous Lion's Gate Mountain, and out over the ocean. It is like a romantic interlude amidst our crazy lives.

As I was wrapping the movie, the studio couldn't have been happier, which only added to my blissful ga-ga state. The transition from taking control of a TV show to taking control of a movie wasn't as difficult as I had imagined. In both cases, you're at the center of this giant decision-making machine and everyone looks to you to make critical choices. Even though, after the movie came out, the media didn't exactly embrace the choices I made, no one knew that at the time. The studio thought that I had really pulled it off as a full-time director. For the moment, they were pumped. I was flying.

Hanging with Howard Lapides on the set of *Freddy Got Fingered*.

The *Freddy Got Fingered* DVD—go pick up a copy!

Basking in this euphoria, I told the studio that I wanted to edit the movie in New York, since Drew was there still shooting. They said, "Sure, anything you want." I set up an editing suite in New York, moved in with Drew, and settled into another blissful six months together. Her loft was the nicest place I'd ever been in Manhattan—it was one of those penthouses where the elevator opened right into the living room—and it felt even nicer when I walked in and saw an entire wall papered with my letters. It made me feel good to know that she was not hiding them in a desk drawer and entertaining other suitors in my absence. A wall full of love letters from your fiancée is a pretty blatant announcement of your unavailability.

Again, I was back to working a normal eight-hour day, this time in an editing studio. I'd awake in the morning in Tribeca, get a cup of coffee, walk to the edit room, work all day, and come home about the same time Drew came in from the movie set. I was still spending 50 percent of my energy on the movie and 50 percent on her.

During my lunch hours, for instance, rather than going out for a bite to eat, I'd retreat to my office and work on a painting I was making her for Christmas. The picture was my amateurish but heartfelt version of Van Gogh's *Starry Night*, Drew's all-time favorite painting. We had visited the real painting at MOMA, which gave me the idea for the fake. I gave it to her on Christmas morning, framed in a gaudy gold ornate frame indicative of something worth a lot more money than the hundred bucks I had spent on oil paints and brushes. She just stared at it for a long time, then started crying. I was thrilled. And proud. If you stood back a good hundred yards, it even looked like *Starry Night*.

At that same Christmas gathering, I helped reunite Drew and her mother, who had been at odds for years. I invited her mother to join us in Ottawa and she graciously accepted. I wanted Drew to marry into my family and I wanted to marry into hers. I wanted to foster as much normalcy and stability as possible in a relationship consisting of two career-crazy people.

Back in New York, we were breezing along, eating out every night and doing more than our share of drinking and cavorting around town. It was not something that bothered me at the time. In New York, you can drink a little over the limit, take a cab, and not realize the repercussions. In L.A., you invariably have to drive home. In N.Y., they drive you. You have a good time, stumble into a cab or town car, go home, wake up the next day, and do it all over again. As long as it doesn't interfere with your work, it didn't really register. We weren't falling down—we were having fun, living the life, neither single nor married but somewhere blissfully in between.

IT WAS A PERIOD of high points. I was asked to host *Saturday Night Live* as a way of starting the promotional drumbeat for *Freddy Got Fingered*. It was amazing. As a joke, I pretended that Drew and I were going to get married on the show, that night. We were going to tie the knot on air, just like Tiny Tim and Miss Vicki had done on the old Johnny Carson show. Throughout the program they would catch Drew, backstage, prepping for the big moment. At the finale, she was nowhere to be found; she had left me at the alter, heartbroken. It was a great joke. My life, as usual, was the stuff of my comedy, only on a much larger stage.

Probably one of the bigger "who-the-hell-am-I-turning-into moments" of this period was eating dinner with Prince Charles. When I think about it now, it's one of those blurry memories that seems impossible to be true. It was the day after I hosted *Saturday Night Live*. You'd think I'd sit around for a month and marvel at that piece of good fortune. But there was no time. Prince Charles wanted to have dinner.

For some godforsaken reason, the future King of England wished to dine with Charlie's Angels. They were having a royal premiere in London, and although I was in the movie, I was basically just along for the ride.

Taking a bath with Lorne Michaels for a *Saturday Night Live* skit.

Still bleary from the *SNL* after-party, where I avoided Tom Hanks all evening because I was too nervous to talk to him, I jumped on a private jet to England with Drew, Lucy Liu, and fourteen assistants. The minute we touched down in England, I heard from Howard Lapides that the *SNL* show got a great rating and even a nice mention from Hollywood's premiere columnist, Army Archard. I was excited to tell everyone, but they were getting dressed for dinner with royalty and didn't much care. After all, it was "just" hosting *SNL*. What's the big deal?

So I put on my fancy tux, we got into our fancy British limo, and drove over to St. James Palace. There were about fifteen people dining with the prince that night, an intimate affair. For some reason, Cameron Diaz couldn't make it. She obviously had more important things to do and I suspect, in her mind, would have many other chances to eat with royalty. I guess I was filling in as the third angel. I was happy to do it.

Although normally uncomfortable in these formal social settings, I felt this one was of a much greater magnitude. Butlers met us at the palace gates and led us into the royal waiting area. I remember the inside of the palace being very red. The carpets were red, the doors trimmed in gold. The ceilings were very high and the walls were covered with oil paintings of people I didn't particularly recognize.

We were led into a large room where we would meet the prince. Everyone was given champagne and we waited. I'm sure I was more impressed by this than many of the others. After all, I grew up in the Commonwealth of Canada. The queen is on our money; the British royals are a much bigger part of our lives. I was starting to get the impression that I was the only person who thought drinking champagne in a tuxedo at St. James Palace was weird. Maybe if I had been a movie star my whole life, it wouldn't have seemed as mind-boggling. Regardless, it was times like this I suspected that Drew and I might never relate on the same level.

Then the prince strolled in. He was with his partner, Camilla Parker Bowles, and you could immediately feel his royal presence. The room became hushed as he walked slowly among the small group of us. It was clear that this is a man who knew how to entertain. He spoke with each person individually, making everyone feel welcome. He moved around the room, chatting away, while

Camilla Parker Bowles spoke to Drew and me. She told me something about her nephew being a big fan of "your movie *Road Trip.*" It was strange.

Then I turned around and there he was. Prince Charles . . . son of the queen . . . heir to the British throne. Somebody introduced me to him as "an American comedian" and soon I was in a full-on conversation about comedy with the prince. He asked me if I liked British comedy and I told him about my love of Monty Python and Peter Sellers. He seemed to light up when he talked about "getting to meet" Sellers. I later found out that the prince was a huge fan of Mr. Sellers and as a teenager would phone his office and invite him on pheasant shoots. Later Sellers boycotted a royal premiere of one of his own movies, and he was scratched from the royal Rolodex.

Our conversation ended and we were then led into an intimate dining area. We ate dinner in a room plastered with antique rifles and swords. There must have been several hundred of them on each wall. Drew and Lucy sat on either side of the prince. I sat across the table next to Ms. Parker Bowles. She talked about "the French" and someone's trip to Brazil; her British accent was so thick I could hardly understand what she was saying, and when I did, I had no idea how to respond. I kept thinking, What in the hell am I supposed to chat about with this woman? Hockey? Skateboarding? College radio? We ended up talking about pulling pranks on my parents, a universal subject, I guess. It was all so surreal. Every seat had a small card with a name on it. At the end of the night I took mine and, unable to resist, took hers as well. I'm sure she didn't miss it. It wasn't her first or probably last royal dinner.

DREW AND I RETURNED to New York and our generally blissful life. When her movie wrapped and my editing reached a certain stage, we moved back to L.A. We had two movies to launch and a marriage to plan. That's when the problems started.

11.

THE FIRE AND *FREDDY*

—

"**W**ell, you know, I thought it [*Freddy Got Fingered*] was hilarious. Now, maybe there's something wrong with me. I mean, anyone who thought that that was a real baby he was wringing around over his head, you know, has to be certifiable. It was a cartoon, for heaven's sakes."

—Mary Jane Green,
on *Freddy Got Fingered*

"**T**here are a lot of times when you rise that quickly that the press doesn't have a chance to get you and when they have that chance, they make up for lost time. Was that stuff justified? Absolutely not . . . and by the way, he survived that because *that* cancer wasn't real."

—Howard Lapides

WITHIN WEEKS OF RETURNING TO L.A., MY DAD CALLED from Ottawa. He had just been diagnosed with prostate cancer.

We had barely settled in when we got this news. Before we had left town for Vancouver and New York, I was still renting the William Shatner house but spending most of my time at Drew's house off of Coldwater Canyon in Beverly Hills. It was a big wood-framed farmhouse stuck in the woods, far enough from civilization that Drew often felt isolated when she was alone there. That's why she was living in the Chateau Marmont when I first met her during the production of *Charlie's Angels*.

After our return, I dropped the rental place and moved into that house. I had a small recording studio that I set up in one guesthouse and moved all the rest of my stuff, which wasn't that much, into the main house. The plan was that we were going to stay there as long as we wanted and eventually buy another house together. We were in no hurry. I had just signed a deal to star in a movie called *Stealing Harvard*, again for more money than I ever imagined making in my whole life, and there was still a lot of work to do on *Freddy Got Fingered* and *Riding in Cars with Boys*, respectively. We just wanted to stay put for a while and move at our leisure.

My dad's cancer, of course, was a crisis we weren't prepared for. First of all, there was the problem of the Canadian health-care system. Ostensibly a universal plan that covers everyone and any medical contingency, in reality it is full of holes. A lot of Canadian doctors move to the United States to earn more, and the hospitals are often backed up, understaffed, and overstressed. In my dad's case, once his cancer had been diagnosed, his first surgical appointment was set three and a half *months* in the future. When I had testicular cancer, my first operation to get my testicle removed was two days later. To me, that was a frightening difference.

So, having had a little experience with the mysteries of cancer, I could talk to my dad with a certain authority. My first piece of counseling was, "Fuck, you're not going to wait three and a half friggin' months." So we decided that my parents would fly to L.A. and my dad would be treated at the USC/Norris Comprehensive Cancer Center and Hospital, the same facility where, only a few months earlier, his son had had two successful cancer operations. And it would take three weeks to get in, not three and a half months.

This was, needless to say, weird. It was weird because I felt like I was reliving my own cancer trauma only months after I had lived it. And it was weird because, for the first time in my life, I was in a position to help my parents financially at an absolutely critical time. My father didn't have any medical insurance that would cover a cancer operation in the States, an expensive proposition. Fortunately I had been insured for my own cancer and had the money to help pay for his. Little did I know when I was doing that underarm-deodorant commercial whacked out on Vicodin that the money would be going to such a worthy cause.

My parents came down, my father had his surgery, and then they moved into the other guesthouse at Drew's farmhouse to recover. It was incredibly stressful for everyone. Neither Drew nor I was prepared for having *another* person with cancer living in our house. It was both a worry and a distraction, especially for me. I was trying to finish the biggest movie project of my life and at the same time pay attention to my father, a couple of hundred feet away, lying in bed with tubes coming out of him, in the same state of pain and confusion I had just experienced firsthand. I knew exactly what he was going through. I felt his level of distress all over again.

"THE HOUSE BURNED DOWN, HOW DO YOU THINK WE FEEL?"

MY PARENTS WERE STAYING IN THE STAND-ALONE guesthouse the night of the monstrous fire that demolished Drew's farmhouse and added another cruel and bizarre twist to our lives. It was a Saturday night, in fact Molly Shannon's last appearance as a cast member of *Saturday Night Live*. Drew and Molly were friends, so she wanted to stay up and watch the show. I wanted to see it too, but I flaked out about halfway through and fell asleep.

The next thing I remember was Drew screaming and shouting. It was four in the morning. The fire alarm had gone off somewhere in the house, and one of her dogs was barking maniacally. I woke up in a complete daze. I looked at the window. The blinds were closed, but there was an orange glow leaking through. We ran to the window, opened the blinds, and stood there in shock. At the other end of the house were shooting out what seemed like one-hundred-foot flames. It was a massive blaze.

While two of Drew's dogs were sleeping in the bedroom, her dog Flossie was trapped outside the room. She didn't normally sleep out there, and it was her bark that alerted us to the fire. We quickly opened the door to let her in and as I looked down the stairs—the bedroom is on the second floor of the main house—I could see smoke but no fire. It was only out the window that we could see the fire engulfing the house. It was like a forest fire. We knew at once that we weren't going to be able to spray some water on it and put it out.

I closed the bedroom door behind Flossie and we escaped through a patio door off the bedroom. The way the house was configured on a hillside, that door led to solid ground. We ran down the driveway to wake up my parents in the guesthouse. Drew called 911, then the phone went dead. The fire had consumed the main wires. Nevertheless, the fire department got the message and was there in a matter of minutes. Unfortunately there wasn't much they could do. The house was pretty much gone by the time they arrived. The structure was all wood. It burned like a grove of trees.

I remember standing on a hillside not far from the house, waiting for the fire trucks to arrive. I was standing behind Drew, my arms around her, watching the fire, whispering, trying to console her. She was calm, her mouth agape and eyes wide in their sockets, stunned. Other than the thundering rumble of the fire and the cracking of burning wood being consumed, it was quiet. It felt oddly peaceful, almost as if we lay in a dream. At the same time, I remember asking myself, How could yet another thing be going wrong in my life? It was like living under a curse.

As the distant sirens grew closer, we watched the enormous blaze at one end of the house flow with unstoppable speed toward the opposite end. It was hard not to picture the specific items being destroyed inside, and it felt as though the fire and the approaching sirens were racing each other to an obvious finish. The carroty inferno continued blasting hundreds of feet into the air. Even standing a ways up the hill, the heat was powerful.

By the time the fire trucks arrived, the fire had won, the entire house was engulfed, and it was obvious that everything inside was destroyed. Holding

Drew close, I could feel her memories that lay inside that home, her house, being pulled from inside her. I knew this was going to be another event in our lives that would not just wash away easily. When these ghastly events occurred, which seemed to be more and more frequently, I would feel almost an instinctive urge to protect her. Now, here we stood on the hillside, with my family, witnessing everything in her life destroyed. It was very sad.

There were news helicopters flying over reporting live to all of L.A., or at least the audience watching the news at four in the morning. There were huge lights and fire trucks and firemen and water everywhere. It took a couple of hours before it was safe for us to get close to the house. It was around six, the sun was coming up, and the fire was sort of simmering.

We walked back into the bedroom from the same door we had exited. The bedroom, it turned out, was saved from the fire because I had run back in and closed the door closest to the fire before we left. I think I faintly remembered the fire drill at school where they said to always close any door you go through. In any case, in nothing but my boxer shorts, I had gone back in to do just that.

And I know why. The rest of the house was in the process of being destroyed—and with it essentially Drew's whole life. I had been in the house only a short time and was living out of a suitcase. Drew had a lifetime of treasures and mementos in danger. The only things that I really cared about were the things that had grown out of our relationship—the marijuana-freak-out painting, the lobster "PETC" montage, our still cameras. I remember thinking about running downstairs and grabbing one of the paintings. Then I thought, No, that's insane, that fire is deadly. In the bedroom, Drew had this series of scrapbooks that she had collected that were filled with the history of her family. John Barrymore had apparently collected all of his press photos and other material in these large, leather-bound books, and they had been passed down to Drew for safekeeping. By closing the bedroom door, I knew there was a chance those books would survive. And they did.

Except for the *Starry Night* painting, it felt like the fire had erased the history of our whole relationship along with Drew's own history. I left with little else than the pair of pants I had quickly put on, but I didn't care. Looking back, it seems only right that probably the most important historical and family items of all, those leather-bound books, were preserved: Drew no doubt had a spiritual bond with her acting forefathers, especially her grandfather, and at least the mementos of that weren't lost in this horrendous act of destruction.

The official cause of the fire was an electrical short located by inspectors in one of the walls at the far end of the house. We had been in New York for about seven months, and the house had sat dormant. Maybe a little mouse had snuck in and chewed through a cable and screwed up our lives. We'll never really know.

We finally got our wits about us and decided to get away from the fire and find a hotel to check into. The house was surrounded with local news units, "entertainment reporters," and public gawkers. Drew was subject to panic attacks under much-less-stressful circumstances, like hearing a weird sound in the middle of the night. And I don't mean, "Oh, I'm nervous" panic attacks; I mean full-on crying and hysterics, i.e., total insanity. So when the house burned down, it wasn't just, "Okay, let's go check into a hotel, this is really sad, this is crazy, and we're crying. . . ." This was a volatile situation in which I was panicked myself, wondering if either or both of us was going to fall apart.

I tried to lighten this up a little, even though the media hounds had us surrounded and Drew was freaking. "Let's just drive through them with the top down and make a joke." She agreed that was a good idea. As we were trying to drive away, someone yelled, "How do you feel?" I yelled back, "The house burned down, how do you think we feel?" Drew broke down laughing. We were in shock, but we were trying to make light of a horrible situation. We were doing what media objects are suppose to do—maintain a sense of cool and composure in all circumstances, no matter what. I was sure if we weren't surrounded by cameras, we would have been shaking and crying. Instead, we made a joke and got the hell out of there.

The premiere of *Freddy Got Fingered* was only a few weeks away. As we drove through the media gaggle and I was trying to think of something witty to say, it crossed my mind to shout out, "Go see *Freddy Got Fingered!*" It would have been as stupid and irrelevant as all the inane questions being shouted at us. It would have been a great media joke, as if I had set our house on fire so I could get maximum exposure for my new movie. I didn't say it, of course, but in retrospect maybe I should have. It would have fit the absurdity of the situation perfectly.

We ended up checking into the Hotel Bel-Air and collapsing. I remember checking into this five-star hotel with my father in his bathrobe, hooked up to a rolling IV. The place cost a fortune, and we ended up staying four days as we tried to figure out our next move. Because of the fire, we were instantly thrown into a radical new situation. We were not only getting married in a few months, we were not only dealing with another cancer trauma in the family, but we would now be buying a new house together and starting over. Our lives were changing very fast, and we were completely disoriented.

Of course things would have been a lot easier if the house hadn't burned to the ground. We could have gotten married, stayed in that house, and argued for months about the next house, "our" house—where to buy, how much to pay, two- or three-car garage, etc. I was still relatively new to L.A. I didn't really understand the subtle but, to some, life-altering difference between an 818-area-code house and a 310-area-code house. I didn't get why one house, on one side of the hill, cost three times as much as, and had fewer amenities than, an equally attractive house on the "bad" side of the hill. This was my first house, after all. I think Drew bought her first house when she was six.

We were distraught, confused, and in a hurry. We moved into a succession of rental houses, three in all, and every time we moved, it just added to the general disorientation. The stress was intense, and I think it had a profound effect on both of us. I began to see a different person emerge from the person I had fallen in love with a year and a half before. After all, she had just lost everything she owned, and we were both being thrust into a strange new state of affairs.

And then *Freddy Got Fingered* came out.

"A CULTURAL FATWA"

EVEN BEFORE THE HOUSE BURNED DOWN, THE SAGA of *Freddy Got Fingered* was starting to look like a tragedy, but for the longest time, it didn't appear that way. The euphoria of the production continued well into the editing. I had an early screening of a two-and-a-half-hour-long rough version for friends only in New York. People were laughing, having a great time. Then I cut another half an hour, and the studio weighed in with their comments. Their attitude was not, "Oh, God, we're fucked." Maybe we were all deluding ourselves, but the general consensus was that we had something extreme, but also entertaining. Things had to be whittled and shaped and enhanced, but the movie was there. Or so we thought.

First, I had to get an R rating from the movie ratings board, the MPAA, or Motion Picture Association of America. An NC-17 rating was totally unacceptable, since the primary audience for the movie was around sixteen. I wrote a succession of long-winded letters to the head of the MPAA, Jack Valenti, explaining why certain jokes had to stay in the picture. I also knew that the whole process would be a terrible struggle. From the MPAA's point of view, many American parents might not want their impressionable sixteen-year-old seeing a baby being extracted from a woman's womb, then seeing the umbilical cord being ripped apart by teeth, then seeing the comatose, lifeless fetus being brought back to life by being slung around like a tether ball on a rope. Since the baby lives, I argued that this was a life-enhancing scene. It took some convincing.

I knew the movie was going to be branded initially with the dreaded NC-17, so I purposely cut a two-hour version of the movie to send to the MPAA. After we got the NC-17, the MPAA suggested cuts that would bring the movie up to the R level. I then cut twenty minutes of offensive material that I was going to cut anyway and wrote the board to explain the very difficult decisions I had to make to meet their criteria. This went on until they were sufficiently impressed to hand us an R rating. They thought masturbating a horse for two minutes was simply outside the community standard for good taste. So did I. When the scene came back as five seconds of screen time, we were all happy.

After months of editing, we had a screening at Fox in L.A.—a very intimate screening for only Arnon Milchan and the other Regency executives. This was not the finished film—it had a lot of weird temporary music, like the soundtrack from *The Thing*—but it was close. I couldn't have been more nervous. The movie ended, and everyone was very quiet, waiting for Arnon, the boss, to react. Arnon stood up and started clapping. You could hear every person in the room take a deep breath, especially me.

He then made a short speech praising both me and the movie. He said he had been making movies for thirty years and that this was one of the proudest moments in his career . . . "to take a kid who's never directed a movie, writes a script, comes in, says 'I want to direct this movie,' and goes out and does it." It was a very, very positive moment. Everybody walked out of the room thinking, Holy shit, we've got a fuckin' hit movie here. Tom really pulled it off. This thing is going to be huge!

That lasted for about four exhilarating days. The next step was to show the film to a preview audience of regular moviegoers and get their focus-group-type response, a very common practice for studio films. After these screenings, filmmakers often go back and re-edit the ending or play up some aspect of the film that people really responded to. It's like test-marketing a new Cajun chicken sandwich at McDonald's. Which is why, I guess, most movies come out looking like McMovies.

We did our first big preview screening in Phoenix. People are asked to fill out little response cards after the screening, and the marketing people then come up with a mathematical score indicating how well the movie played. A perfect score would be 100. We thought we'd get in the high 90s.

We got a 17.

Every woman in the audience freaked, and the men weren't too happy, either. Many walked out during the umbilical cord-swinging scene. It was just too gross for them to sit there and watch. And that's why the score sucked. The studio chiefs had every other movie score to compare it to. "Okay," they would say, "*American Pie* got a seventy-eight score and made this much at the box office. Mathematically, that means *Freddy* will make about . . . uh-oh. How do we get this movie to a seventy-eight?"

There are, of course, wild success stories that contradict this bean-counter logic. I've heard that *Austin Powers* got only a 48 score with the focus crowd. Audiences didn't get it at first, obviously, and it had to slowly seep into America's comic skull before it first became a cult hit and then, with the sequel, a box office hit. All we had to do, we figured, is get from 17 to 48—from an F, say, to a strong D—and we'd be cruising.

We also had to account for the aggressively hostile comments that showed up on the little cards. "This was the biggest piece of shit I've ever seen" was one of the nicer ones.

Reading those cards for the first time was a big moment for me, a kind of watershed event in my so-called career. I had been making over-the-top comedy for fourteen or fifteen years and had certainly had my share of people screaming, cursing, even vomiting on the occasion of a particularly offensive joke, but this was different. This was the first time that I had seen outright hatred—almost homicidal loathing—coming from an audience. And in such large quantities. This wasn't just one disgruntled grandmother or moral crusader. This was a whole town of bloodthirsty vigilantes, ready to string me up to the nearest tree.

The plane ride back to L.A. was like flying home with the team that had just lost the Super Bowl. As I flipped through the stack of vicious, vituperative hate cards, everyone on the plane was completely silent. The joy and exhilaration of four days ago was totally out the window. The people, or at least a theater full of people in Phoenix, had spoken. The scores don't lie. *American Pie* had a 78 and we had a 17, and we were flying home knowing—with mathematical certainty—that this movie was going to bomb. The movie was months from coming out—we hadn't done one ad, walked onto one talk show, gotten one review—but we were, in the studio's eyes, dead meat.

It was depressing. We went back into the editing room and tried to make some audience-pleasing changes that would perk up the score without gutting the whole movie. We showed it to another focus group a week later, and the score went up to 20. This went on for a while without much improvement. To me, it was baffling. We would play the movie to an audience in Las Vegas, say, and they would react vocally—not booing, but laughing, screaming, covering their eyes—throughout the entire movie, in fact, more so than at any movie I've ever been to in my life. When I bit that umbilical cord in half, the reaction was so loud you couldn't hear the person next to you. Then we'd be handed a sheet of paper by a guy with a calculator in his hand and a frown on his face: "You got a nineteen. This movie is fucked."

And the downward spiral began. I remember reading the first review that came out. It was in the *Hollywood Reporter*. It was the worst review anybody could ever get. It was certainly the worst review I'd ever gotten. In part, it read:

In a year that has seen no shortage of potential candidates, Tom Green's *Freddy Got Fingered* has the dubious distinction of being quite possibly the worst comedy ever made. It's not just bad; it's jaw-dropping, head-pounding, tumor-inducing, apocalypse-summoning bad. . . . Aside from maybe the kind of people who get off on 22-car pileups, it's unlikely that many others will venture into this torturous laugh-free zone . . . a pathetic, unparalleled abomination.

How do I explain the huge disparity between this kind of reaction and our own take on the movie? I don't really know—wrong movie, wrong time, wrong audience, wrong something. Because it was a studio film, you couldn't just sneak it out there as a cult item. You couldn't just let kids discover it; you had to get them to fill out focus-group questionnaires with an adult pacing around like a teacher at the front of the classroom. And most people, even kids, go to the movies to see something they already expect. Finally, there must be an invisible line between using fake jissum as a hair tonic, à la *Something About Mary*, and pleasuring a real horse. In the mass movie market, we crossed that line.

For what it's worth, *Freddy* survived the critical drumming and went on to make $30-plus million on DVD alone. Not bad for a movie that cost half that much to make. Obviously there was an audience for it. I hear from *Freddy* lovers all the time. Unfortunately that audience didn't make itself known in the early days of its release. We got murdered.

"OH, YOU DO THAT 'GENERATION X' COMEDY"

ON THE SAME DAY THAT THE FIRST SCATHING REVIEW came out, I was invited to tape a segment of the *Primetime Glick* show on Comedy Central, starring Martin Short as a grossly fat, unctuous, and offensive celebrity talk-show host. Despite the review, I was excited. I had been a fan of Martin Short since SCTV. Two or three years before, I was a guest on his first, straight talk show and had a great time; Steve Martin was also a guest, and I remember how exciting it was to sit between Ed Grimley (Short) and The Jerk (Steve Martin).

I looked forward to a similar experience with his unctuous alter ego, Jiminy Glick. I had a short preshow chat with him, half-dressed in his fat suit, and everything seemed fine. The review was out of my mind. I was ready to goof around and have some fun.

The interview began, and I immediately sensed a distinctly negative vibe. I played like I didn't know what camera to look at, and Jiminy Glick snapped back with something like, "You've got two cameras, idiot, look at that one." I took his reaction not to be funny-aggressive, not fucking-with-you-aggressive, but just plain aggressive. And hostile.

I had never seen the show before, so I guess I didn't understand the rules. He threw out some obscure comedic references and, assuming that I didn't know who these people were, trashed me before I had time to answer. He pegged me as having "that Generation X comedy," whatever that is. It was all happening very quickly. His job was to put me on the spot and make me as uncomfortable as possible. It got to the point that every attempt at humor I tried, however, became a target of his not-too-subtle invective. He clearly had me on the ropes—it was his show, he was in the fat suit, he could do or say anything under that disguise, and he flat-ass didn't like me.

About the time I stopped trying to play along, he went for the cancer. Coming so soon after the real event, this was too much. He started in on the fact that I only had one testicle. Maybe he misread my feelings about this because I had made so many jokes myself, i.e., "Hey kids, feel your balls, squeeze your balls, so you won't get cancer." But it's one thing to make fun of your own cancer, more or less as a defense mechanism, and it's quite another for a faux talk-show clown in a fat suit to make fun of it. Richard Pryor could always get away with using the *N* word in his act, but no white comic would ever touch the word. Cancer is a joke best told by people who have had it.

I was pissed at this point and began to respond to his jabs with one word, yes-and-no answers. In character, he said, "Well, I don't think we're gonna be able to use this." That was my cue. I said, "Okay, well, thanks a lot," got up, and walked out of the studio, not saying anything to anyone. My publicist looked at me like I was crazy. This had never happened before. I had done every talk show in America and Canada five times over, and I had never taken a hike.

I got into the limo, and as we pulled away, I saw Martin Short waddle out in his fat suit, trying to catch up to the car. He probably wanted to tell me that

I'd never work in this town again. I didn't care at that point. I hadn't signed a release form and knew the segment would never air. And it never did.

Coming on the tail of that disaster was the critical blitzkrieg waged against *Freddy Got Fingered*. Just for the record, the movie got a very good review in the *New York Times*:

> Mr. Green stage[s] his gross-outs with a demented but unmistakable integrity. Like it or not, he's an artist.... The movie's comic heart consists of a series of indescribably loopy, elaborately conceived happenings that are at once rigorous and chaotic, idiotic and brilliant. Some of these ... may show up some day at the Museum of Modern Art.

But that was like trying to ward off a herd of thundering elephants with a flyswatter. Entertainment editors competed with one another to come up with the stupidest review title: "Freddy Gets Fingered and So Will You," or, "Tom Green Gets Fingered," or, "Let's All Give Tom Green the Finger."

If they had just hated the movie, that's one thing. I'm sure the makers of *Ishtar, Pluto Nash,* and *Gigli* all had a bad day or two, then went back to their lives. But in the case of *Freddy* the attacks were personal. They would say things like ... "The only good thing about Tom Green is his goatee, because it covers his ugly face." Or, "Now that I think about it, what is that Drew Barrymore doing with *him?*" It wasn't "This guy made a bad movie"; it was "This guy's a bad guy."

Reading this bile, I became deeply, deeply upset. I was sad, depressed, scared, and panicked, all at the same time. This was the second time in my turmoil-filled relationship with Drew where I needed her support badly. I had given her as much support as I could muster through the fire, her family problems, her career problems, the whole gamut. And now I needed some emotional backup. I had needed it during the cancer ordeal, of course, but now I *really* needed it.

Whatever I needed, from my point of view, I wasn't getting. It was very confusing at the time and also added to my high level of distress. Self-centeredness is an occupational hazard in Hollywood, and, remember, she had been in the occupation of movie star since the age of five. Her entire life had been spent worrying about herself. And she was surrounded by people whose only job was to worry about her. So it was difficult, to say the least, for her to respond to my needs.

Of course, I'm all of thirty-two years old and am telling my life story in a book. How self-centered is that? Attention and adulation can and does screw with your head. To stay sane, and to treat others with some modicum of compassion, you have to constantly check yourself. In some ways, it was a great experience for me to taste both illness and failure. They both have helped clear away the narcissistic fog of Hollywood.

I didn't think that at the time. I felt like the American entertainment press was calling for my death. Overnight I had become the Salman Rushdie of the movie business. There was a cultural fatwa issued with my name on it. And there seemed to be joy in this character assassination. This really bothered me. Why couldn't these critics just dismiss the movie like they dismiss dozens of box office flops every year? Why couldn't their attitude have been "Didn't work, Tom, better luck next time. . . ." instead of "You made a bad movie, Tom, and now you must *die!*"

As I look back now, I think this onslaught had to do with more than just the movie. To many people out there, I represented a brand of humor that they had long despised, and it grated on them that this humor, despite their cries of outrage, had been quite successful. It's very much like rap—something adults rarely listen to but always have a bad word to say about. This media group was looking for someone who overstepped the bounds of good taste and fell on his face. I was that guy.

On top of that, I had gotten too successful way too quickly. I hadn't "paid my dues." The success gods had treated me too well. Now the media gods were going to correct this seeming injustice.

Because of the controversy of my MTV show, and *Jackass*, and even the crude moments in *Something About Mary, Freddy* couldn't just pass unnoticed. Because I had gotten "too much" media exposure, especially relating to Drew, it couldn't just die on the first weekend. And because I was by definition a trickster, it was an easy slam. "Trickster Gets Tricked."

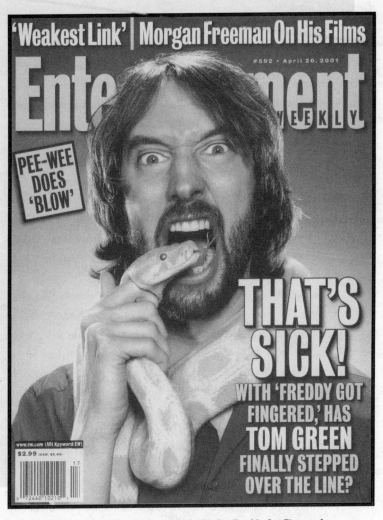

The cover of *Entertainment Weekly* for *Freddy Got Fingered.*
Don't ask me why they wanted me to put a snake in my mouth. . . .
I guess that's crazy or something.

To some, the whole marriage story struck them as an attention-getting device to bolster my career. And we didn't exactly avoid the subject. For example, we had been lying about already being married for a long time before we actually got married. As I mentioned, when I hosted *Saturday Night Live* during the editing of *Freddy*, we hinted to *Entertainment Weekly* that we would get married on the show. Drew came out in the opening of the show, and I said, "We're getting married tonight." The cake was rolled out, and all you had to do was watch the rest of the show to see us get married. When, at the end of the show, Drew didn't appear and I screamed, "Drew! Drew!" and acted like a jerk, it was just a stunt to get laughs. At least to me. To others, no doubt, it was another attempt to milk this celebrity nonsense for all it was worth.

Live by the media, die by the media.

In hindsight I see that I was playing with fire. I didn't understand how the "entertainment press" really worked. "Are you getting married? Are you dating? What's Drew's favorite color? Did you bite an umbilical cord in half? Why did you put a mouse in your mouth? How did the house burn down? Did *you* do it? . . ." As silly as all of these questions seemed to me, I forgot that the people asking them take this stuff dead seriously. This is their livelihood. By making up ridiculous lies, by goofing with them, they got offended. I thought the media as a whole, from marriage to Monica, was part of the comedy. They didn't get the joke. They are like a humorless, media-pack version of my sixth-grade teacher, Mrs. Gaudreau. "Try to watch the 'talking out,' Tommy. It is not appreciated."

Drew was and is a powerful woman in Hollywood. I was a cable-TV clown with a movie about to come out. We were not on equal media footing—I was an upstart, and an unruly one at that, and she was Hollywood royalty. The tendency of the media in situations like this—a powerful woman and a not-so-powerful man—is to make the man look like a loser, a usurper of privilege and beauty, a hanger-on.

The brief marriage of Julia Roberts and Lyle Lovett is a case in point. "Why," the media world wondered, "was she marrying *this* guy?" Before he was an appendage on the arm of the adorable Julia Roberts, Lyle Lovett was a highly respected country singer. He was always quirky, but the press had only nice things to say about him. But as soon as he hooked up with Julia, he became the

Drew and me on New Year's Eve. We were in a bar in Ottawa called Barrymore's.

butt of hateful jokes. "What is *she* thinking?" "What is *he* thinking?" Few people in the media ever said that Julia Roberts "wasn't good enough" for Lyle
Lovett.

That's the extremely mean-spirited edge of the media. And it has its effect.
It eats away at you. You see stories everyday in places like *People* and *Details*
where an actor or someone else married to a media-beloved woman is "secretly
depressed" that his wife is doing better than he is or that she is so consumed

with her career that he feels invisible. I'm sure the women of celebrity-centric men feel the same, but that's more of a "dog bites man" story—i.e., the myth of the faithful wife who shuns the spotlight. Faithful wives don't get the media play of the sad male spouse on the arm of the powerful woman.

And you know what? It can be depressing. Even under the best of circumstances, it can be difficult living in that arrangement and being measured and scrutinized and second-guessed. You aren't just with someone—with the person you care about and want to build a life with—but you are also with her public persona, her press, her yes-people, and her fans. I don't think I identified early enough that I wouldn't be happy in that world.

First, I had to get married.

12.

THE GREENS

—

"It was out in Malibu in a nice place and we walked in, in the traditional way, to be seated last. We were seated in front of Courtney Love, who was smoking a cigarette, or at least I think it was a cigarette, during the whole ceremony, and I thought, 'Jeez, where am I? What is going on here?' "

—Mary Jane Green,
on Tom's wedding

I GOT MARRIED AND FIVE MONTHS LATER I GOT DIVORCED. That seems weird, even to me.

The simplest way to explain it, I think, was that we were aboard an unstoppable train and couldn't get off. Even at the time, whenever I entertained the thought of not getting married, of calling the whole crazy thing off, it seemed much more bizarre and painful than going ahead. We were too far down the track. It's easy to see how people in movies, à la *The Graduate*, can run out on a marriage on their wedding day. In the real world, it's not so easy.

This was not, I repeat, *not* an impulsive weekend-in-Vegas kind of relationship. We lived together for a year before we were engaged, and we were engaged for a year before we got married. There was obviously some chance of this marriage working. We were compatible enough to spend two and a half years together. When you have a public relationship, entertainment writers tend to reset the odometer if it doesn't work out. "Isn't that bizarre, they were together for only five months." It makes a better story. It confirms middle America's (and Fox News's) view of the whole decadent Hollywood milieu.

"These people are so irresponsible, so utterly contemptuous of the institution of marriage, the very bedrock of Western civilization, that they treat it like a new brand of gum. When it loses its taste, they just spit it out." That's the popular talk-radio view.

To be completely honest about this very intimate part of my life is impossible. Or at least it is something I am unwilling to do. On one hand, I am very much aware that the underlying reasons for the failure of our marriage might seem unclearly explained. Yes, I have said that we came from completely different worlds, but unfortunately that alone wasn't the only schism. I don't want to sound coy or cavalier, or come off like another Hollywood prick who laughs at marriage, but it's inappropriate bordering on tacky to say more, so I won't.

The marriage, in short, was more than I had bargained for. Things changed after the cancer, and the house fire, and the movie bomb, and the media onslaught. She began to change, I began to change. After we got married I quickly began to see through the mirage of the two people I thought we were. There were deep-seated issues that I didn't have a clue as to how to fix. It happens in bad marriages every day, I'm sure. In a situation like ours, these issues just get amplified, distorted, gossiped about, written about, and finally poisoned by the public life we both chose to pursue.

At the time, of course, if you actually plan to marry someone you've spent two years with, you don't just throw in the towel at the first sign of trouble, or even the thirty-first sign of trouble. Your instinct is to try to fix the things that are wrong. And even if those problems are getting progressively worse—especially in the wake of cancer, a house burning down, a movie flop, and a few other off-the-chart life experiences—you tend to excuse them as simply a response to the pressures of the moment.

You hear stories—and see movies like *Father of the Bride*—where the couple fights constantly during the planning and execution of the big day, then settles into a life of marital bliss. "It's just the stress of buying a house together, and all the legalisms involved in a high-profile union, and all the party-planning-isms," you think. You can't wait for all of this to end so that you can return to a reasonably happy and satisfying relationship.

In other words, you trick yourself into thinking all of this anxiety and disagreement is normal. If you bail, you are not just ending the wedding, you're ending the relationship. I don't think either of us was ready to do that at that point. So we plowed on.

And of course the wedding wasn't the only distraction at the time. Besides all the time I had spent promoting *Freddy*, only to see both it and me get thoroughly vilified, I was also off for six weeks to do my next movie, *Stealing Harvard*. The wedding was planned for shortly after the movie was completely wrapped. The producers of *Stealing Harvard* had paid me well to star in their movie, and they were probably second-guessing the whole arrangement after *Freddy* came out. I didn't care that much—the wedding was foremost in my mind. I wanted to get back, get married, and stop the infernal bickering with Drew.

Meanwhile, careers aside, we had to buy a house, plan a honeymoon, and organize a wedding, all of which were crazy-making events. Without the fire, a new house would have never been a concern. As it was, it became the first in the string of collisions of two worlds, or at least two worldviews. I had made a lot of money in the last couple of years, but I was still a middle-class kid from Ottawa and very leery of overspending. Drew had been making a lot of money since she could remember and had a radically different view of what things costs. We were coming from much different financial places.

It's one thing to be the big spender and say foolhardy things like, "I'll pay for dinner every night, babe." But when you're purchasing a multimillion-dollar home together—and splitting the cost 50/50—it can get weird fast. Her idea of a fixer-upper and my idea of a fixer-upper were many zeros apart. We'd find a nice place that I thought was in move-in condition, and she'd say, "Oh, this place is great, you know, if we could just tear the whole thing down and build it again." This didn't make sense to me. "Isn't the reason we'd buy the house," I'd say, "to live in it?" This would lead to a massive misunderstanding of what constituted a livable house in a livable zip code at a livable price.

I'm sure millions of just-to-be-marrieds have soul-wrenching arguments over finances and, since buying a house is the biggest financial decision most couples make, arguments over the price of a new home. The only difference, I guess, in our case, was that the argument was over *millions* of dollars. I was way too new to the warped reality of Hollywood to take any of these riches for granted or to spend what I had on a fantasy house that was so far more extreme than what I had known for the first twenty-eight years of my life. Sure, I wanted a big house with all the trimmings. But I feared getting sucked into some kind of Tony Montana/*Scarface* excess that I couldn't escape from.

I mean, they have nice houses in the Valley, too.

Houses, not surprisingly, are a constant source of discussion, comparison, and envy in Hollywood. I have to admit that, coming from a modest home in Ottawa, I was overwhelmed by the excess of it all. The first thing I noticed is the extreme emphasis on expensive appliances. A simple refrigerator is just not good enough. It has to be a Sub-Zero refrigerator, oversized and stainless steel, the kind they have in restaurants. But that's not enough. You need two, one extra-large one with a glass door. This one is used solely for beer and wine and champagne. And you can't just have a normal stove, it has to be a Viking Range, also stainless steel as seen in restaurants. This is very important stuff to Hollywood people. Even though nobody really cooks—eating out is both easier and a potential photo opportunity—a really nice kitchen is a must. *MTV Cribs* might drop by.

And one more thing: tiles. Young rich people in Hollywood are obsessed with tiles. That's right, tiles. Fancy imported ceramic tiles, for either the bathroom, or the kitchen, or the pool. From either Spain, or Italy, or France. I won't name any names, but one particular young actor I knew really stood out. This was a person who was having a bit of a "lucky streak" in the career department. Every time I would work with this person, he was on the phone with his assistant, discussing furnishings, renovations, and tiles.

This dude got so obsessed with tiles and interior design that one day his assistant showed up at the movie set with dozens of different tile samples to pick through. He spent the whole day wandering around the set trying to decide with the crew which ceramic tile would look best in his steam shower. It's as if he was saying to everybody, "Look at me! Look how sophisticated I am! I'm into fancy stuff!" Regardless, this is a kid in his twenties! I mean, I'm no hick, I like to feel as cosmopolitan as the next guy. But this guy should have been thinking about his next beer or which extra he wanted to bang after work. Or even better, he could have been learning his lines.

"GWYNETH ALWAYS GOES THERE"

THE SAME COLLISION OF WORLDVIEWS EXTENDED to planning a honeymoon. Being the concerned, budget-minded guy I was in this relationship, I asked that we agree on a spending limit for our planned, five-week getaway. We both wanted to take a lot of time to escape the rigors of work and the pressure-cooker atmosphere of Hollywood. We both had been working for two or three years straight and figured we'd be doing a similar work stretch when we got back, so why not take the time now. At a price, of course.

This all seemed well and good until Drew said, "Great, let's call my travel agent and put her on the speaker phone." The travel agent was ready to send us to the moon. "Oh, great, you want to go to Greece? I have a great yacht for rent that 'Harrison' always uses, he loves it, it's only a hundred and fifty a week." Drew's right with her. "Oh, that sounds like fun." "It is. It has a staff of twelve, a wonderful cook, you can watch the sun go up and down."

I'm thinking, $150,000? That's more than my parents paid for their house! For a one-week trip with good food? And a whole lot more than our agreed-upon budget ceiling. I didn't know what to do. I didn't want to fight about this and seem like I'm out to ruin her honeymoon, but I sure didn't want to spend $150,000 on a fucking boat trip.

The agent had a better idea. What about a week's stay on an island that Richard Branson owns? "Gwyneth always goes there." Hollywood is an extremely competitive place, right down to who goes to whose island for vacation. I think Drew began to think, Hey, if Gwyneth goes there, then by God I can go there, too, while I was thinking, Gwyneth goes there? Then that's way out of my price range. It's funny how the word "Gwyneth" sent us in completely opposite directions.

In the end, we nixed Greece altogether, including Harrison's yacht and Gwyneth's island. We ended up planning a trip to the Bahamas for a week, then a trip to Paris, then a car tour of Ireland, and a few days of decompression in my parents' cabin in rural Canada. It was . . . well, I'll get to that later.

"DAISIES IN COKE BOTTLES?" "SURE, NO PROBLEM."

AND THEN CAME THE PLANNING OF THE WEDDING itself. I was very much in favor of a small intimate wedding. I didn't really want it to be something that became some sort of Hollywood event. And it didn't seem that she really did, either, but somehow the momentum of the event pushed us in that direction. Again, this produced an argument about money, and though it may seem silly that two people with money would constantly argue about it, everything is relative, even in the most fortunate situations. I just knew I didn't want to spend a million dollars for what I perceived to be a big party. And we didn't. Quite.

I was away for much of the wedding planning, shooting *Stealing Harvard*, so Drew and her crack team of assistants took charge. Everybody here has an assistant or two or twelve. It's amazing how important these assistants seem to become. When you move to Hollywood, all of a sudden you realize that you are surrounded by people who no longer have to really live life: they have assistants to live it for them. If even a minor celeb were to say, "I've got to go Christmas shopping," they wouldn't actually be thinking of going to a store. That would be crazy! Instead they would sit down in their fancy, unused kitchen with an assistant or two and make a list. The assistant would then go shopping. The assistant would also sign the card.

The thing that is really strange about assistants is how close they become to the people they assist. They become "professional friends." It's actually the perfect arrangement—they can "hang out" with these people all day, but whenever something needs to be done, go to it, kid! And they all have the keys to their "master's" (or "mistress's") domain. Car keys, house keys, credit cards, bank cards. Everything that one would usually consider private, like space, is no longer so. There is just something strange about getting out of the shower and running into a gay guy with a bunch of boxes he's dropping off. I remember coming home one day and some assistants were all trying on dresses for some drag party they were going to. "Oh, hey Tom!" they shouted, "You're home! We're all going to The Drag Strip tonight!" Of course I would smile, as these people were supposed to be my "friends." But, I thought, Don't you people have homes! What planet have I landed on here! GET THE FUCK OUT OF MY HOUSE!!!! (You can't really say that; it wouldn't be right, not in Holly-wood.)

Anyway, the assistants plotted the wedding details, and Drew had the lion's share of the pressure of putting on this show, and I'm sure it got to her. On the other hand, as I was slowly learning, she very much liked to be in charge. She was used to being in charge of her work, her production company, and most of the major decisions of her life. My strategy was to watch that I didn't blow all of my money but mainly defer to her judgment and concur whenever possible. Of course that strategy didn't work, either. You can't win.

With the wedding in mind, Drew used her insurance money from the fire to rent a beach house in Malibu for a short period. It was a phenomenal place—four acres on a cliff overlooking the beach with a path to walk down to the water. It came with five pet llamas in a pen on the property. We had our own llama herd.

So I saw this place, and though it was a monstrous amount to spend on the event, I was starting to think, Wow, this is going to be a pretty great party. I had never spent that much on a party before. Usually it was Domino's, a couple of twelve-packs, and you're rockin'. My budget figure was greeted with a disguised disdain by the A-team party planners. We ended up spending much, much more. Just like in the movies, it escalated fast—from 25 close friends to 120 close friends, distant friends, professional friends, or just professional acquaintances. In the end, it made sense; I had a slew of family coming down from Canada—aunts, uncles, and cousins—and Drew's family was largely her group of Hollywood friends. So my side of the aisle was largely "civilians," and hers was largely stars, agents, and lawyers. Another collision of worlds.

As it turned out, there weren't that many famous people at the wedding, but there were enough that I'd never really met, and enough to intimidate my non-Hollywood friends and family—their presence tilted the whole event slightly in the direction of a celebrity gathering with a wedding thrown in. Of course the Hollywood people didn't know my Uncle Don or Aunt Margie, either, but neither of them had just made a $50 million movie.

But, along with everything else, I didn't question the guest list. I really worked at being the get-along guy. "Do you want daisies in Coke bottles on every table?" I was asked. "Sure," I said, "that sounds great." "Do you want a karaoke machine on the stage at the reception?" "Sounds like fun," I said. Everything seemed to be going smoothly for a couple of weeks until I began to notice a lot of anger being directed my way. "Why are you so angry?" I said. "Because," she said, "you don't give a damn. You're not making any decisions here." So then I'd try to make a decision, "Okay, maybe we shouldn't have Coke bottles then." That was not the right decision to make. She really wanted daisies in Coke bottles. "Okay," I said, "then it's set—daisies in Coke bottles." That only made matters worse. "Don't you see? You're not making a fucking decision! That's what *I* wanted to do!"

It was a little insane.

"I GIVE YOU . . . THE GREENS!"

IT WASN'T SO INSANE THAT WE WERE GOING TO INVITE paparazzi and *Entertainment Tonight* to the affair. On this count we scored big. We did a fine job of hiding the fact that we were getting married. First came the trick of leaking into the public gossip stream that we had already gotten married months before. Then, on the day of the wedding, amidst the huge party tents and all the decorations we had put up on the field overlooking the ocean, we hung this huge banner on the roofs of the tents that read: "Happy 50th Anniversary Bob and Frieda!" It was a beautiful tribute.

Any helicopter flying over Malibu, looking for some celebrity-rich event to invade, would look down, see all the trappings of a big beach party, and wonder who the hell Bob and Frieda were to afford such an elaborate affair for their fiftieth anniversary. I think someone got one picture from a boat that made the tabloid press, but for the most part we succeeded in not turning the event into a media circus. In fact, we got married and went off on our honeymoon with hardly a peep. The story became media fodder when someone discovered the official filing of the marriage license in the public records. Hollywood is a sick place. People actually get paid to go through divorce and marriage applications that get submitted daily in hopes of recognizing a famous name. Only the celebrity garbage scavengers are lower on the food chain.

Safe from gluttonous media, people began to arrive. Our disparate tribes merged. For every Cameron Diaz or Adam Sandler, there were multiple Green in-laws from Prince Edward Island, Edmonton, and small-town Barrie, Ontario. Whatever doubts I had about getting married, I couldn't disappoint this extended family. They had spent the time and money to fly to L.A., stay in a hotel, rent a car, and probably buy new clothes. These are normal people who don't do this at the drop of a hat. They could have spent the same money taking a memory-filled trip to Hawaii or Cuba—Canadians regularly vacation in

Me and Phil about one hour before I got married. Don't I look relaxed?

Cuba—but instead they spent it to come down here to help celebrate our wedded love. Far beyond the well-coiffed group on the other side of the aisle, they gave this event gravitas.

I showed up early and mingled with the crowd. I remember Courtney Love, a good friend of Drew, coming up to chat for a second. Her mood would change as the day went along, but right then she was very pleasant. In the course of this brief encounter, she uttered, matter-of-factly, a telling phrase, "Well, if you guys stay married." I was getting married in ten minutes, and she was talking about "if" we stayed married. And that bothered me. "Oh, no," I said, "we are going to *stay* married." She looked at me with more than a hint of skepticism. In hindsight, of course, she clearly knew something I didn't know.

As I walked down the aisle surrounded by this strange mix of humanity—Ottawa normalcy and Hollywood royalty—I had to make a joke. I shook a few hands and kept walking. At one point I shrugged my shoulders and announced to no one in particular, "Wow, this is a really important moment in my life." It got a good laugh, which only helped me feel slightly less awkward. I mean, it wasn't like we were fighting on our wedding day, but I was definitely uneasy about making this very serious commitment. Or maybe I was just uneasy because I didn't know half the people at the event.

We had an, uh, unconventional Hollywood minister suggested by a friend of Drew. (This was not an area where I was going to weigh in.) She was a spiritual vegan minister with long gray hair and some kind of elaborate tie-dyish robe. The hair said to me, "I've smoked a lot of dope in my life, sonny." I don't know how to describe her other than she looked like she had been living on Charlie Manson's commune too long.

I had absolutely nothing against this woman—in fact, she was very nice, almost comforting—but it just didn't strike me that this was the sort of person who was going to officiate at my one-and-only wedding. I'd never visualized that I'd be married by someone who looked like she had been screwing in the mud at Woodstock, you know what I mean?

A lilting version of a very popular love song played as Drew walked down the aisle. It was a beautiful song—an obscure ballad by John Lennon from his post-Beatles period. The Hollywood people were in tears. What a bold choice. I think it was the first time I'd heard that particular song. My relatives were already confused. "Is it starting?" "When does it actually start?" "Is it already over?" "Are they married?"

The minister had suggested that we pick an appropriate verse to read at the wedding and print it up so that the audience could read along with us. I decided to come up with my own "verse"—a long poem about drag racing. Instinctively I wanted to throw some sort of lightness and ridiculousness into this solemn ceremony. Given all of the bickering and dissection that had been going on between us, I knew that I would have a tough time expressing my more tender emotions in this public arena. In the best of circumstances, which these weren't, I would still have a tough time exposing my deep feelings in front of my Uncle Don, let alone Lucy Liu or one of the Beastie Boys. It was a lot easier to do something silly.

It wasn't really a poem. There were no rhymes. In fact, it was just a highly detailed analysis of the types of oil that goes in the engine of a top-fuel drag racer and other such arcana of the sport.

> Drag racing: Top fuel dragsters represent the pinnacle of drag racing performance. Utilizing a supercharged engine producing over 5,000 horsepower from 500 cubic inches of displacement, these engines can accelerate from a standing start to 100 miles per hour in less than one second. . . . Pro modified is one of the most popular divisions in the sport. Pro modified embodies the true spirit of hot-rodding, offering a widely diverse group of race cars and a variety of 2000 horsepower engines.

Everyone read along dutifully, and certainly the cognoscenti among them immediately got the joke. Again, my Canadian relatives were probably wondering what drugs I had taken right before the ceremony. Hippy-dippy ministers, pop music, drag racing . . . what next? Daisies in Coke bottles?

As the minister announced our blessed nuptials, she suddenly stopped and peered out at the ocean. "Oh, look," she said, "the dolphins have graced us." We all looked out, and sure enough, a school of dolphins was cruising by, jumping through the water and genuinely "gracing" us. Everyone there thought this was an epiphany of nature—the pièce de résistance of this romantic union.

Everyone except me. I think those dolphins were there to either play a cosmic joke on us or curse the marriage outright. They were probably running for their lives from a tuna trawler.

As soon as we were officially married, some crazy country song kicked in, we walked back down the aisle, and the minister yelled, "Everyone! I give you . . . the Greens!" Everybody cheered because they thought that was so ridiculous, so rich in nuptial irony. Everyone, including even my most distant relatives, knew there was no way in hell that Drew *Barrymore* would ever change her name to Drew *Green*, or even Drew Barrymore-Green, or Drew Green-Barrymore. Of course it's not the Greens, you crazy New Age priestess, they thought; if it's anything, it's the Barrymores. That's hilarious.

We walked out into a greeting area. I kept looking at my ring, kept playing with it, as the throng approached to congratulate us. I was really happy to be married. I was thoroughly overwhelmed by the whole situation.

"A PERFECT COPULATOR"

THE RECEPTION WAS HELD IN THE NEXT TENT OVER. Sure enough, it was wall-to-wall Coke bottles with daisies. My friend Phil served as emcee. He gave a weird little intro speech, then introduced my friend Derek. Derek was a little nervous, for obvious reasons. A lot of Hollywood types with their arms crossed were judging his every word. It felt like, "Oh, I don't want to bomb up here—six movie stars and the biggest comedian in the world are watching me!" Phil and Derek were clearly too local-yokel for Courtney Love. Derek wasn't halfway through his little speech before she started to heckle him.

Then my dad got up. He has always thought of himself as a bit of a jokester cum after-dinner speaker—he always had something smart to say when we woke him up in the middle of the night. I'm sure he thinks, and rightly so, that he had something to do with starting me out on the trail of comedy. He was more than up to the task of toasting his first-married son.

He made a joke that probably would have killed if he had told it in front of an army group and not in front of a room full of self-centered cynics. "When I first found out that Drew and Tom were getting married," he said, "I asked

Drew what they wanted as a wedding present. She said they wanted a coffee percolator. But I think I misheard her—I think what she actually said is that she wanted a 'perfect copulator.' "

Bada bing.

I thought it was funny. Corny and blue, but given that it was so far outside of the "ironic" school of jokes most of the Hollywood crowd would chuckle at, I thought it fit the occasion to a T. But it clearly made a lot of people uncomfortable and embarrassed for me, I guess.

It was kind of quiet, and then the attention-starved Courtney, the Simon Cowell of this crowd, weighed in with some serious heckling. "Get off the stage!" "Go back to Canada!" That kind of stupid drunk-in-the-third-row level of derision. I couldn't believe it! Courtney Love was heckling my dad at my own wedding! It was a perfect clash of the two worlds, the relatively innocent "copulator" world of my family and the cutting, snide, status-obsessed world of show business. It was funny. It was sad but funny.

I don't think the A-listers knew how to take my father. At one point, he made a reference to the effect that before he had met Drew, he had never really met a movie star before. He said this in a mock-yokel tone, but the movie stars and the talent agents missed the "mock." They like to see themselves as "normal people" and not self-involved celebrities, though there is nothing normal about them. I'm sure they thought, Who are these poor people? Abnormal people who think themselves normal often have a hard time actually recognizing genuinely normal people. And they often don't get the joke, especially when the joke is on them. They are blinded, I guess, by their own reflection.

Phil Giroux got back on stage and launched into a hysterical routine. Full of an inflated sense of the occasion, he pulled a rock out of his pocket and said, "See this rock? This rock symbolizes love. Drew and Tom are in love, and this rock is a symbol of Drew and Tom's love."

"But," he went on, reaching into his pocket again, "all the love that Drew and Tom have can't be contained in a single rock." He pulled out a second rock. "They need a second rock." Beat. "But all the love that Drew and Tom have can't really be contained in this second rock, or even the two rocks combined. That's why in my pocket I have a third rock. Is there more love than three rocks? Yes, there is." And on he went, rambling about our love and pulling rocks out of his pocket until he reached sixteen. This took what seemed like hours, and everybody loved it. Well, almost everybody.

The Heckler could take only so much of this shaggy-dog joke. Between cat-calls like "Get on with it!" she made some nonsensical reference to a six-million-dollar house. Phil, not the least bit intimidated by any of these people, had found his opening. He stopped what he was doing and looked directly at The Heckler. No one had really acknowledged her behavior up to this point, and I guess as emcee, Phil felt a responsibility to do this.

He started in on the house. "Oh, a six-million-dollar house. Boy, that sounds like a pretty big house." She didn't know what to say. I don't think Courtney was used to having people talk back to her. "What about a four-million-dollar house?" Phil went on. "Is that, like, a really big house, Court-ney?" Whatever she might have tried to say in response was muffled by his barrage of sarcastic questions. "Okay, what about a twelve-million-dollar house? That has got to be a really, really big house, wouldn't you say?" He was relentless. "Would you pay two million dollars for a car even though it only costs two hundred thousand?" He would have probably razzed her for the rest of the afternoon if someone hadn't leaned over and told her to shut the fuck up. She finally quieted down. She had been seriously burned, and she knew it.

Everyone then got up and sang karaoke songs. Cameron Diaz sang the Janis Joplin hit "(Lord Won't You Buy Me a) Mercedes Benz." I think the Cana-dian crowd was looking at one another, thinking, She probably can afford one, can't she? Is she rubbing our faces in it? Then I got up and sang—and I am em-barrassed to admit this now, because it sounds so sappy—Drew's favorite song, John Lennon's "Imagine." I'm embarrassed by that now because, looking back, I recall staring out at a lot of people listening to me in that audience who I felt didn't like me very much. When I looked into one of those star's eyes, singing "Imagine" to my wife on my wedding day, I saw a person looking back who didn't know me, wasn't happy for me, and was probably at that very moment thinking, This guy's an idiot; poor Drew.

Well before the party was over, the important people started to slip out, one by one. It was actually interesting to watch this process—the higher profile the person, the sooner they left. There was a definite pecking order at work here, and it was fun to watch them leave in what appeared to be a prearranged

My buddies Derek, Glenn, and Phil.

procession. "You should leave now." "Oh, no, after you. Your last movie did much, much better than mine."

There was one notable exception—Adam Sandler. He stayed to the end of the night, danced with my mom, and talked to my brother, a huge fan, at length. In fact, he was still there when Drew and I snuck out. There were a couple more weird incidents to cap off the evening. Apparently one of the assistants was caught sodomizing one of the caterers in a service tent. Pretty classy, eh? Also, a friend of mine from Canada and his estranged girlfriend got into an enormous physical fight—kicking, scratching, trying to claw each other's eyes out—in front of a bunch of the guests. I remember opening the bathroom door as we were dressing to leave, and there was my friend, blood pouring down his face. "Sorry, Tom," he said. A nice way to end a wedding.

We stayed in a Santa Monica hotel that night before taking off to the Bahamas the next morning. Before we left, we went for a walk out on the beach.

We both had our wedding rings on, and I think we were both a little surprised that we'd actually gotten married, to be honest, because of how stressful it had been up to that point. There was almost a little bit of a jumping-out-of-an-airplane feel to it. "Whoa, we got married."

We stayed in the Bahamas for ten days and spent much of the time playing Scrabble. I had never really played before, so Drew usually won, but after a few dozen games, I started to get a little more competitive. Scrabble, ostensibly a game you play to while away the hours, became kind of a battlefield for this honeymooning couple. It became something to argue about, an extension of the emotional turmoil that began long before the wedding and failed to subside afterward.

One fight was sparked by her very name. Late in one game, Drew proudly arranged the letters B-A-R-R-Y-M-O-R-E and started counting up the points. With nine letters and a *Y*, that was a lot of points, since it was also linked up with another word. You get a score like that, and it's a guaranteed win.

"Sorry," I said, "you're not allowed to use proper names. Everybody knows that." "Yes, you can," she replied, "you can use anything that's in the dictionary." "Fine," I said, "Barrymore's not in the dictionary." "Yes, it is," she said.

She then walked out of the room, went down to the front office, and came back with a dictionary. And there it was—"Barrymore, John," American actor, etc. And it wasn't in the back of the dictionary under proper names. It was right there in the *B*s. Technically, I had just had my ass whipped.

I lost, but more to the point, I felt burned and I felt stupid. The message I heard was, "My name is in the fucking dictionary, didn't you know that?" I checked in the Scrabble dictionary later and the name wasn't there, so technically *I* won the game. But lost the marriage, I guess.

Other than the Scrabble battles, we had a good time in the Bahamas, reading, walking around, taking literally thousands of pictures, just like our early dates. Then we went on to Paris for ten days—this was a long honeymoon, probably too long. I don't think we were in Paris for five minutes before we got into a silly argument about whether we would check into the hotel or go to an ATM first. Paris was followed by a road trip around Ireland, where we had fun but also had to fight off the stress of being recognized everywhere we went. It was still strange to get recognized in America, but when you're sitting in a little cafe in Kilkenny, it's even stranger. Alone, we both probably could have donned a baseball hat and been fine. Together, we were often on display.

The fighting continued, and the relationship at times got so negative that I started to resent the very things that I had initially found so endearing. If somebody has just screamed at you for an hour and a half and then you climb a mountain and they sit cross-legged and start crying because the sky is so blue, it doesn't seem endearing anymore. When you're madly in love, you haven't had a fight in six months, you can't think of anyone in the world you'd rather be with, and they cry at the beauty of the universe, you think, Oh, isn't that sweet and philosophical. But when you're angry, or just trying to get over the frustration of a long argument, you think, Oh, stop with the bloody ode to nature. I'm still pissed!

I think, by that time, I had started to come to a sad but profound realization: Maybe I was too cynical for this person. Maybe I needed to find someone who I could sit with and talk about how stupid or absurd or strange everything was, not how great and perfect it seemed. Or perhaps I was just cynical about my predicament—entangled with someone I cared deeply about but couldn't quite figure out or get along with. I had a star-crossed marriage.

"OH, MY GOD, THERE'S ANTHRAX IN ROCKEFELLER CENTER!"

AFTER OUR FIVE-WEEK-LONG HONEYMOON, WE RETURNED to Los Angeles and attempted to assume a normal married life. I had started a movie production company—Bob Green Films—and opened an office to develop new properties. Despite *Freddy Got Fingered*, New Regency was willing to back me in the film business, and I was more than ready to prove them right. Drew's new movie, *Riding in Cars With Boys*, was scheduled to come out in October. It was a movie she was very proud of and secretly hoped might garner her an Academy Award nomination. Right after that, she was scheduled to start another movie, *Confessions of a Dangerous Mind*.

Then 9/11 hit.

The events had a massive impact on everyone in America, and that certainly includes Drew and me. In retrospect, I can see that it created a whole other set of problems to an already problem-filled marriage. There was of course the fear and uncertainty that surrounded the entire event. But, on a more mundane level, there was the immediate impact on Drew's working life. This may sound oh-so-Hollywood, but movies are a big corporate enterprise, and Drew had a movie premiering within weeks after 9/11.

Of course no movie people were doing anything right after the attack. Like everyone else, they were in shock, and no one wanted to go out and look like they were trying to do business and promote themselves like nothing had happened. Unfortunately, Drew found herself in a position where she had to be one of the first high-profiled movie stars to go back into the marketplace. She was caught in a terrible bind. She wanted the movie to do well, but no one at the time was out pitching their movie. It was a very awkward period for her.

Drew was scheduled to be the second host for *Saturday Night Live* after Rudolph Giuliani reopened the show after the tragedy. When you host *SNL*, you spend the preceding week in New York writing and rehearsing with the rest of the company. Drew went to New York, and I stayed in L.A. to jumpstart Bob Green Films. On Thursday of that week, I was sitting in my office when someone came running in. "Oh, my God," they shouted, "There's anthrax in Rockefeller Center!" It was the day they announced that anthrax had been found in Tom Brokaw's mail. Tom Brokaw was in Rockefeller Center. As were the offices of *Saturday Night Live.*

Almost at the same time Drew called with genuine panic in her voice. She was at Rockefeller Center at that moment and was scared. I was scared, too. This was my wife, there was anthrax in the building, the hysteria of 9/11 was still very much in the air, and people had already died in this anthrax scare. At this point, remember, no one had any idea what might be happening. For all we knew, a massive biological attack might have been underway.

The *SNL* people were telling Drew to stay and host the show. My advice was, "Listen, why don't you leave. Go back to the hotel, wait a couple of hours, and feel it out." She said she would do just that and hung up. The next call came from the lobby of her hotel. She was still very shaken. As I tried to calm her down, all of a sudden a famous Hollywood actress who'll remain nameless took the phone from her and started talking to me. I didn't know this person, but there she was, scolding me of behalf on the *SNL* people for freaking out my wife and sending her back to her hotel. I'm telling myself, Wait a minute. This is the fucking world I'm in? I don't even know who I'm talking to!

I couldn't find Drew for a few hours after that and through her publicist finally discovered that she was out riding around in a limo, trying to regain her composure. Of course I felt completely stupid, like I was not doing my job as a husband to comfort his wife in a time of need. Instead, people I didn't know from Adam had assumed this task.

Drew called me about an hour and a half later and said she wanted to stay and wanted me to come to New York to be with her on *SNL*. Her movie studio was going to charter a jet and fly me out immediately. "Could you please come?" "Of course," I said.

The anthrax scare subsided and the show went off without a hitch. I even ended up being incorporated into the show. Drew, during her opening monologue, went on about how she was initially afraid of being there, but that she wasn't afraid now and wanted to thank everyone there for also not being afraid. The camera then cut to the audience and, as everyone clapped, it panned over to me; I was sitting there in a gas mask. I took the mask off, continuing to breathe into my shirt, and got a big laugh.

"I WANT A DIVORCE"

THE MOVIE *RIDING IN CARS WITH BOYS* CAME AND went without much fanfare. The studio ran trade-paper ads hyping Drew "For Your Consideration" for an Oscar, though it was pretty clear that it wasn't going to happen. But there was always more work, specifically a new movie directed by George Clooney called *Confessions of a Dangerous Mind*, about the strange life of game-show host Chuck Barris. The movie was to be shot in Montreal. I think after all the constant fighting in our fragile marriage, before and after the wedding, she probably was happy to be out of town for a while. On top of this, I wasn't the stable rock that I may have seemed in earlier times. I was still stinging from the onslaught of my big movie and more than a bit depressed.

Christmas was on the horizon as Drew prepared to go to Montreal for her movie. Hollywood shuts down at Christmastime. You are almost forced to take a two-week vacation because you can't call your agent or meet with studio people. They're all out of town. So a weird predicament presented itself. We had been fighting more or less constantly for six months, and all of a sudden there were two weeks where we couldn't go off to work every day and sidestep our problems. We had, in fact, two pressure-free weeks to go someplace and try to resolve a few issues.

My idea was to meet in Ottawa for Christmas. We had done that in the past and had had a wonderful time. The timing was perfect. Drew was to be in Montreal right before and after Christmas, and Montreal was all of an hour's drive from Ottawa. Away from anything that even remotely resembled "the business," I thought, maybe we could recapture some of that carefree affection that had brought us together in the first place.

As we sat in our bedroom discussing this plan, I started to feel very strange. I wanted to drive down from Ottawa, pick her up on her last day of shooting, and drive back. She didn't want that. She wanted an extra day in Montreal before I came. "Why?" I asked. She didn't say. This precipitated a larger discussion of whether or not she wanted to go to Ottawa and spend Christmas with my family in the first place. It turned out that she didn't. She wanted to go to Hawaii for two weeks with one of her close friends.

Well, fine, I thought, maybe Ottawa is too boring for her. I understand that. So I proposed that rather than going to Ottawa, I'd come to Hawaii with her and her friend. We went around about this for a while until it became clear that she didn't want me to go to Hawaii. In fact, she wanted to go to get away from me.

This was a breaking point. We had two weeks where we might be able to turn things around and she was set on getting three thousand miles away from me.

At this point, the unstoppable train suddenly stopped and I was ready to get off. I said, "That's unacceptable. I want a divorce." She said, "Fine."

And that was that.

13.

HOLLYWOOD CAUSES CANCER

—

"**H**e is, in my opinion, a full-blown entertainer. . . . He has the ability, the great gift to entertain people, and so he keeps going and doesn't let fires, cancer, divorces, Bar Mitzvahs stop him. . . . If you have the talent and dream, show business is about showing up. And he's showed up."

—Howard Lapides

I HAD MADE THE DECISION—I HAD TO LEAVE. LONG before she realized that I meant it, I had contacted a lawyer. I then began the very sad and painful process of preparing the legal forms. I remember driving down into Beverly Hills and taking the long elevator ride up to some busy law office to meet with some powerful Hollywood divorce lawyer, a man who handles the wreckage of lives every day of the week. It was an amazing clash of sentiments. Here I was, just a normal, thirty-year-old guy—if not normal, then naïve—going through the most gut-wrenching heartbreak one can go through, meeting with a guy in a suit who was just spending another day at the office.

To me this was a pivotal moment of my life. As far as the lawyer was concerned, I was just doing what people in Hollywood do when they get married. I was getting a divorce.

Have you ever been to a funeral where the minister had never known the deceased personally? He can see the sadness in everyone else's eyes, but he's not sad himself. He's just doing a job—putting this obviously nice person in the ground. After all, he trades in births, marriages, and deaths. Divorce lawyers trade in misery.

In a sense the lack of emotion from these people actually makes the whole process a lot easier. The cavalier attitude they have toward rubber-stamping the rearrangement of lives actually makes divorce seem almost normal. They treat it like you're going in for a driver's license or applying for a library card. In my situation, you have to compound the silliness of it all with the fact that everyone in the office recognized me. I remember walking through the hallways of this law firm, past the secretaries, legal aides, and interns, and staring into their not-so-surprised-to-see-me faces. I could hear them chuckling inside their own heads: Oh, well . . . it's that Tom Green–Drew Barrymore thing . . . *that* didn't last long.

Everyone knew why I was there. Some were probably dialing *People* magazine as I walked by. I popped into the big corner office, met this lawyer referred by my entertainment lawyer, and started filling out forms. He asked me when I wanted to file. Suddenly I felt weak and breathless. It was as if all the air had been sucked from the room. I was on the verge of crying.

"Right, when did I want to file?" I sat there with no answer for what seemed like minutes. It was one of those rare passages in life where time seems to stand still, seconds pass by like minutes, and everything around you seems like a cloudy dream. Ironically, the last time I had felt this was when I proposed to Drew on one knee in the sand on the beach. I remember kneeling there, breathless, holding the ring, and waiting for her to answer.

I snapped out of this daze. When did I want to file? I pondered the question, and then for some reason, perhaps caught up in the romance of my thoughts, I told the lawyer that I was still not entirely ready. I told him to keep the papers here in his big office-that-divorce-built until I gave him the word. I wanted to go home and talk to my wife.

The conversation, to put it mildly, did not go well. It was another endless argument going nowhere that led me once again to that almost incantatory word, *divorce*. I was ready to file. Things had become so difficult that I don't think it came as a great surprise to her. The opportunity to escape this insanity was probably a relief to her as much as it was to me.

The next day I called the divorce lawyer and he went down to the court-house and filed for divorce on my behalf. I don't think my ex-wife-to-be had realized I was as far along in the process as I was, and at this point I didn't feel the need to tell her. She was traveling that day and found out what I had done from her publicist as she got off a plane in Montreal, still wearing her wedding ring I had given her. Welcome to Hollywood. I have not seen her since, and that was over two years ago as I write this.

I recall feeling numb for a long time. It was just before Christmas that I filed for divorce, so I went home to Ottawa to be with my family. It was a very somber holiday, easily the worst Christmas I have ever experienced. I spent much of it curled up in a ball of sadness in the dark room in the basement where I would sleep when I visited home, the same room where I had spent months waiting for that CBC pilot to be picked up seven years earlier. I think I was still surprised that I was in that bed alone, as I was used to her being there beside me. Only a year earlier we had spent a very romantic Christmas in Ottawa together. Her mother was with us, and I had surprised Drew by having her dog Flossie flown up to greet her unexpectedly on Christmas Eve. It was almost normal. Having a family, I think I was trying to say, isn't out of reach. Perhaps in the world she came from, the world that I had entered, she knew better.

So I lay in this dark room in the basement and the sadness made my body throb and head pound. It was my childhood bedroom, once decorated with spray-painted hieroglyphics and skateboard posters. Now it was tastefully redone in flowery wallpaper and respectable antique furniture. It made its point. I was no longer a child. I was divorced.

As much as I had told myself that I would never be divorced, that I would never be "that guy," I had also not come close to predicting what I would get myself into. I had never prepared for the world that I had actually entered. I had always dreamed of being a comedian, but never really understood all the psychological strings attached to succeeding, especially succeeding at the age of twenty-seven. I had worked so hard at my craft, at trying to make funny TV, at trying to make people laugh, but I had never thought of the extra pressures that came with the job.

I had a lot of time to think now.

THE *NEW* TOM GREEN SHOW

AFTER CHRISTMAS I RETURNED TO LOS ANGELES. I returned to the house that we had bought together. It seemed much more peaceful now. There were no more fights and there were no more Hollywood assistants/friends/hangers-on showing up unexpectedly and tracking through the living room unannounced. It was quiet. In a gesture that unnerved me, Team Barrymore had entered the house while I was out one day and rounded up the dogs, Flossie, Vivian, and Templeton. I came home from the office and they were gone. They were her dogs, but it was upsetting that they were pilfered without either my knowledge or consent. It may sound silly, but I never really got to say good-bye to them. I was sad to see them gone.

It was more than a little creepy that these assistants were just entering my house and taking stuff. I made the uncomfortable move of changing all the locks. Although the solitude was a big shift, the emptiness began to feel like I was back in my own world. The Hollywood machine had whirlwinded its way out of my life, complete with entourage in tow. Now I had time to ponder the aftermath of a three-year tornado and maybe reclaim some pieces of myself that had been chipped away in the process.

I did miss those dogs, though.

I decided that dogs were something I definitely needed in my life. Over the next few weeks I searched for and eventually adopted two Siberian huskies. Annie and Steve, both girls, quickly became a very big part of my life and made things far less lonely in my new post-whirlwind life.

My routine completely changed. I began taking my new dogs for walks, usually in the canyon near my house. It was a daily ritual, which I found was very productive, and necessary, giving me time to think. I would do this every morning, without fail. I was at a crossroads once again and had some important decisions to make.

As I said, I had started a company, Bob Green Films, named after a nonexistent uncle who supposedly was the financier of the whole operation. In reality I was very fortunate. Despite a critical and commercial bomb, I was still in the movie business. I liked to write and direct. I'd be back, I said to myself. That one just missed. The next one—like *Organized Rhyme*, the radio show, the community cable show, the Comedy Network show, the MTV show, and *Road Trip*—will hit.

Although I had been working on two scripts that I had sold to the studio, I wasn't sure this was the right next move. I began to think more about what it was that I truly wanted to do, and in my newly reclaimed world I was beginning to think more clearly. I was no longer surrounded at home by movie people all day and night, no longer spending my evenings discussing the creative genius of Woody Allen or Hal Ashby through a blurry haze of pot smoke and red wine. I no longer had to impress anyone or live up to someone's perception of who I was or what I should do next. I had time to think about what I thought was funny again. I had time to do what I wanted to do, what I had always wanted to do before being sidetracked. I wanted to make television.

I love talk shows. Since moving to L.A., I've had the pleasure and privilege of appearing a number of times on Jay Leno's *Tonight Show*. As the world knows, Jay is a genuinely outgoing person; he constantly encouraged me to take risks on his show. On one appearance I decided to test the potency of the liquor in the famous Jay Bar, a cart of drinks rolled into each guest's dressing room before the show. Remembering some boozy moments from *The Tonight Show* of the sixties, I decided to booze it up a little myself.

I wandered on stage with the rolling bar and proceeded to knock back a dozen shots of Jagermeister, a German liquor. I told the producers I was going to do this, but ended up getting a little more soused than I had planned. I spilled my drink on the beautiful young actress Rosario Dawson and got so carried away that they had to edit out some of my blotto antics. On the way home, I'm told, I emptied the contents of my stomach into the *Tonight Show* limo. I woke up the next day completely embarrassed and figured that was it for me and Jay. Not so. In fact, Jay graciously called me at home that morning to see if I was okay. We had a good laugh and he invited me back. A couple of weeks later I showed up in a suit, somber as a preacher, head hanging low, and apologized to America for making a fool of myself.

While I was becoming intrigued again by TV, my longtime television agent (and friend) at the powerful William Morris agency, John Ferriter, was approached, almost by coincidence, by a major television network. John and I had been working together for years and he was a big factor in my decision to return to television. It had been a few years now since I had been on TV and the network wanted to know my level of interest in doing a weekly show. Walking in the canyon with my dogs, I pondered all of these possibilities. I suppose if I had really wanted to make a movie out of one of my scripts, I could have. I knew from experience, from a lot of waiting and doubting and false starts and second guesses, that perseverance in this business usually paid off. These scripts we had written were both really funny, but did I want to spend the next two years of my life trying to get them made? Maybe, but would the jokes that are funny now be received as funny two or three years in the future? When I threw the prospect of more critical lambasting into the equation, I thought maybe it would be best to get back to something I really understood. I opted to go in and meet with this network. I wanted to do a TV show.

Without boring you with the details, before we made a new commitment, my agents and I felt that we had made a previous commitment to MTV those two years before. When I became sick with cancer, I had left MTV to make a couple of movies, but had agreed that if I wanted to work in television again, I would talk to them first. After our meeting with this major network, we felt obligated to let the people at MTV know our plan. And thus began the next phase of *The Tom Green Show,* which we aptly titled *The New Tom Green Show.*

We met with MTV and told them what we wanted to do, a nightly hour-long talk show. This would be a place, I felt, where I could regain my comic equilibrium and get back to a comfortable creative forum. I wasn't the same person I had been the last time I was on the air. I had more to say, had experienced so much more—I had grown up. A nightly show was really what I had always wanted to do, and now, for the first time in my life, I was probably capable of pulling it off. I had been around now, married, divorced; I had survived both cancer and a public lynching. For the first time in my life, I felt confident

In Texas for *The New Tom Green Show* on MTV. This is a real county . . . named after someone else, apparently.

that I could go out on TV and talk for an hour every night. For the first time, I felt I could talk about almost anything and not just Monty Python movies and Tony Hawk moves.

I spent the next months studying all of the masters. I had grown up a huge fan of David Letterman and *The Tonight Show,* but now I wanted to look at the whole medium under a microscope. I began to pore over the lives of TV greats. I read countless biographies of Johnny Carson, Jack Paar, and Steve Allen. I read probably a dozen books on the history of *The Tonight Show* alone. It became almost an obsession. When I wasn't reading, I was at the Museum of Television and Radio in Beverly Hills, screening old shows. It was a mesmerizing experience looking at early episodes of Ernie Kovacs, a TV legend I had read about but never seen. I spent months practically living at that museum.

We teamed up with a new producer for the show. Burt Dubrow created both the *Jerry Springer Show* and the *Sally Jesse Raphael Show* and now, the new Tom Green show. He was himself a fanatic television historian and with him I learned so much about early TV history. Burt and I would spend hours talking

Hanging out on *The Tonight Show.* How cool is that?

in ridiculous detail about obscure Johnny Carson trivia of the likes I had never heard. And we wouldn't just dissect talk shows—we'd break down *Howdy Doody, Amos and Andy,* and *The Lone Ranger.* In fact, Burt is so into all this stuff that his living room is filled with TV memorabilia, including the original Howdy Doody himself encased in a glass box. After working with him for almost two years, I now consider him not only my producer and TV history teacher, but also a very good friend.

I would be lying if I didn't say that all that old TV-watching was therapeutic at the same time. I was still reeling from the divorce, and a public one at that. There was hardly a day that would go by where I didn't walk past a magazine or newspaper with something about my now "ex-wife." I wasn't surprised to see that within what seemed like minutes she had turned her undying devotion to some new flame of the month. Marriage in Hollywood is often easy come, easy go, including, it seemed, my own.

Me and Glenn in El Paso for *The New Tom Green Show.*

For a while, the media continued to take a particular delight in pummeling me at every opportunity. It was as if Hollywood itself were breathing a collective sigh of relief to see that their "little girl" was no longer married to this interloper, this "bad man." I don't want to sound like John Bobbit or Tammy Fae Baker, but it became a fun story to kick "Tom Green" while he was down. It was a cheap and easy joke. It's strange how these things play themselves out. These people didn't know me, but they had concluded that I was crazy, or talentless, or both. I guess if you play a crazy guy on TV, then that has to be true. Regardless, I became good at ignoring it, and as I suspected, it eventually went away.

The New Tom Green Show on MTV lasted only eleven weeks, but it was a great experience. It opened up to critical raves unlike any I had ever received. It was exciting to again be receiving some positive recognition from the media that I had grown fearful of. The *New York Post* gave the show a four-star review:

> Someone at MTV deserves a laurel and a hearty handshake for having the imagination to hand Green an hour every weeknight to do whatever he wants. . . . Based on just one show . . . it's not far-fetched to conclude that Green is a force to be reckoned with, a creative talent and natural broadcaster in the tradition of the young David Letterman."

Both the *New York Times* and the *Los Angeles Times* also said great things. I must admit, with all the accolades, it was a bit of a surprise that the show ended so quickly. But it was very expensive to produce and not really the type of show that MTV has been traditionally known for.

"HOLY CRAP! WHAT THE HELL ARE YOU DOING HERE!?"

WHILE I WAS WAITING FOR THE TALK SHOW TO GET going, I decided to contact the USO. I wanted to go overseas and visit with the troops. I wasn't at first sure why. I think I was more curious than anything else. Many of my comedic idols had done the same thing; I had just finished reading that Jack Paar had spent his military service performing for troops at Guadalcanal in World War Two. Also, I had grown up on an army base and remember what it was like to be separated from my father when he went on year-long tours to Vietnam or Cyprus. So I called the USO and they sent me on a "handshake tour" to Kosovo.

That trip led to a second one after *The New Tom Green Show* was canceled. This one was much more extensive—five different African and Middle Eastern countries, including Iraq. We went to Bahrain, then Abu Dhabi in the United Arab Emirates, then on to Djibouti in Africa, then Kuwait, and finally Iraq.

Getting my hair cut for my USO tour to Iraq. This photo was taken at an airbase in Abu Dhabi. The soldiers seemed to get a kick out of it. Not sure if I did.

After nearly twenty-four hours in airplanes and airports, Glenn and I hobbled off a plane on the other side of the world. It was head-spinning.

Bahrain is like the Las Vegas of the Middle East. Muslims say that a black cloud hangs over Bahrain that Allah can't see through. Alcohol is allowed, and the city is filled with Arab sheiks ready to party. I had my first Middle Eastern dining experience at Kentucky Fried Chicken. I could have chosen Dairy Queen, McDonald's, or Cinabon. I had flown halfway around the world to order a three-piece chicken combo. It was a little depressing.

Bahrain is one of the several jumping points for U.S. troops headed for Iraq, so the next day we ate lunch with a thousand soldiers. The thing that you instantly notice is that they are all very happy to see you. As I was led around the base, they would come running up to shake my hand and thank me for coming. To be honest, it throws you a bit. I'm thinking, What are you thanking me for? You're the ones risking your lives over here! It's as if these soldiers have an underlying anxiety that what they are doing over there has been forgotten in America. The mere presence of someone they recognize from back home does more for their morale than any of us could understand.

On a daily basis, an officer would approach and in a ceremonial manner present me with a coin of excellence. These unique brass coins marked with units' insignias are awarded to soldiers for excellent behavior. Except for a slew of "Razzies" for *Freddy Got Fingered*, I'm not someone who gets many awards. I wanted to say to the officer, "Give this to someone who deserves it," but they would insist that what we were doing was a great help to the soldiers. You could see it in the troops' faces. They smiled and laughed twice as hard as any joke deserved.

All of them wanted to talk about other USO tours, and you could tell it had been the highlight of that week for them. "I got Robin Williams's autograph!" or, "When Bruce Willis was here he bought us all beers! Are you gonna buy us all beers?" One British officer I chatted with in the lobby of the Baghdad International Airport explained to me that every day over there starts to feel like *Groundhog Day*. Every day is exactly the same, same job, same tasks. Just a minor variation is a really big deal, and these tours positively affect morale long after they end.

Before Iraq, when we had made a quick trip to Djibouti in the East Coast of Africa, at one point we drove off the military base into the surrounding countryside. Before we knew it, literally dozens of starving children surrounded our car, begging us not for money, but for water. This was a curveball I wasn't expecting, a level of extreme despair that I have never seen. When you have fifteen or twenty starving kids tugging on your shirt, with tears running down their faces, looking in your eyes and desperately screaming the word "water"— the only English word they know—it changes you. Especially when you don't have any water to give them. It was so overwhelming that at one point I began to cry. Embarrassed, I walked out into the desert and wiped my eyes where nobody could see. We drove back to the base that day in guilty silence. The whole thing was a revelation.

The trip into Iraq was intense—people were getting ambushed and blown up daily—but there were light moments. Flying in, the pilot got on the headset to say, "Hey, I loved you in *Joe Dirt*." I responded, "Uhh, I wasn't in that one, that was David Spade." The pilot broke up laughing. "I've been waiting to do that all day!" It was moments like this that made you pause. You're flying over the Iraqi desert into Baghdad with reserves from the Illinois National Guard, and you're laughing about shit like *Joe Dirt, Road Trip, American Idol,* and *Freddy Got Fingered.* It hits you that these young enlisted men and women are just regular, iPod-blaring-Christina-Aguilera-MTV-watching kids. Their relatability is a surprise that makes what they do seem that much more impressive.

The three days in Iraq were amazing. Flying through Baghdad in a Blackhawk with machine gunners hanging out the windows. Walking through one of Saddam Hussein's many grandiose marble and gold palaces, only to be told that this is in fact the maid's quarters and the actual palace is "that big one up the hill." One young soldier showed me his metal breast plate from his flak jacket. There was a bullet lodged in it. Only a few days before he had been knocked fifteen feet when he was shot in the vest by an enemy AK-47. The force knocked the wind out of him and he lay on the ground assuming he was dead. Now, only a few days later, he was back at work, lined up in the mess hall for his Salisbury steak and beans. As a reminder he hangs the metal breast plate in his tent beside his bed.

Toward the end, we visited Nasiriyya, both the location of the famous Jessica Lynch rescue and the home of a four thousand-year-old ziggurat, or pyramid, said to be the second oldest man-made structure on the planet. This area was the birthplace of Abraham, and the ruins of his home were only a few feet away. You realize you are in the Garden of Eden . . . the actual Garden of Eden! There are no tour buses, there isn't an entrance fee, and you are there by yourself. We climbed to the top, and in the distance across the dry desert plains we saw a Humvee driving toward us. Two air force guards hopped out, seemingly sightseeing themselves. As they climbed the long ancient staircase toward us, the younger of the two recognized Glenn and me. His eyes widened with confusion. "Holy crap! Tom Green?! What the hell are you doing here, in the cradle of civilization?" I looked back at him and the other soldier and said, "We're here to say thanks."

After that trip, Hollywood no longer seemed like the center of the universe.

WHILE OVERSEAS, I KEPT thinking about the title of this book. Hollywood causes cancer? What does that mean, exactly? Maybe after reading this far, it's apparent, but I'd like to add a few more details.

Yes, it's ironic that I got "real" cancer so soon after moving to Hollywood, but the cancer Hollywood causes is more emotional, or maybe spiritual, in nature. I was jettisoned into this community, and this business, from a small town and was completely unprepared for the emotional craziness I was about to experience. Arnold Rifkin, the famous agent I met early on, was right. "Everything," he said, "that you consider to be normal now is not going to be normal in a few years." I didn't know what he meant at the time. Now I do.

Maybe things would have been different if I had lived in Hollywood for a few years before getting that "big break." I certainly worked to make it happen, but I worked in Ottawa, a world away from Hollywood. It is not a world filled with young people trying *desperately* to be rich and famous. It is a world where people are perhaps a little more content with themselves the way they already are. When you suddenly find yourself surrounded by these strange new Hollywoodites, perhaps it is better to blend in, pretend you are one of them, and just spend time watching their behavior.

254 | Tom Green

Being an actor, an actress, a comedian, or any type of entertainer is, needless to say, a very self-centered occupation. It takes a certain personality to want to stand in the spotlight and say, "Look at me!" Entertainers are in the business of marketing and promoting themselves to the biggest audience possible. When you get close to it, it's a pretty annoying thing to be around. I think the biggest problem that affects people in Hollywood is that they stop noticing the abnormalities of their own personalities. They begin to honestly believe that the most interesting thing that one could possibly talk about, think about, and obsess about is themselves. It's a professional shortcoming that makes some people crazy, others insufferable, and the rest just fatuous and boring. Dull.

And if you actually plant a foot in Hollywood, other people change as much as you do. Arnold Rifkin mentioned this, too: your friends stop being your friends. Some of my best friends from home are now distant and removed. This is a very sad side effect of chasing a dream, an effect I don't quite understand. I'm sure I've had something to do with it, and if not me, my ambition. Is it just the inability for friends to relate to one another after people's lives change so rapidly? Or is it simply the complex human traits of jealousy, greed, and envy that make succeeding (or failing) in Hollywood very difficult for relationships to weather?

For instance, without naming names, I find it interesting how many high-profile actresses do not speak to their mothers. Do some research and you'll find that an abnormal percentage of highly successful Hollywood types have very rotten family relationships. Of course these glaring personal tragedies are glazed over or minimized by the public personas they so carefully craft. And such serious family fractures would be inconsistent with the "normal" public persona that everyone in Hollywood attempts to achieve. Another example is divorce. Why do so many high-profile marriages in this business end in divorce? If these people we watch on TV and in movies are so normal, why can none of them keep it together? Sure, there are few exceptions, but give them time, they'll come around.

One thing that is particularly interesting about Hollywood is that everybody is always right. In personal conversation, everything that one celebrity

During a renovation of my pool in L.A., with the dogs.

says to another is always a stroke of genius. An actor friend of mine, my own undisclosed source, told me a great story. When he first moved to Hollywood, he ended up living in the guesthouse of a very popular actress. She would often throw dinner parties for all of her very popular actor and actress friends. At these affairs, my friend would sit and observe, and the thing that struck him most is that no one would ever disagree with anything that anyone had to say. If someone told a joke, no matter how good or bad, everybody would laugh as if it were the funniest thing they had ever heard. If someone were to dare bring into the conversation politics, or philosophy, or art, anything they said, no matter how clever or stupid, would be treated as genius. My friend, of course, being a shit disturber himself, would sometimes disagree with these famous Hollywood types, just to see what happened. It would invariably leave them distressed and confused.

I feel fortunate that I've had the time to step back a little after the cancer and the divorce. I wouldn't have thought so at the time, but the break has given

me a chance to recalibrate my life. For many of the people I've met in Hollywood, *reality* is just another imaginative construct and *normalcy* just a state of
pretend. I wish them well in their bubble.

I'M NOW BACK IN Hollywood and excited about the future. With the
talk show a critical success, I look forward to doing it again someday. It is exciting to have been given the opportunity to do a nightly show. It answered a lot

of questions that I had been asking myself since I was a sixth-grade kid in my school gym pontificating about the nature of humor. Sure, I loved watching talk shows, but would I ever be able to do it? Could I write and perform a daily monologue? Could I interview a serious guest? Could I be reasonably funny every night for an hour? Could I keep up with the daily grind? Would people like me?

I really do have good reason to thank a lot of entertainment people, especially the people at MTV. They gave me the opportunity to succeed on my own terms. I sometimes think about what would have happened if MTV hadn't put me on the air in the first place. Without them, I would probably be living back in Canada, happily married, with two testicles . . . because Hollywood, you know, causes cancer. Certainly, I wouldn't have suffered many of the difficulties and disappointments that this new life brought with it. But then again, I would have never met David Letterman or hung out with Tony Hawk. In hindsight, although I remain hurt and confused by many of the twists and turns, I don't think I'd want to replace them with anything else. It's all a part of this ridiculous journey that is life, and I have a feeling that the stupidity of it all will inevitably end up leading me somewhere that I may have never found. I wonder where that will be.

Stay tuned and I'll keep you posted.

Sincerely,

Tom Green

PHOTO CREDITS

ABOUT THE AUTHOR

Tom Green was the host of
MTV's *The Tom Green Show* and
The New Tom Green Show and
has starred in the films *Road Trip,*
Freddy Got Fingered, Stealing
Harvard, and *Charlie's Angels.*

Allen Rucker is the author of the
#1 *New York Times* bestseller
The Sopranos Family Cookbook,
The Sopranos: A Family History,
and two books with Martin Mull,
The History of White People in America
and *A Paler Shade of White.*